IMAGES
of America

MILLVALE

ON THE COVER: Baeuerlein Brewing Company, established by Adam Baeuerlein in 1845, moved to Evergreen Avenue in Millvale around 1868, when the borough was incorporated. Workers stand proudly with their delivery horse before the brewhouse, then known as the Star Brewery. Baeuerlein merged into the Pittsburgh Brewing Company in 1899 and was one of its main plants until closing at the onset of Prohibition in 1920. (Janine Vecenie.)

IMAGES
of America

MILLVALE

Bill Stout and Jean Domico

ARCADIA
PUBLISHING

ISBN 978-1-4671-2134-7

Published by Arcadia Publishing
Charleston, South Carolina

Printed in the United States of America

Library of Congress Control Number: 2013946978

For all general information, please contact Arcadia Publishing:
Telephone 843-853-2070
Fax 843-853-0044
E-mail sales@arcadiapublishing.com
For customer service and orders:
Toll-Free 1-888-313-2665

Visit us on the Internet at www.arcadiapublishing.com

To our parents—Mary Marlovits, Bill Stout, Caroline Marlovits, and Regis Hilderbrand—and our sisters, Mary Ann Stout Alexander and Janet Hilderbrand.

Contents

ACKNOWLEDGMENTS

This book sprang out of a natural inquisitiveness my cousin and I share regarding history. After living for many years elsewhere, we both recently moved back to our hometown of Millvale, where Bill has since been elected to the borough's council. When he was approached to write this book on the town, I asked if I could join him in the endeavor, as research has always been my forte. So, off we went on our quests, though there was certainly no yellow brick road to follow!

Given Millvale's history of floods, we knew that the task of finding old photographs would be difficult, but Tropical Depression Ivan in 2004 made it daunting. So many of the town's residents and businesses, believing that Girty's Run had been tamed by the Army Corps of Engineers, stored old photographs and documents, the treasures we were seeking, in their basements. Luckily, borough officials, neighbors, friends, and family members searched albums and found gems. In addition, the books created for Millvale's centennial and 125th anniversary were invaluable. We could not have completed this project without help from the following people and organizations, listed here in no particular order: Jennifer Cohen, Mary Ann Knochel, Carol Szwedko, Ann Conners, Borough of Millvale, Vincent Cinski, Jack Cavanaugh, Arlene Carr, Al Atkinson, Nancy Schaper, Bill Marlovits, Nancy and Vince Jaksic, Debra Stoltenberg, the late Richard Mikus, Sudie Schindler, Dorothy Pfischner, Becky Stout, Elsie and Nick Grubic, Jean Anson, Michele Rheam, Janine Vecenie, Frank Vecenie, Suzanne Salhany, Karen Wittmer, Panza Gallery, Flo Silbach, Barb Treusch, Sister Marilyn Joyce and Sister Florence Brandt of Mount Alvernia, Heinz History Center Archives, Ron Baraff and the Rivers of Steel National Heritage Area, Miriam Mieslik and the Archives Service Center at the University of Pittsburgh, the Society to Preserve the Millvale Murals of Maxo Vanka, the Carnegie Library, and Pastor George of Christ Lutheran.

Many thanks to anyone we may have forgotten, most especially the current and previous residents of Millvale.

INTRODUCTION

Millvale was built along the valley formed by the creek called Girty's Run. The site was originally home to the Seneca Indians, one of the five tribes of the League of the Iroquois. Indians and traders, traveling from Shannopin's Town (two miles above the forks of the Ohio River, about Thirtieth Street in Pittsburgh), crossed the Allegheny River and followed the Venango Path northward up Girty's Run.

Returning from delivering Virginia's ultimatum to the French at Fort LeBoeuf (Presque Isle) to leave the forks of the Ohio, George Washington, with his guide Christopher Gist, may also have followed the Venango Path, in December 1753. Crossing the Allegheny River near Girty's Run, Washington was thrown into the icy stream but managed to escape to an island later known as Wainwright's Island (now Lawrenceville).

In 1784, after the American Revolution, 3,000 acres, across the Allegheny River from Pittsburgh ending at Girty's Run, were purchased from the Iroquois by the Commonwealth of Pennsylvania. These acres were reserved for land grants in lieu of money as payment for soldiers in the Continental army. One such soldier, James Semple, from Cumberland County, settled along Girty's Run around 1790. He built a log cabin, farmed the land, and operated the first gristmill in the area. Semple later changed his last name to Sample to comply with an error on the patent granting his land.

An early story relates how, in 1791, James Sample's wife and children were taken prisoner by Indians two weeks after the birth of a son, Thomas. He was the second white male child known to born north and west of the Allegheny River. The family was rescued through the assistance of an Indian woman to whom Mrs. Sample had given clothing the winter before. The woman ferried the three oldest children across the Allegheny and then gave the canoe to Mrs. Sample, who paddled across with her infant son, arriving safely at the Ewalt farm.

Thomas Girty, brother of the infamous Simon, moved his family here from Squirrel Hill in 1792. It was by his name that the creek would thereafter be known. About 1797, Benjamin Herr purchased land along the Allegheny River and the island known by his name. His daughter, Elizabeth, was born in a hewn log house on his farm in Millvale in 1814. Herr's house was moved to his island to make way for the Pennsylvania Canal, which opened in 1829.

Slowly, the valley along Girty's Run was settled. With the growth of Allegheny City (now Pittsburgh's North Side), access to Millvale became easier with the 1819 opening of the Pittsburgh and Butler toll road running along the Allegheny River. Millvale was civilized enough by 1831 that widow Mary McCalister Dempsey rented 30 acres of land from William Sample and, with her six children, built a house and farmed the land.

To provide work and housing for its indigents, Allegheny City purchased 166 acres of John Sample's farm along Girty's Run for a poor farm in 1844. Industry soon moved northwest from Pittsburgh. Men who lost positions in the labor strikes and riots of 1849–1850 built a small rolling mill called the Mechanics Iron Works. This mill passed ultimately to Graff, Bennett & Company in 1863. Five years earlier, in 1858, two Prussians, Anton and Andrew Kloman, had established a small forge making superior railroad axles. Needing capital to expand, the brothers turned to Miller, Phipps, and Carnegie as partners. Kloman and Company became the birthplace of Pittsburgh's steel industry.

By 1859, there were houses along Girty's Run for the mill workers, including the puddlers, iron rollers, nail cutters, bricklayers, and blacksmiths. The J. Giles Hotel and the Williams Hotel provided rooms, meals, and locally brewed German lager.

In 1866, Allegheny City moved its poor farm to Claremont Station (near Blawnox). The Millvale property was laid out into streets and lots, and the first sale took place on September 4, 1867. The Borough of Millvale was incorporated by Act of Assembly on February 13, 1868. It comprised a portion of Shaler Township and that part of the Borough of Duquesne not included within the limits of Allegheny City set by the Act of Consolidation on March 12, 1867.

Local history credits M.B. Lyon with naming the town for its "mill in a valley." The Graff, Bennett & Company mill became Millvale's primary employer for the next 25 years. Millvale and Bennett were to become synonymous. Millvale's first post office, established in 1869, was the Bennett Post Office, and the freight station on the Pennsylvania Railroad was called Bennett Station. In fact, advertisements sometimes referred to the town as "Bennett, PA." The borough's street names reflect its Northern sympathies during the Civil War: Lincoln, Grant, Sherman, Stanton, Butler, Sheridan, and Hooker (now North).

A new wooden covered bridge, built in 1870, connected Butler Plank Road (now Route 28) to Forty-third Street (formerly Ewalt Street) in Lawrenceville. The bridge brought tremendous growth in population and industry. From a population of 668 in 1870, Millvale grew to 1,824 by 1880. Within that decade, Millvale's citizens built a Presbyterian church, the First Methodist Church, the German Reformed Church of Girty's Run, St. Ann's Roman Catholic Church, the First Ward School, and a German Catholic school conducted by the Sisters of St. Francis. The first fire department, called the Franklin Fire Company, was organized by Graff, Bennett & Company.

Besides the mill, Millvale's businesses in 1872 included the following: three breweries—Baeuerlein & Brothers, Willow Grove, and Hoehl; Oesterling & Company Sash and Door Factory; Gerdes Paint Factory (later Gerdes Leather Company); and the Riverside Oil Refinery, destroyed by lightning in 1875. The last lot from the Allegheny Poor Farm was sold in 1875 for a grand total of $292,396.72, realized on the original purchase price of $12,000. Millvale had its own weekly newspaper, the *Bennett Star*; a narrow-gauge railroad from Butler Plank Road, out Grant and Hooker Avenues, to Evergreen Hamlet; and a graveyard out on Stanton Avenue toward Hoffman Hollow. In August 1879, as a result of two days of heavy rain, Girty's Run overflowed its banks. In the end, 30 houses were flooded, stables and outbuildings were carried away, and bridges and culverts were destroyed.

Over the years, Graff, Bennett & Company expanded and modernized the mill, and it became one of the first iron mills to use natural gas in place of coal. On December 11, 1881, the mill was totally destroyed by fire. Though only partially covered by insurance, the mill was rebuilt in 1882, bigger and better. Unable to meet its obligations in 1883, Graff, Bennett & Company was granted an extension on its million-dollar debt, which was finally paid off in 1887. However, further expansion of the mill consumed all profits, and in February 1888, the firm went bankrupt, throwing hundreds of men out of work. The mill was sold at auction to a syndicate of the firm's creditors. It would remain in business intermittently until 1898, when it was dismantled. The facility was sold and moved to Massilon, Ohio, in 1901.

By the mid-1880s, businesses had moved uptown, including the following: the Baeuerlein & Brothers Foundry, on Hooker Avenue, north of Lincoln Avenue; the Watkins Preserving Works, on the corner of Hooker and Lincoln; and the Walker Rope Factory, in a building two blocks long, from Hooker Avenue to William Street. The latter business was called a "rope walk," because workers walked backward, braiding rope as they moved. The Second Ward School was dedicated on July 23, 1885. The building, grand for its time, had nine classrooms and a principal's office. Millvale had its own town hall, later known as the Opera House, on the corner of Grant Avenue and Sheridan Street.

Millvale's German Catholics split from the English-speaking members of St. Ann's and, in 1887, built a frame church called St. Antonious, where Mass was performed in German. Also in 1887, the First German Evangelical Church (later First United Church of Christ) was formed.

In June 1889, the water in Girty's Run rose 10 feet in 30 minutes, flooding some of the culverts under the streets and washing out the railroad.

In June 1893, the Third Ward was added to the town from portions of the Sample farm and Shaler Township. Beginning at Elizabeth Street and ending in Bauerstown, the land was developed into residential areas by Klopfer, Friday, and Schmitt. The Lutz and Schramm jelly factory, a competitor to Heinz, was destroyed by fire in May 1894. The Penn Saw Works of E.T. Lippert & Son moved to Millvale and erected a three-story building that still stands today. In the spring of 1896, a petition, signed by the requisite number of borough citizens, asking to be annexed to the city of Pittsburgh was presented to the common pleas court, but it was refused and declared unconstitutional.

By 1900, Millvale had six bakers, eight barbers, two dentists, two dressmakers, three druggists, one general store, twenty-one grocers, three horseshoers, eleven hotels serving meals and drinks, seven meat markets, four physicians, six realtors, four shoemakers, three tailors, nine tobacco merchants, and three undertakers. The town's major businesses included its three breweries, Ed Vero's coal company, Bennett Lumber & Manufacturing Company, and Lippert's Penn Saw Works. In the early 1900s, Standard Box & Lumber Company and McDowell Manufacturing moved here to expand. Pittsburgh Railways purchased the old mill property and built a carbarn for its streetcars, which operated in Millvale until 1952. Millvale was the first borough to own its own water and electric power company, and by 1900, it had its own bank. The town had made the transition into a Pittsburgh suburb, where people lived and shopped but did not necessarily work.

In 1900, the Croatian community of Allegheny City moved to its new church, named for St. Nicholas, on a hill overlooking Millvale. The Sisters of St. Francis, who served as teachers and nurses, moved into their new motherhouse, Mount Alvernia. A new church for the Christ English Evangelical Lutheran community was built on the corner of Lincoln Avenue and Sedgwick Street. E.T. Lippert purchased the Millvale Methodist Church building, at the corner of North Avenue and Elizabeth Street, donating it to the congregation of the German Evangelical Lutheran St. John's Church (formerly the German Reformed Church of Girty's Run). By 1906, beyond where North and Evergreen Avenues meet, Millvaleans could enjoy Vermont Park and its pavilion. The Third Ward School, known as Sample School, was built in 1908.

By 1911, Millvale had four nickelodeons on Grant Avenue, serving a population of 7,861. The town also had one architect, four attorneys, and ten building contractors. Millvale again experienced devastating damage in September 1911, when a storm hit Millvale, Etna, and Sharpsburg, causing $500,000 in damages. Though the effects were not as severe as in Etna, where the streets were flooded to 12 feet, scores of people in Millvale had to flee for their lives. The cornerstone on the new St. Anthony's Church, designed by the architect John T. Comes, was laid in 1914. After fire destroyed McDowell Manufacturing in 1916, a new fireproof, concrete building was erected. In 1918, Jacob A. Haser started his "trucking" business, delivering ice and coal in Millvale and Etna with his horse and wagon.

By 1920, Millvale's population reached 8,031. In 1922, the last remaining wooden river crossing, the Forty-third Street Bridge, was removed. In 1924, on the anniversary of George Washington's crossing the Allegheny River, the Washington Crossing Bridge was dedicated. Millvale High School opened for classes in January 1926. Prior to that, students used the upper floor of the Third Ward School. The first class of seniors to graduate from the new high school numbered 38, out of the 98 students who had begun as freshmen, a reminder that education was often a luxury, as families needed the wages earned by their children.

Prohibition spelled the end to Millvale's breweries. In 1921, American Brewing Company sold out to Fried & Reineman Packing Company, which mainly slaughtered and processed hogs. A cigar factory was operated in the stables of the Baeuerlein Brewing Company but, after a few years, it, too, ceased operations.

Millvale's population continued to grow. In March 1924, the new St. Ann's was dedicated. The Grant Hotel (now Grant Bar), purchased by Matthew and Maria Ruzomberka in December 1925, provided rooms for railroad and mill employees working along the Allegheny River. In 1928, the Lincoln Pharmacy was established by Oscar and Joseph Cohen.

In 1929, Millvale's businesses included Anchor Box and Lumber, Bennett Lumber, Duquesne Mine Supply, Evergreen Motor Sales and Service, Lippert Saw, McDowell Manufacturing, Medick and Nethling Chevrolet, Millvale Hardware, Millvale Service Station, North Avenue Garage, Pittsburgh Insulating, Steel City Machine and Manufacturing, Ed Vero Coal and Builders' Supplies, and Yundt Motor. There was only one restaurant and one hotel, the Grant, and no bars. But, of course, this was during Prohibition. Local stories tell of at least one speakeasy where illegal spirits could be obtained and "other services" purchased.

With the end of Prohibition in 1933, Frank Vecenie opened his beer distributor business, delivering local brews to taverns and homes. Greb's Bakery, located on Grant Avenue, was also started. In the 1930s, Millvale was home to a Bell Telephone Company switchboard office on the second floor of the Lippert building. The exchange in Millvale was "Taylor." In 1938, Ester Mehler started Esther's Coffee Shop at 303 North Avenue, selling ice cream and candy. The shop moved to its present location in 1954 and later expanded to include hobbies and toys.

Floods were a major problem in the 1930s and 1940s. The First Ward would flood sometimes two or three times a year. The worst one was the St. Patrick's Day flood on March 18, 1936. The Allegheny River crested at 46 feet, 21 feet over flood stage. All of Millvale's First Ward and part of its Second Ward were flooded; some of the First Ward buildings had water four to five feet above the second floor. On January 26, 1937, the river crested at 34.5 feet, the eighth-highest on record. On April 27, 1937, the river crested at 35.1 feet, the seventh-highest on record.

During World War II, Millvale's factories worked three shifts a day, seven days a week to help the war effort. These businesses included McDowell Manufacturing on Stanton Avenue, Victory Engineering on Sedgwick Street, Duquesne Mine on Hansen Street, Standard Box on Lincoln Avenue, and Safety Guard on Lincoln Avenue. McDowell Manufacturing made shipping bands for bombs, fins for fragmentation bombs, parts for ammunition boxes, and lug bands for rockets. It also did machining on 1,000-pound bombs and 4-pound butterfly bombs. E.T. Lippert Saw made cannon barrels, shells, and packing boxes. Haser Trucking transported most of the material for the war effort. The First Ward School, which closed its doors in 1938 when the Millvale Fire Company took over, was used as a ration center for food and gasoline stamps.

In 1968, Millvale celebrated its centennial with weeklong activities, including a visit from Vice Pres. Hubert Humphrey. Millvale High School closed its doors for the last time three years later. In June 1972, Hurricane Agnes hit Millvale with rain for 30 days, causing flooding when the Allegheny River backed up into Girty's Run. Fortunately, this was the last time flooding was caused by the Allegheny River.

After floods swept through Millvale three times in 1973 and 1974, the Army Corps of Engineers built a flood-control project along Girty's Run. For almost 30 years, the work to straighten out the stream and stabilize its banks kept the flow out of the backyards and basements of those who lived along the creek. But Millvale got muddy and flooded again in the wake of Tropical Depression Ivan in September 2004. Once again, the town's citizens and businesses banded together and recovered from the disaster. With its population declining (3,752 in 2010), Millvale is attempting to regenerate itself, especially along its waterfront, now home to a bike and hiking trail, Kayak Pittsburgh, and the Three Rivers Rowing Club. In August 2013, Millvale opened its first public library in the borough's 145-year history, hoping that it will be an agent for positive change.

One

IN THE BEGINNING

The story of any town, while packed with facts and dates, is really the story of its people. In the case of Millvale, the names of the vast majority of its residents are not known to history, but their character is unmistakable. They were hardworking, prudent men and women seeking a better life for themselves and their families and were willing to face the challenges of a new life in unfamiliar circumstances. This, of course, is true of the early settlers, like James Sample and his family, who came to Girty's Run and faced the threat of hostile Indians. But it is also true of the immigrants who came from virtually every European country to work in the factories and mills of Pittsburgh and its neighboring towns.

Often, they started their own businesses. Some were successful, like the Kloman brothers, who developed a new process for making superior axles in their little forge in Millvale. Others, like the men who built the small rolling mill called the Mechanics Iron Works following the labor strikes of 1849–1850, were not. Some entrepreneurs would try again and again. Eventually, John Graff, James Bennett, and Robert Marshall purchased Millvale's mill in 1863 and became the town's main employers for 25 years. Bennett was the innovative business leader willing to take risks, such as using gas instead of coal for fuel and installing automated Danks puddling furnaces. There were hands-on workingmen, like John I. Williams, who became the mill's supervisor. He understood the art of making iron, refined the new technology, and made it successful. However, the so-called ordinary Joes working 10-to-12-hour shifts remained nameless, unless some special circumstance occurred. Such is the case of James Burns and John Henderson, two workers at the open-hearth furnace. A crane toppled over and struck the natural gas line, igniting the gas. Hemmed in between the fires from the furnace and the gas line, they dashed through the flames and were badly burnt. Their story was reported in the *Somerset Herald* on November 24, 1886.

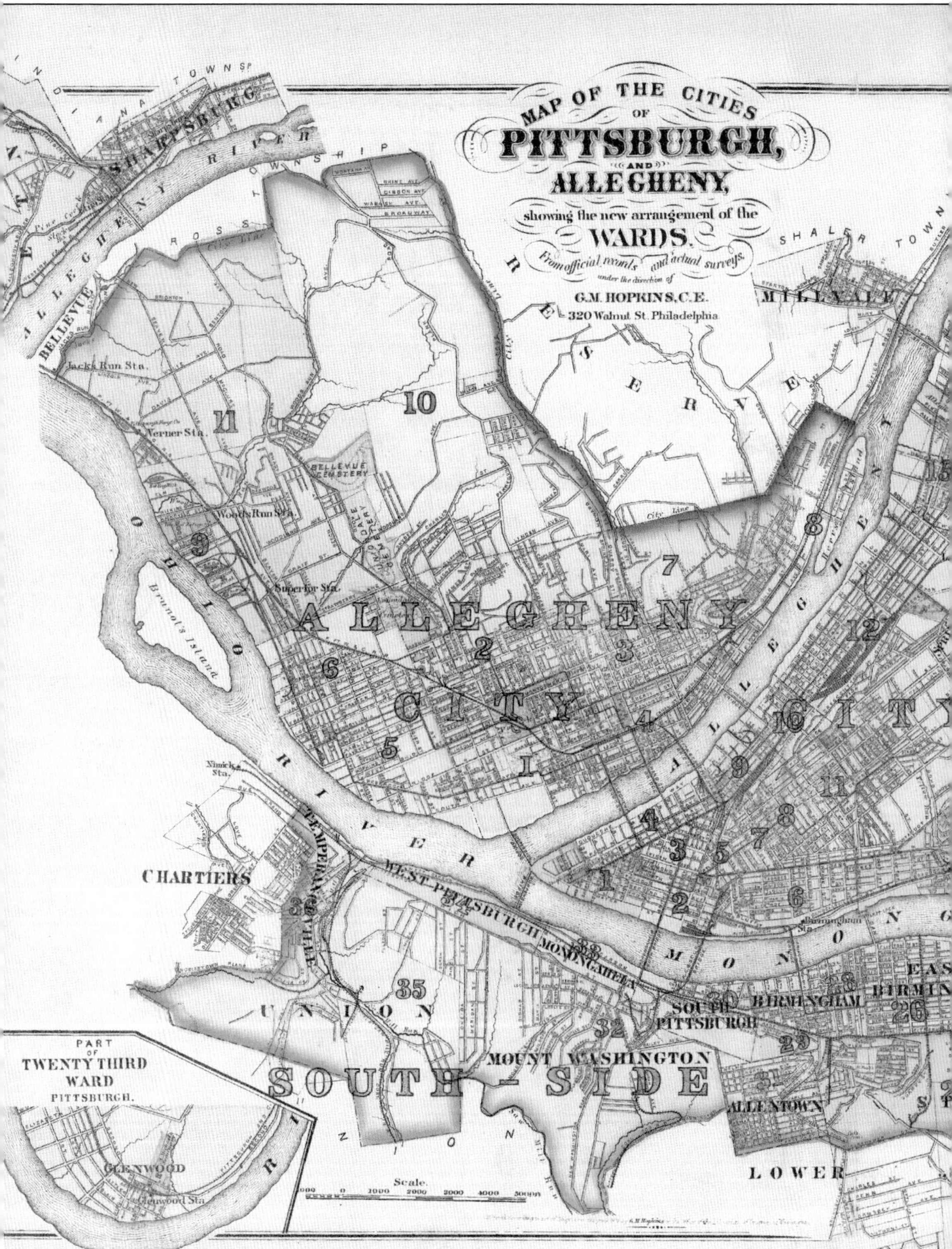
MAP OF THE CITIES OF PITTSBURGH, AND ALLEGHENY,
showing the new arrangement of the WARDS.
From official records and actual surveys.
under the direction of
G.M. HOPKINS, C.E.
320 Walnut St. Philadelphia
ALLEGHENY CITY
SOUTH - SIDE
MOUNT WASHINGTON
CHARTIERS
BIRMINGHAM
SOUTH PITTSBURGH
ALLENTOWN
MILLVALE
SHARPSBURG
BELLEVUE
PART OF TWENTY THIRD WARD PITTSBURGH.
GLENWOOD
Glenwood Sta.
OHIO RIVER
ALLEGHENY RIVER
MONONGAHELA
Brunot's Island
Scale.

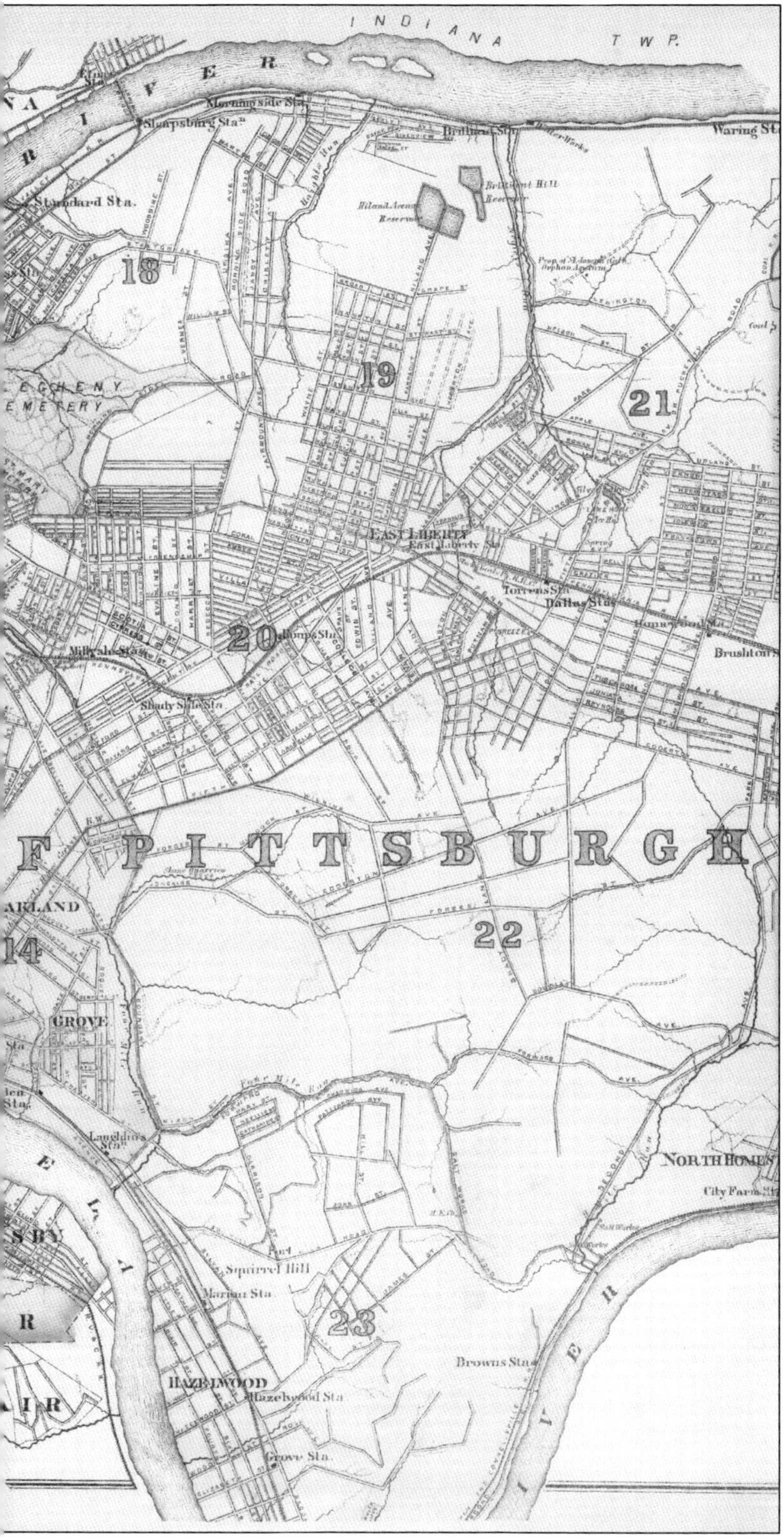

This 1872 G.M. Hopkins map of Pittsburgh and Allegheny City and the adjoining boroughs shows the relatively small size of the Borough of Millvale. The large portion of land marked "Reserve Township" was originally part of the land reserved after the American Revolution for land grants to soldiers as payment for serving in the war. It is easy to see how people and businesses desiring more space would move west along the Allegheny River. Little by little, Allegheny City would grow to encompass all the land to the boundary of Millvale before ultimately becoming part of Pittsburgh itself. (G.M. Hopkins Company Maps, 1872–1940, Archives Service Center, University of Pittsburgh.)

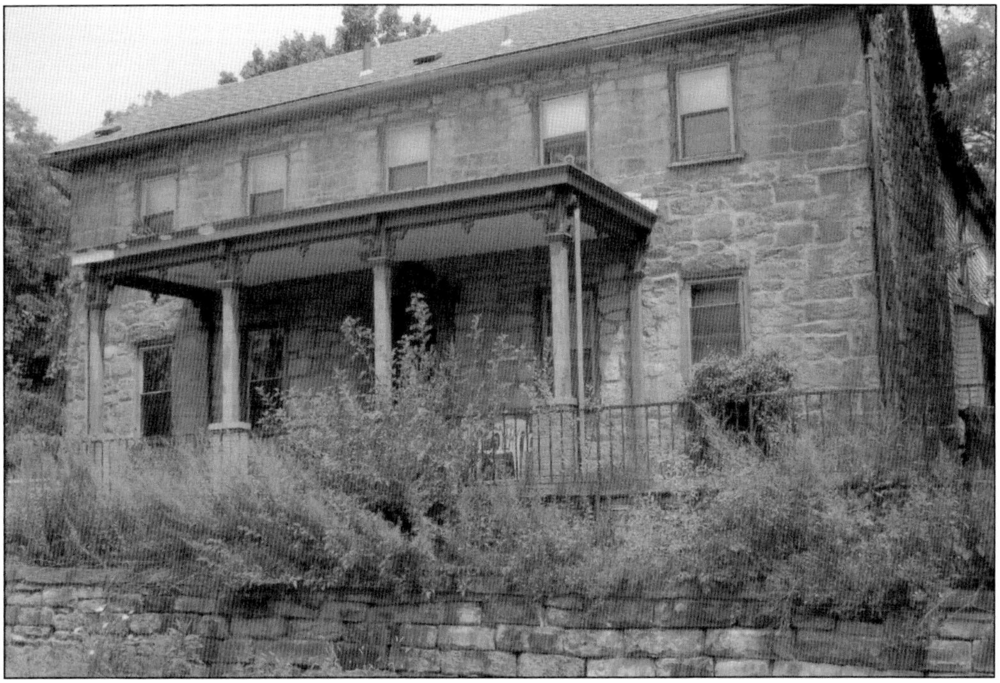

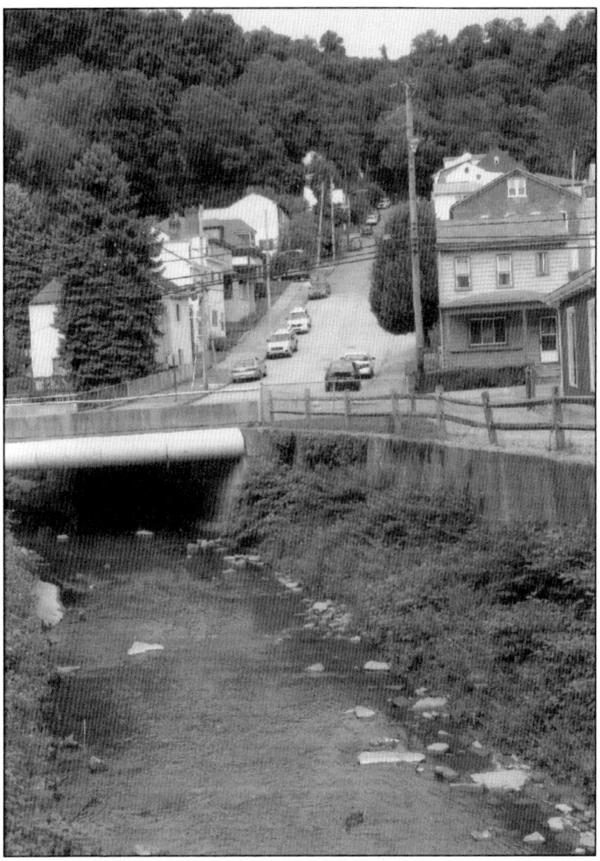

The house at 144 Evergreen Road, built before 1826, is a five-bay example of Western Pennsylvania stone architecture. It is situated on the 230-acre tract originally granted to John Wilkins, one of three grants comprising Millvale. The other grants were to Peter Shafner and George Wallace. The house is shown as the property of H.K. Sample on 1872 and 1886 maps. (Bill Stout.)

Whether named for the notorious "white savage" Simon Girty or his patriotic brother, Thomas, Girty's Run is a small creek that meanders through McCandless and Ross Townships and Millvale Borough, ending at the Allegheny River. Through the years, the buildings in Millvale have been built on or near bridges that span Girty's Run. (Bill Stout.)

Andrew Carnegie's steel empire began in a small forge in Millvale operated by two Prussian brothers, Anton and Andrew Kloman. Opened in 1858, the Kloman Forge produced durable iron railcar axles using new and improved iron-making methods discovered by Andrew Kloman (shown here). The brothers added a second trip hammer to their small forge in 1859. (Jean Domico.)

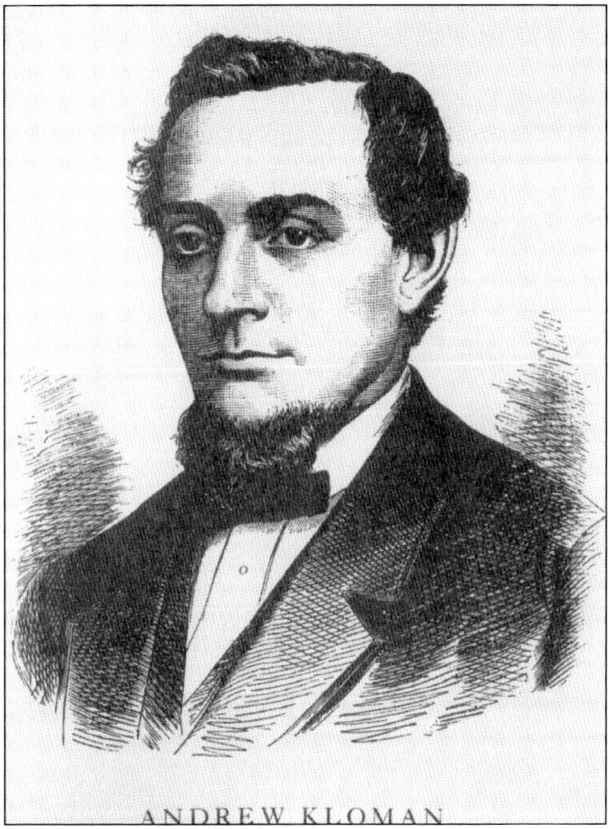

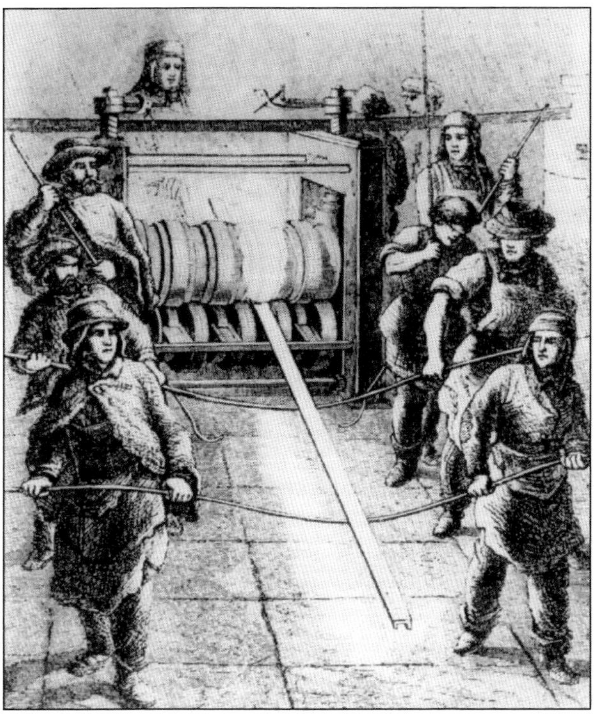

The Civil War created a greater demand for their railroad products than the Kloman brothers were able to meet. Needing capital to expand their business, they turned to Thomas Miller and Henry Phipps, boyhood friends of Carnegie, for funds to purchase more equipment. In 1863, Carnegie himself invested in the business, the Union Iron Works, which had moved from Millvale to a site in Lawrenceville. (Carnegie Library.)

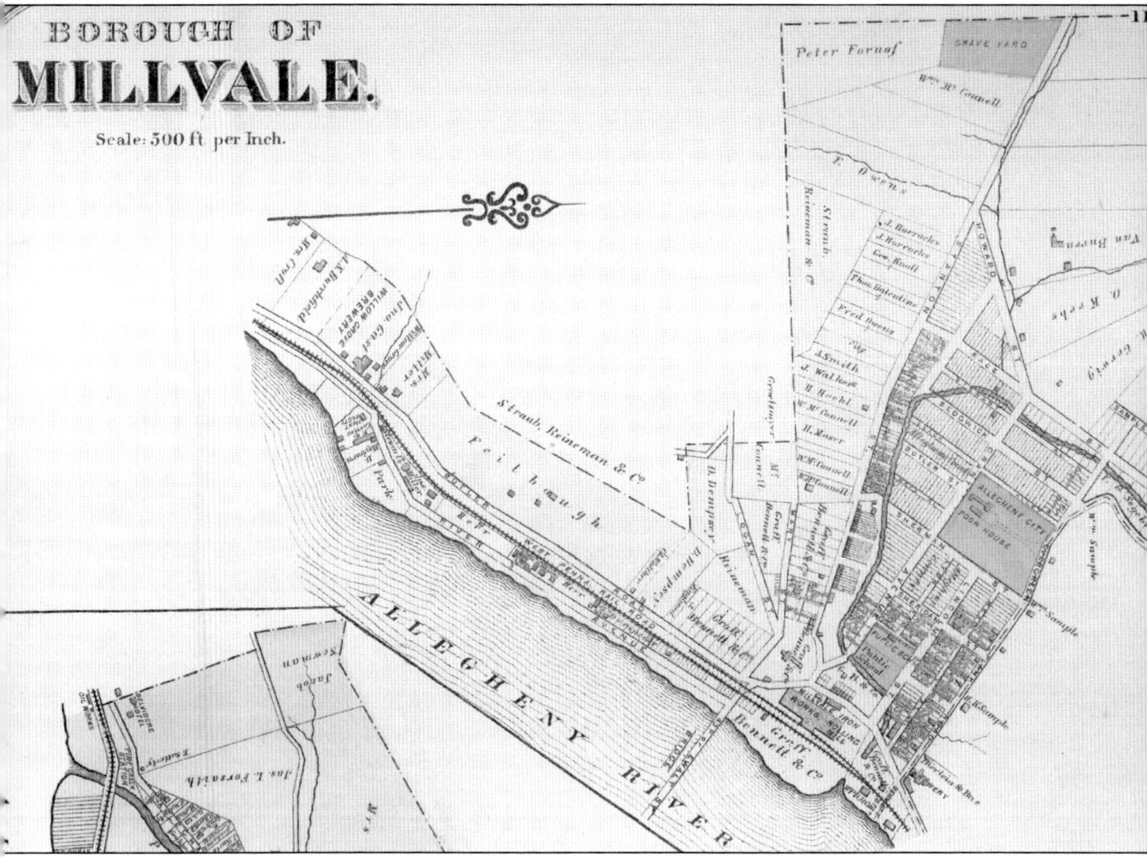

This 1872 G.M. Hopkins map was produced just four years after Millvale's incorporation as a borough. The extent of the Graff, Bennett & Company holdings, evident here, shows how much the town and its population relied on the mill. All three of the town's breweries are also visible: Baeuerlein (Bierlein and Bros.) on Evergreen Plank Road, Willow Grove Brewery on Butler Plank Road, and Hoehl Brewery on Stanton Avenue. Plank roads were actually roads lined with wooden planks to make horse and wagon travel easier, though the wood deteriorated quickly in bad weather. The present-day North Avenue is here named Race Street, and Allegheny City's poor farm spans a large section of town. (G.M. Hopkins Company Maps, 1872–1940, Archives Service Center, University of Pittsburgh.)

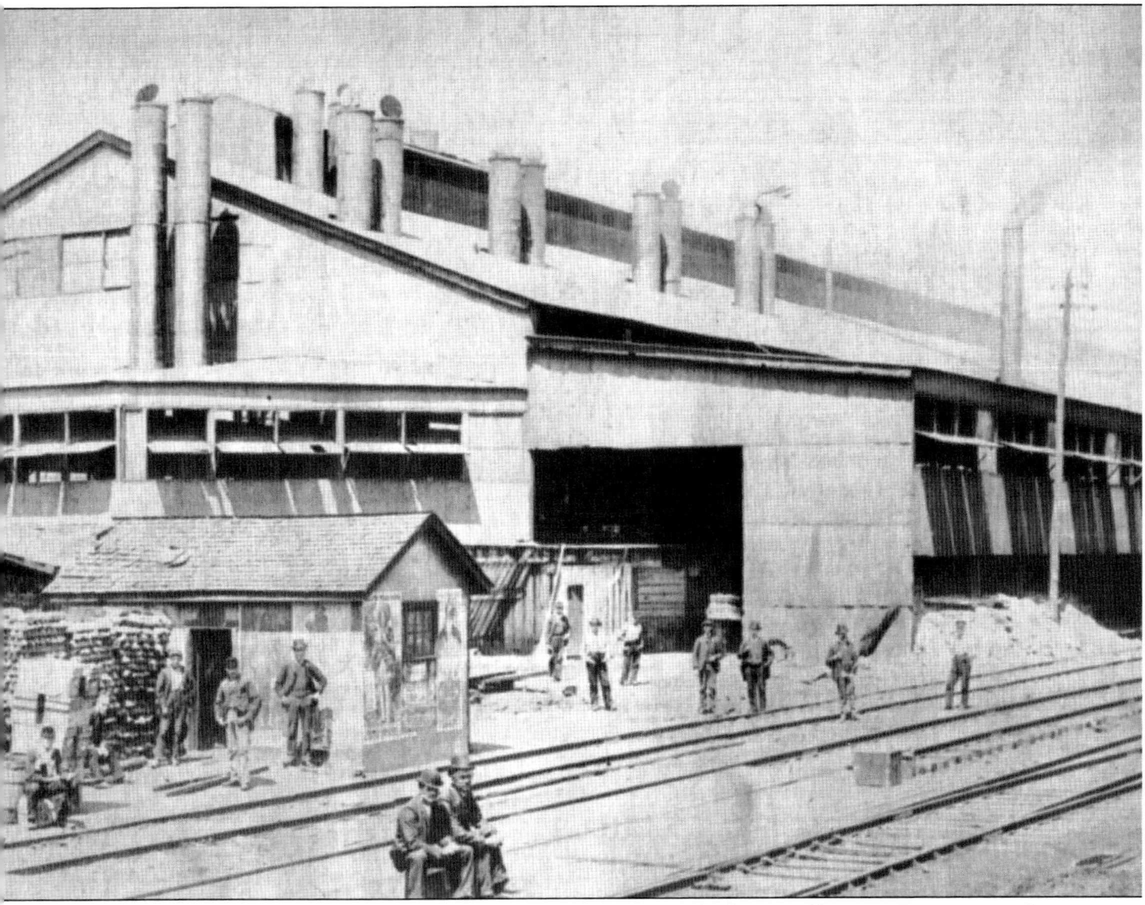

The Millvale Rolling Mill was part of the industrial holdings of John Graff, James Bennett, and Robert Marshall, which also included the Clinton Mill and Furnace on Pittsburgh's Southside and an interest in the Isabella Furnace in Etna. The iron mill of Graff, Bennett & Company was the "mill in the valley" for which Millvale was named in 1868. The mill was modernized over time, becoming one of the first to use natural gas instead of coal. On December 11, 1881, the mill was totally destroyed by fire, but it was rebuilt and expanded. It was Millvale's largest employer for 25 years. After declaring bankruptcy, the Millvale Rolling Mill and the Clinton Mill and Furnace were sold at auction. The purchasers were a syndicate of its creditors, including James Friend, James Bailey, and James Pickand. Judge John Bailey, brother of James, was appointed as trustee during the liquidation. Accusations of fraud and duplicity arose during Judge Bailey's later run for mayor of Pittsburgh. (Jean Domico.)

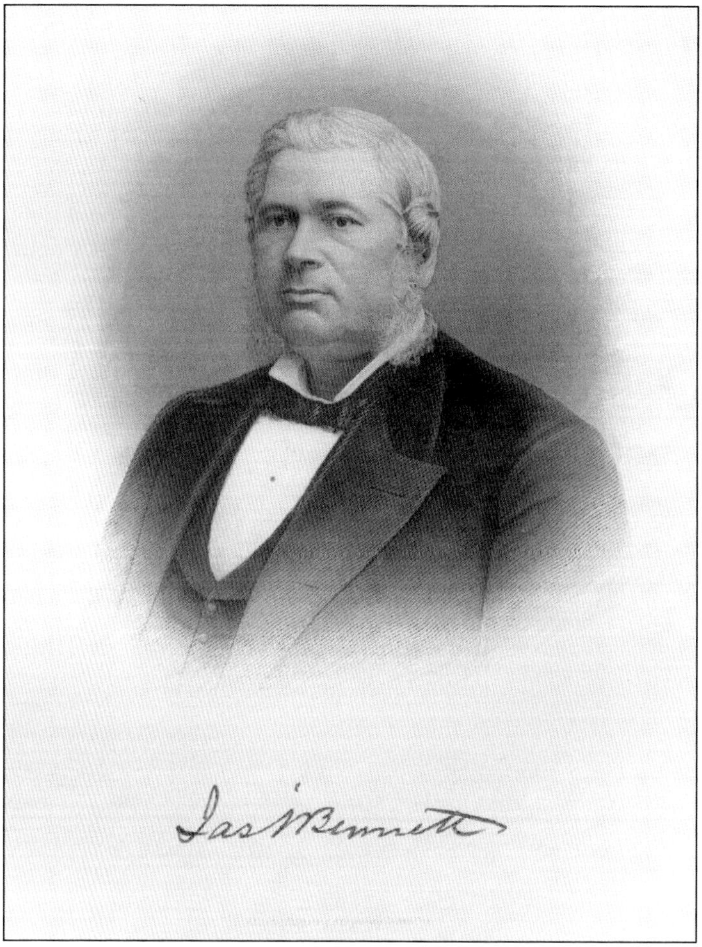

James Israel Bennett advanced from a clerkship in a Pittsburgh grocery store to become a Pennsylvania iron master, then president and director of railroads, foundries, banks, and other institutions, including the Ewalt Bridge Company. With John Graff and Robert Marshall, Bennett owned and operated the Millvale Rolling Mill, which they substantially expanded and improved until 1888, when expenses outstripped income, resulting in the firm's bankruptcy. (Heinz History Center.)

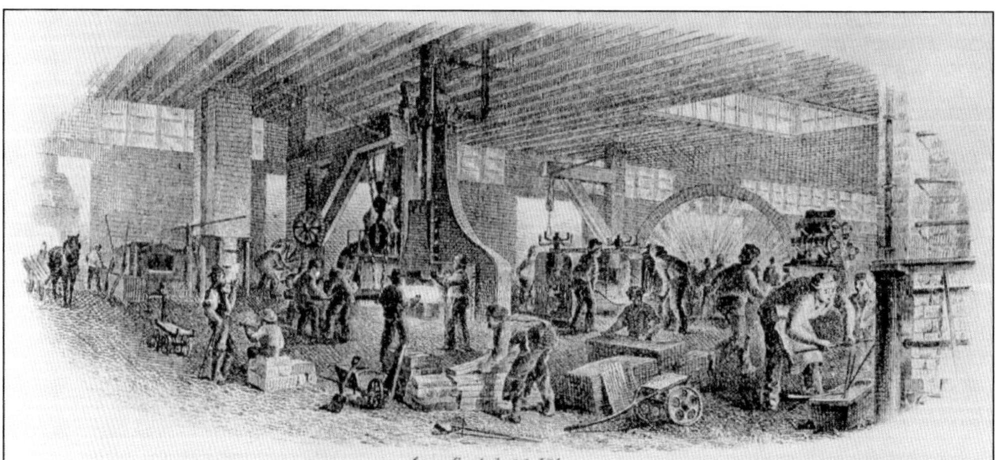

The Millvale Rolling Mill, owned by Graff, Bennett & Company, manufactured iron rods, sheet, plate, and nails, initially using a process like that depicted here. Red-hot iron puddled balls (blooms) were shaped into bars and ultimately into plates by successive passes through the roughing and finishing rollers. (Carnegie Library.)

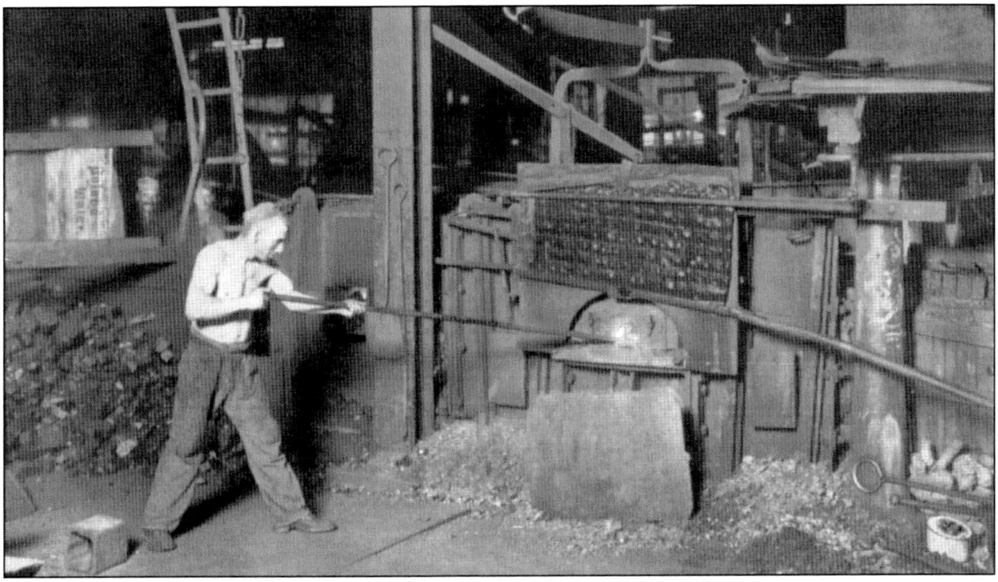

Puddling, the process of making wrought iron from pig iron by heating and stirring it in the presence of oxidizing agents, was more art than science and required the skill of an experienced puddler. Graff, Bennett & Company was one of a few American mills to successfully use Danks mechanical puddling furnaces, thus reducing its reliance on skilled labor. (Rivers of Steel National Heritage Area.)

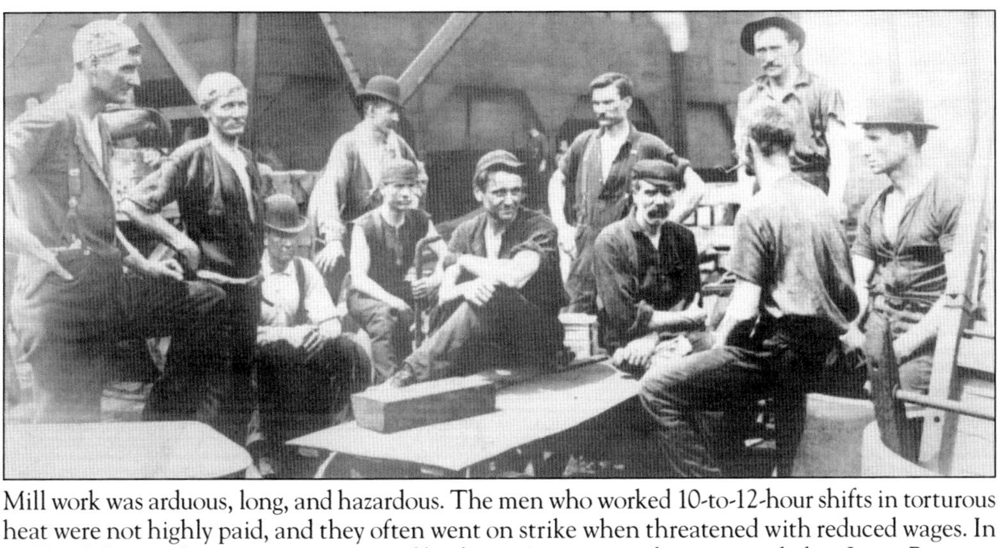

Mill work was arduous, long, and hazardous. The men who worked 10-to-12-hour shifts in torturous heat were not highly paid, and they often went on strike when threatened with reduced wages. In 1865, a sliding-scale agreement was signed by the city's iron manufacturers, including James Bennett, that kept the mills running for almost 10 years without a major strike. (Carol Szwedko.)

1868-1916

64 PLATE MILLS IN 48 YEARS—ONE EVERY NINE MONTHS

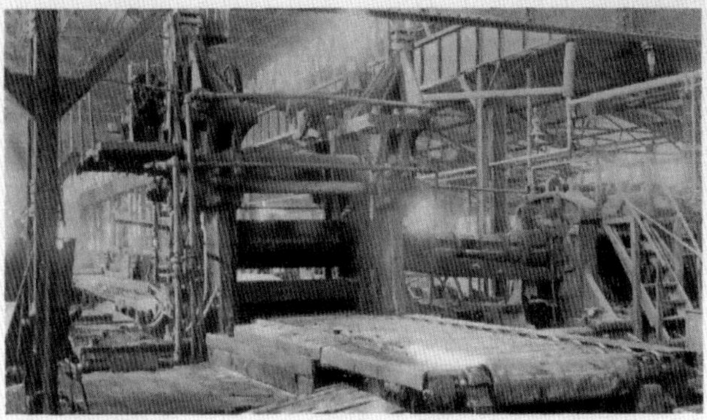

Year	Company
1868	Singer-Nimick & Co.
1871	Wyandotte Rolling Mill Co.
1872	Graff Bennett & Co.
1872	Graff Bennett & Co.
1873	Bay State Iron Co.
1873	Graff Bennett & Co.
1874	Union Iron Co.
1874	Bay State Iron Co.
1875	Lewis Bailey, Dalzel & Co.
1876	Pembroke Iron Co.
1877	Central Iron Works
1877	Pottstown Iron Co.
1879	Chonteau, Harrison & Valle
1879	Chonteau, Harrison & Valle
1879	Naylor & Co.
1880	Oliver Brothers & Phillips
1880	Singer-Nimick & Co.
1880	Cincinnati Rolling Mill Co.
1881	Shoenberger & Co.
1881	Hussey, Howe & Co.
1881	Moorhead & Co.
1881	Central Iron Works
1881	Huston & Penrose Co.
1882	Spang Steel and Iron Co.
1882	Patterson Iron Co.
1882	Springfield Iron Co.
1882	Republic Iron Works
1883	Maunee Rolling Mill Co.
1883	Pottstown Iron Co.
1883	Republic Iron Works
1883	Park Brothers & Co.
1884	Linden Steel Co.
1885	Singer-Nimick & Co.
1886	Chester Rolling Mills
1887	Bessemer Rolling Mill Co.
1888	National Rolling Mills Co.
1889	Birmingham Rolling Mill Co.—Republic Iron and Steel Co.
1889	Chas. Huston & Sons
1889	Carbon Steel Co.
1889	Paxton (Central Iron and Steel Co.)
1889	Moorhead, McCleane Co.
1890	Illinois Steel Co.
1890	Chester Rolling Mills
1890	Wellman Iron and Steel Co.
1890	West Superior Iron and Steel Co.
1891	McCormick & Co.
1892	Carnegie Steel Co.
1893	Nova Scotia Steel and Forge Co.
1894	Birmingham Rolling Mill Co.—Republic Iron and Steel Co.
1894	Shoenberger & Co.
1895	Worth Brothers Co.
1895	Bethlehem Steel Co.
1899	Lukens Iron and Steel Co.
1900	Spang, Chalfant & Co.
1901	Lukens Iron and Steel Co.
1902	Chrome Steel Works
1902	Moorehead Brothers & Co.
1903	Lorain Steel Co.
1903	National Tube Co.
1903	Carnegie Steel Co.
1905	Colonial Steel Co.
1905	Portsmouth Steel Co.
1910	A. M. Byers Co.
1916	Societe Anonyme Accearierie Ferriere, Lombarde of Milan

Just think for a moment of the tremendous tonnage of products these Mills have rolled, and will roll, for ships, cars, tanks, stacks, boilers, bridges, buildings, automobiles, etc., etc.

These Mills have done their share of the World's Work

From its warehouse in Pittsburgh, Graff, Bennett & Company sold commercial iron products. The Millvale mill produced nails early on, but its later products were specially crafted iron pipe and sheets. While the largest and finest universal mill in America was that of Andrew Carnegie and Andrew Kloman, the second-largest universal mill was at Graff, Bennett & Company's Millvale works. It operated with reversing engines and automatic rollers for carrying the bloom to and from the rolls. This equipment was used for rolling Danks furnace blooms, about 1,000 pounds each, into bars for subsequent rolling into thinner bars and plates. For the Centennial Exposition of 1876 in Philadelphia, Graff, Bennett & Company displayed iron that had been rolled 1/3,000 of an inch thick, along with an iron ball weighing 2,034 pounds, a bloom weighing 1,914 pounds, and two pieces of muck bar (iron that had been through the rolls only once) weighing 1,660 pounds. The iron from which these specimens were made was puddled in the company's Danks furnaces. (Archives Service Center, University of Pittsburgh.)

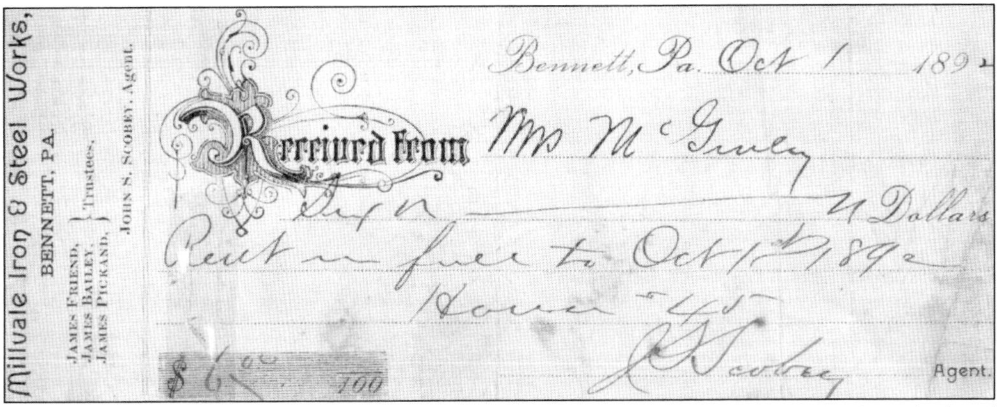
Millvale Iron & Steel Works,
BENNETT, PA.
James Friend, James Bailey, James Pickand, } Trustees.
John S. Scobey, Agent.
Bennett, Pa. Oct 1 1892
Received from Mrs McGinley
Eight ——— Dollars
Rent in full to Oct 1st 1892
House 45
$ 6 00/100
J S Scobey Agent.

Graff, Bennett & Company built housing for its skilled mill workers. After the firm declared bankruptcy, the Millvale Iron & Steel Works, under its trustees James Friend, James Bailey, and James Pickand, continued to rent these houses, as illustrated by this receipt for rent paid by a Mrs. McGinley in 1892. Some of these mill houses can still be seen on Stanton Avenue. (Jean Domico.)

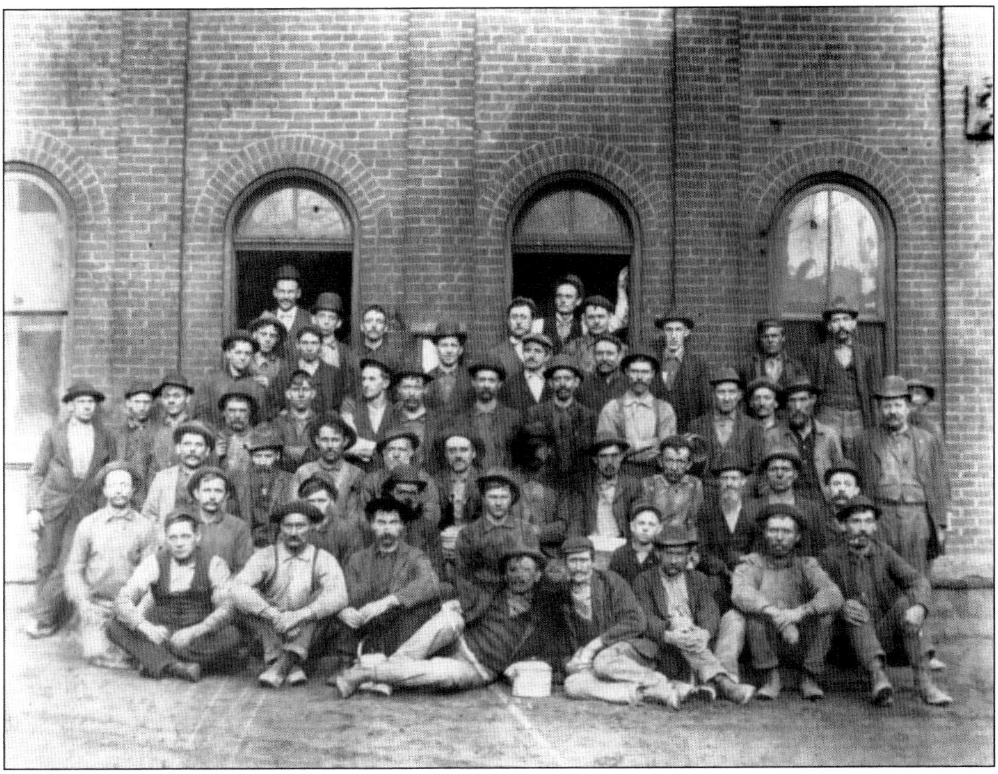

Working long hours for low wages, mill men, like those seen here, formed a labor union called Amalgamated Association of Iron and Steel Workers in 1876. Though the Iron City Forge of the Sons of Vulcan was the first labor union organized in Pittsburgh, it represented only puddlers, the highest paid and most skilled mill workers. Amalgamated, made infamous by the Homestead Strike, represented all workers. (Rivers of Steel National Heritage Area.)

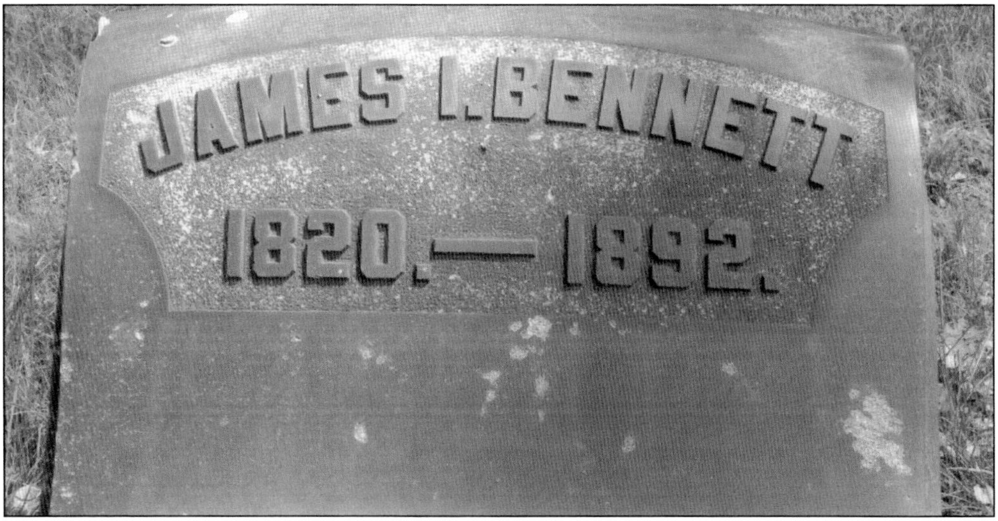

While James Bennett was at one time a millionaire and the recognized head of one of the largest and most solid iron-manufacturing firms, his gravestone in Allegheny Cemetery emphasizes his humble Protestant beginnings. During the Civil War, Bennett took an active interest in the welfare of soldiers and was a prominent worker for the Pittsburgh Sanitary Fair. Until his death, he maintained interest in business and charities. (Bill Stout.)

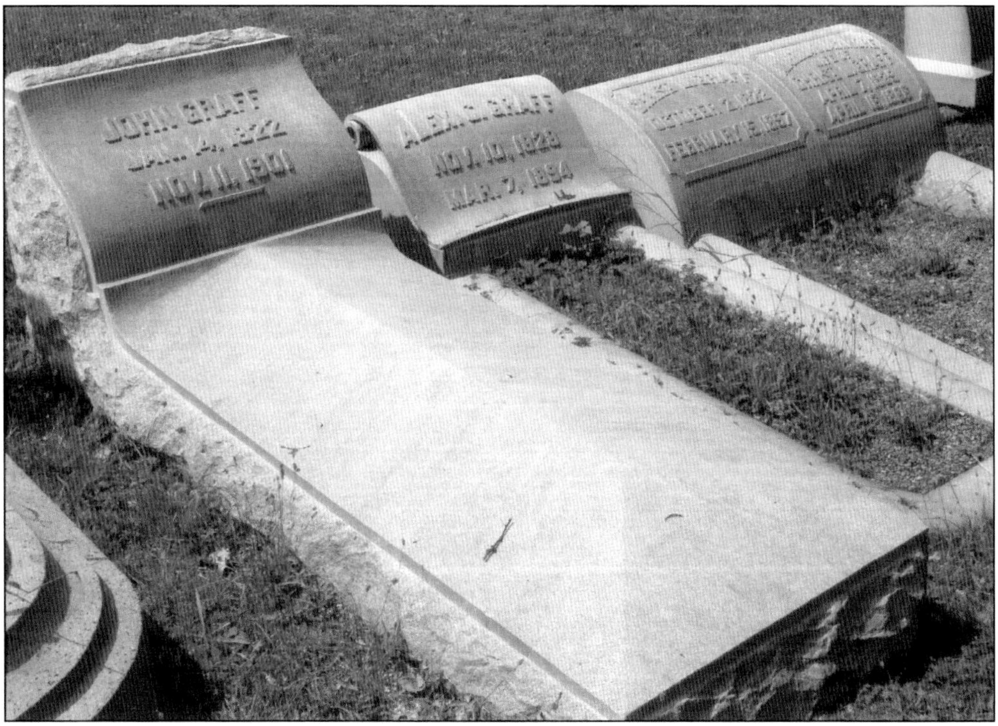

Henry Graff and his sons John, Matthew, Thomas, and Christopher were prominent in Pittsburgh's iron industry. After Henry's death, John took over the Clinton Rolling Mill, taking in James Bennett as a partner. They later owned the Millvale mill. Thomas organized Graff, Hugus & Company, stove manufacturers. Matthew was a partner in the Graff & Woods Rolling Mill, Christopher in the Pennsylvania Iron Works. (Bill Stout.)

Two

Birth of a Borough

The Borough of Millvale was incorporated by an Act of Assembly on February 13, 1868. It comprised a portion of Shaler Township and that part of the Borough of Duquesne not included in the limits of Allegheny City set by the Act of Consolidation on March 12, 1867. Its governing structure was a burgess and town council. The Graff, Bennett & Company mill played an important role in the town's development; after all, the mill provided most of the town's employment and the houses for some of its workers. The area was known as Bennett, Pennsylvania, before and even after its incorporation, as can be seen in advertisements of the day. The first post office was called Bennett Post Office, and the town's first fire department was organized and equipped by the mill. The man serving as burgess for two terms from 1868 to 1878 may have been John I. Williams, supervisor of the mill.

However, little by little, the town grew on its own, aided, of course, by the new Forty-third Street Bridge over the Allegheny River, improved roads, and rail transportation. Then, in 1888, the mill went bankrupt, and although it struggled on intermittently for years as the Millvale Iron & Steel Works, it was no longer closely tied to the town's identity. More and more businesses, needing room to expand, moved to Millvale. Among those firms were McDowell Manufacturing Company, the Penn Saw Works of E.T. Lippert, and the Standard Box & Lumber Company of George Loeffert and Son. Workers and their families followed, and Millvale became a pleasant town in which to live, with its own water and electric power company. The town's population grew, and, with it, newer and bigger churches and schools were built. Then, in 1893, the Third Ward was annexed from Shaler Township, thus enlarging Millvale to its present size of 0.625 square miles.

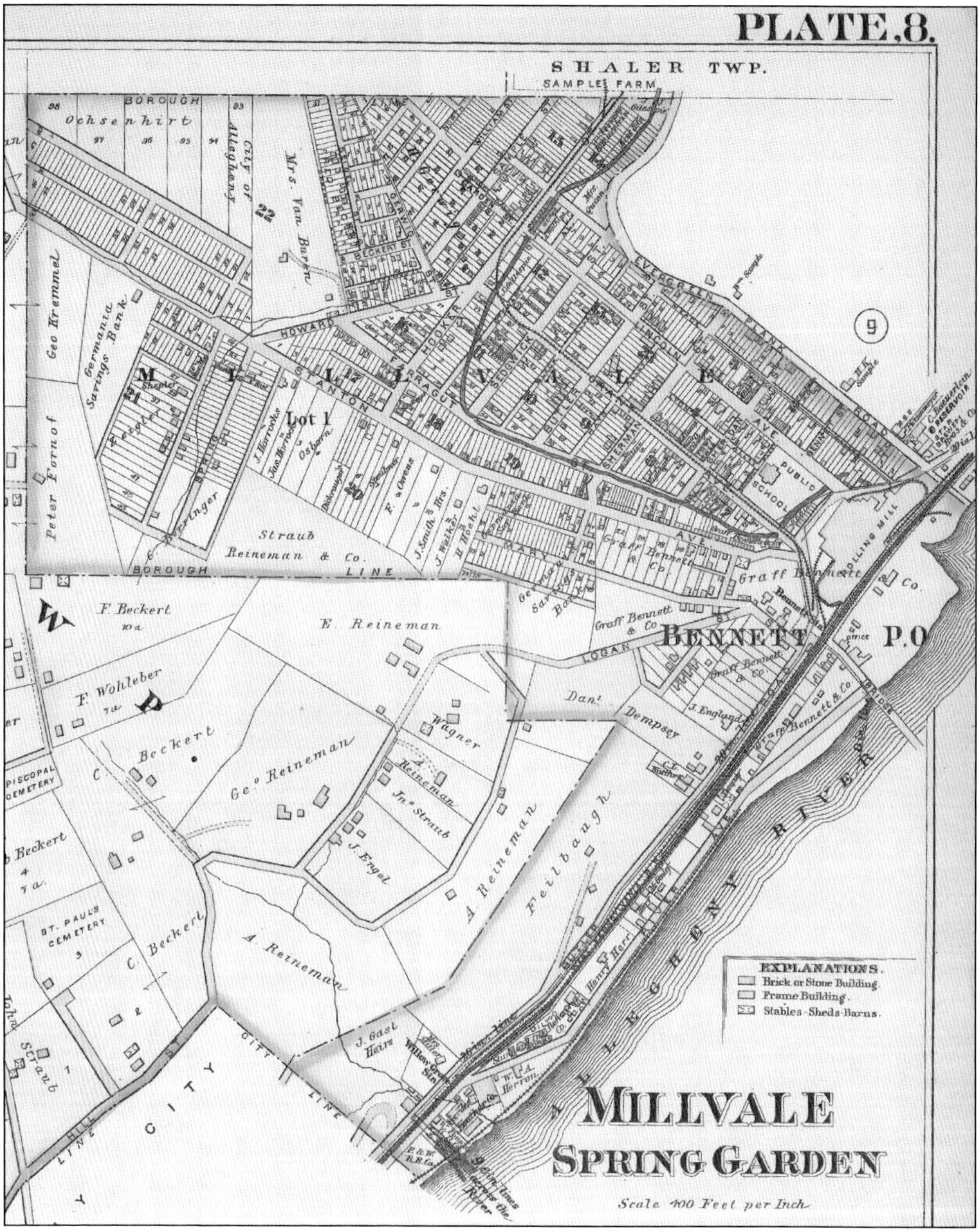

This 1886 G.M. Hopkins map illustrates how much Millvale changed in less than 20 years since its incorporation. Allegheny City's poor farm has been divided into streets and lots. Lincoln Avenue goes straight through to Hooker Street (now North Avenue). More and more people are moving to the town and building frame houses. While the Graff, Bennett & Company mill still maintains a huge presence in the town, small businesses are cropping up, like the Walker Rope Factory, the Watkins Apple Butter Company, and the Baeuerlein Foundry. A narrow-gauge railway runs along Grant and Hooker Streets to Evergreen Hamlet, providing transportation to Millvale and beyond. (G.M. Hopkins Company Maps, 1872–1940, Archives Service Center, University of Pittsburgh.)

AN ORDINANCE

Authorizing the Directors of the Poor to sell certain lots in Old Poor Farm Plan, and make deeds for the same.

SECTION 1. Be it ordained and enacted by the Select and Common Councils of the City of Allegheny, and it is hereby ordained and enacted by authority of the same, That the Directors of the Poor be and they are hereby authorized to sell the following lots in the Old Poor Farm plan, and make deeds for the same, viz.: Lots Nos. 1 and 2, block 10, to Mrs. Margaret Madden, for three hundred and fifty ($350) dollars.

SEC. 2. That so much of any ordinance as may conflict with or be supplied by the foregoing be and the same is hereby repealed.

Ordained and enacted into a law, in Councils, this 22d day of May, A. D. 1883.

In 1866, due to the increasing number of its indigents and the expansion of its boundaries, Allegheny City secured another location and moved its poor farm to Claremont Station (near Blawnox). The Millvale property was laid out into streets and lots; the first sale occurred on September 4, 1867. Each sale required an ordinance be approved by Allegheny City, as shown here. (Archives Service Center, University of Pittsburgh.)

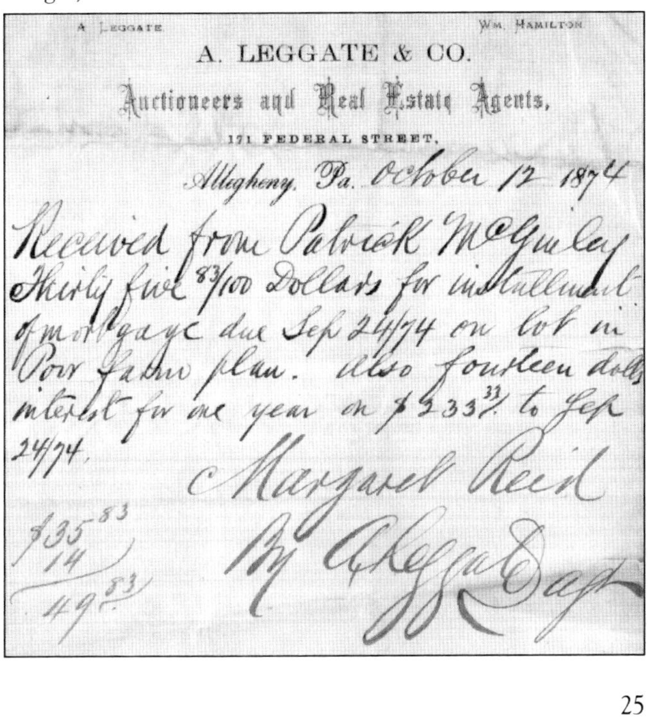
A. LEGGATE WM. HAMILTON
A. LEGGATE & CO.
Auctioneers and Real Estate Agents,
171 FEDERAL STREET.
Allegheny, Pa. October 12 1874
Received from Patrick McGuley Thirty five 83/100 Dollars for installment of mortgage due Sep 24/74 on Lot in Poor farm plan. Also fourteen dolls interest for one year on $233 33/ to Sep 24/74.
Margaret Reid
By A Leggate & Co
$35.83
14
49.83

This receipt, dated October 12, 1874, records the payment of $35 plus $14 annual interest on a lot in the poor farm plan. By the time the last lot was sold in 1875, Allegheny City had realized $292,393.72 on the original purchase price of $12,000 paid to John Sample. (Jean Domico.)

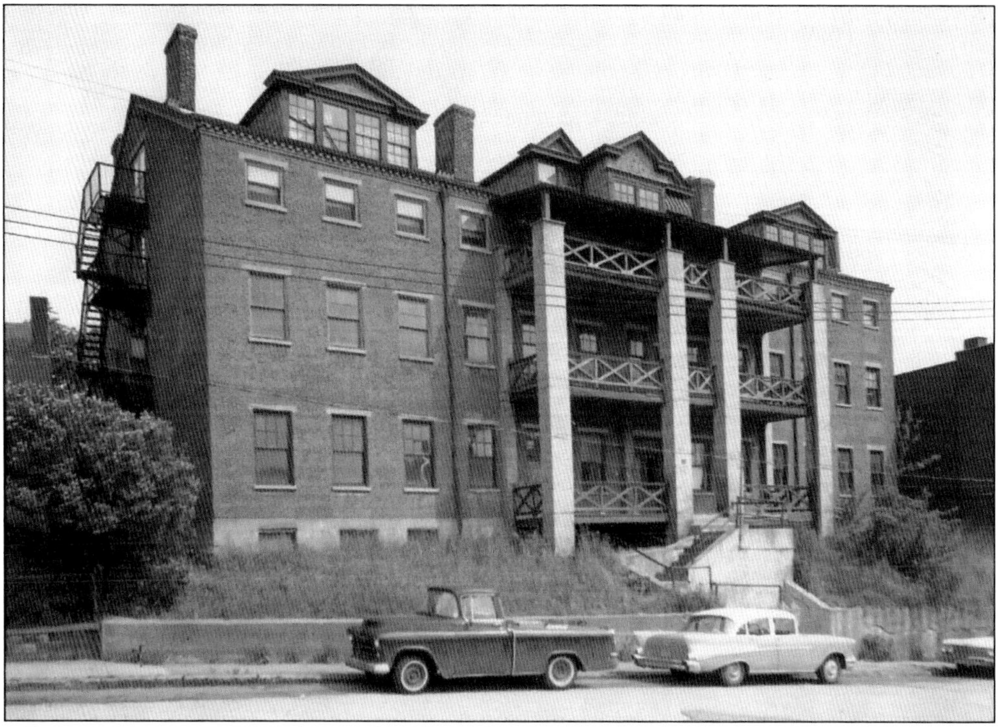

Allegheny City, now Pittsburgh's North Side, purchased 166 acres from John Sample's farm on Girty's Run in 1844 for a poor farm to provide work and housing for its indigents. The cost of the land was $12,000. Renovated over the years, the building shown here, now the Chrismar Apartments, is one of the few remaining structures built as part of the poor farm. (Jennifer Cohen.)

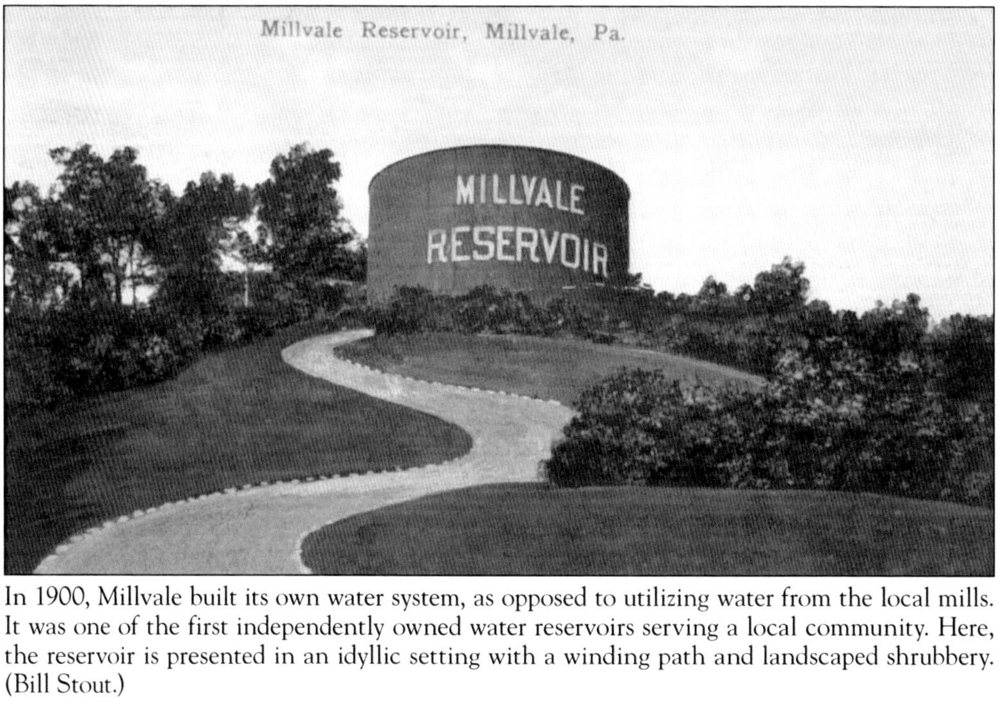

In 1900, Millvale built its own water system, as opposed to utilizing water from the local mills. It was one of the first independently owned water reservoirs serving a local community. Here, the reservoir is presented in an idyllic setting with a winding path and landscaped shrubbery. (Bill Stout.)

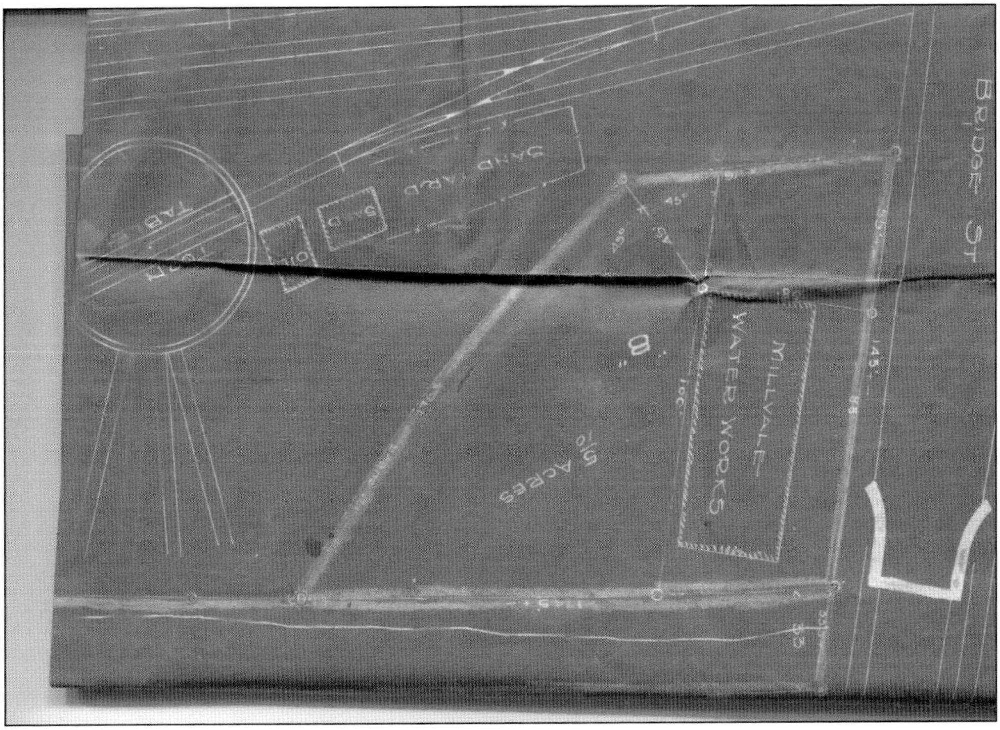

In 1894, Millvale purchased a pump house and water lines from Baeuerlein Brewing Company. The pump house, on the Allegheny River, afforded excellent filtered water for its residents. Less than 10 years later, Millvale was the first borough to own its own water plant, which was adjacent to Bridge Street, as shown by these blueprints dated June 6, 1903. (Millvale Borough.)

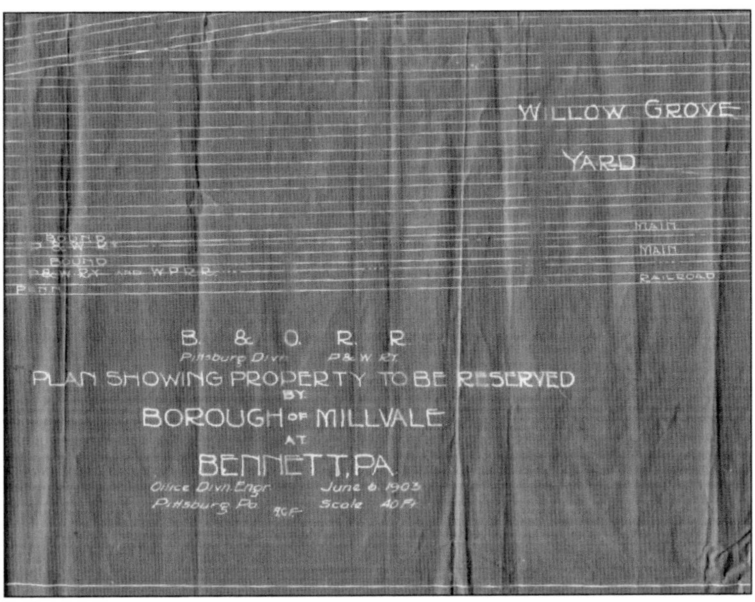

Willow Grove was the name of the station on the Baltimore & Ohio (B&O) Railroad at the boundary of Millvale and Duquesne Boroughs, near the end of Herr's Island. Willow Grove would give its name to the brewery operated by the Gast Brothers in 1866 and the Enz Brewing Company in the 1880s. (Millvale Borough.)

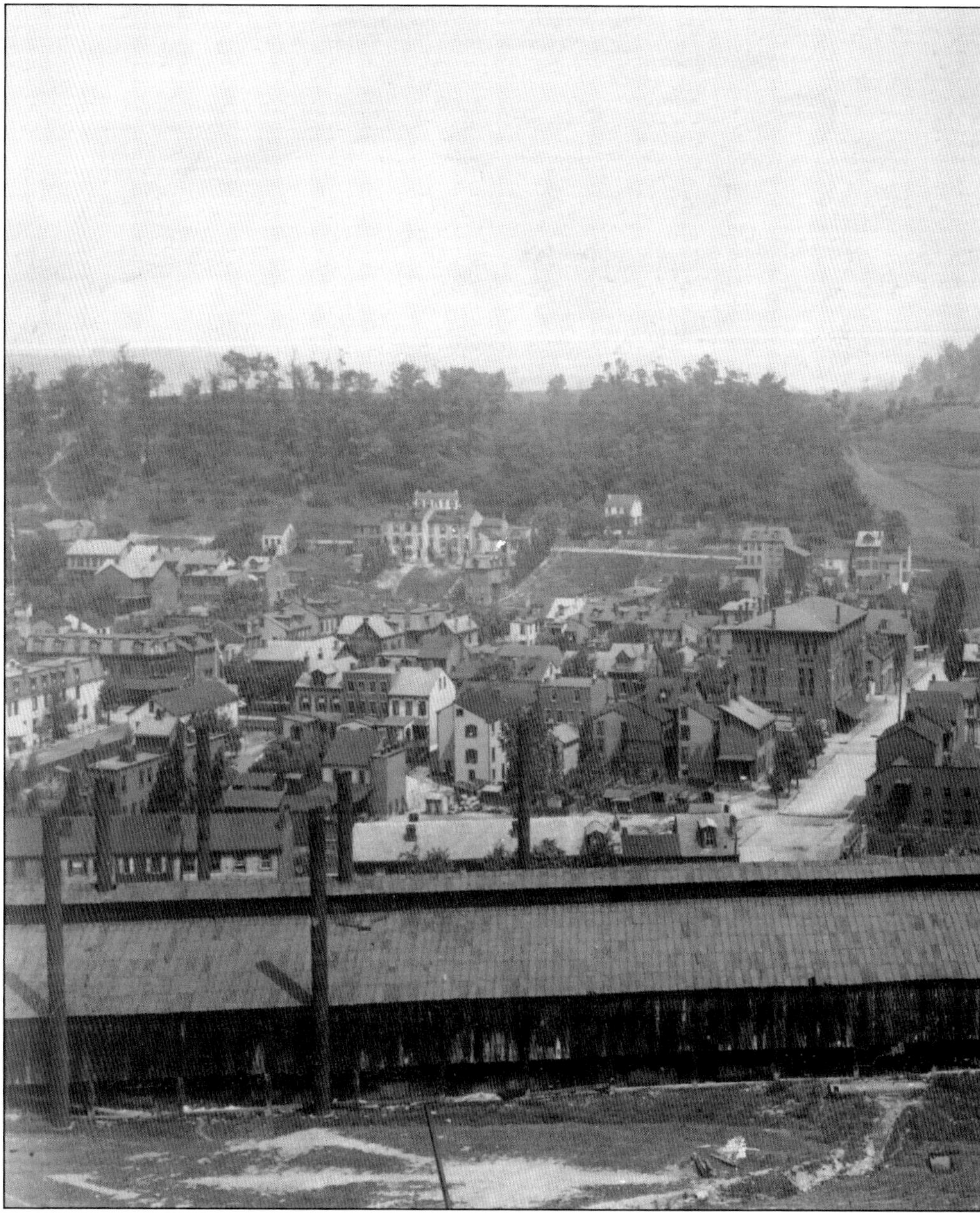

Looming large along Stanton Avenue in the foreground of this photograph is McDowell Manufacturing, which moved to Millvale in the early 1900s to expand its operations. From 1901 to 1912, McDowell was one of the prime producers of stampings for the telephone industry. The product line was later expanded to include bases and housings for electric fans and casings for car-starter batteries. In 1916, fire destroyed the McDowell plant, but it was rebuilt as a fireproof, concrete building. Despite the fire, McDowell was one of the largest producers of booster casings for shells during World War I. After the war, McDowell expanded and began manufacturing simple, yet high-quality, steel toys, like the clockwork Loop the Loop and the Mac Mystery Gun. During World War II, the firm made shipping bands for bombs, fins for fragmentation bombs, parts for ammunition boxes, lug bands for rockets, and it did machining on 1,000-pound bombs and 4-pound butterfly bombs. (Richard Mikus.)

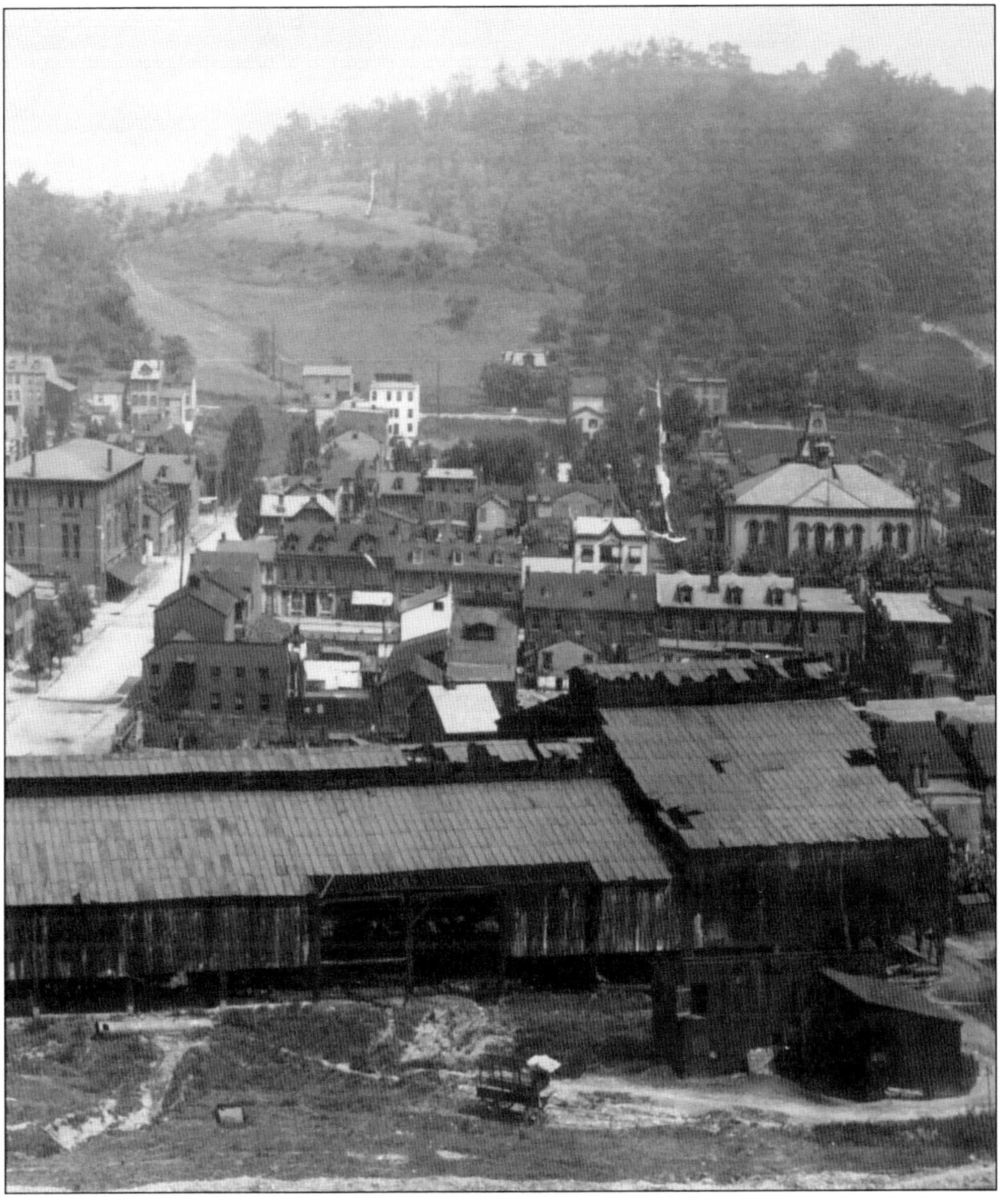

In a newspaper article published in the *Pittsburg Leader* in April 1904, Millvale is described as one of the thriving, sober, and industrious boroughs in the Greater Pittsburgh district. To the author, the pressed-brick houses presented a uniform neatness and evidence of comfort and a modicum of taste and refinement. There was scant evidence of riches or luxury, for in Millvale there were no millionaires. The bulk of the citizenry were wage earners. During the late 1890s and early 1900s, Millvale was much modernized. The main streets—Grant Avenue, Butler Street, North Avenue, and Evergreen Avenue—were paved and sewers were installed. Most notable to the article's author is the town's comparatively deserted appearance during the day. The explanation for this lies in the fact that two-thirds of the inhabitants worked elsewhere in Pittsburgh and Allegheny. From 5:30 p.m. onward, trolley cars poured in hundreds of people from the city. At 8:00 p.m., Millvale became a busy, lively place. Its streets were alive with people and its stores brilliant with electric bulbs. (Richard Mikus.)

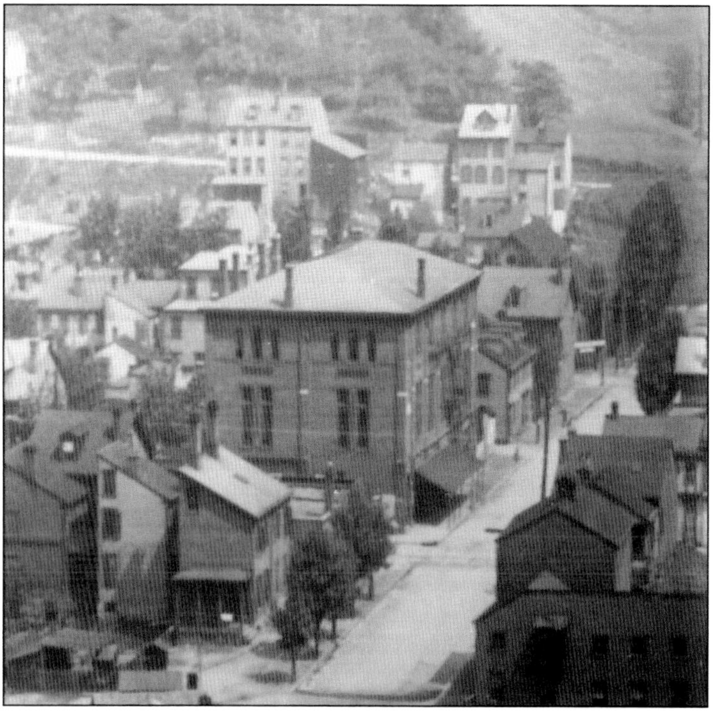

The Opera House, an impressive, four-story brick building decorated with pilasters, stood along Sheridan Street at Grant Avenue. It was originally Millvale's town hall. The first floor held a variety of businesses, including the Mannequin Club; the second floor was a double-height auditorium; and the fourth floor held borough offices. In its last years, the building was used as a cold-storage plant. It was demolished in 1969. (Richard Mikus.)

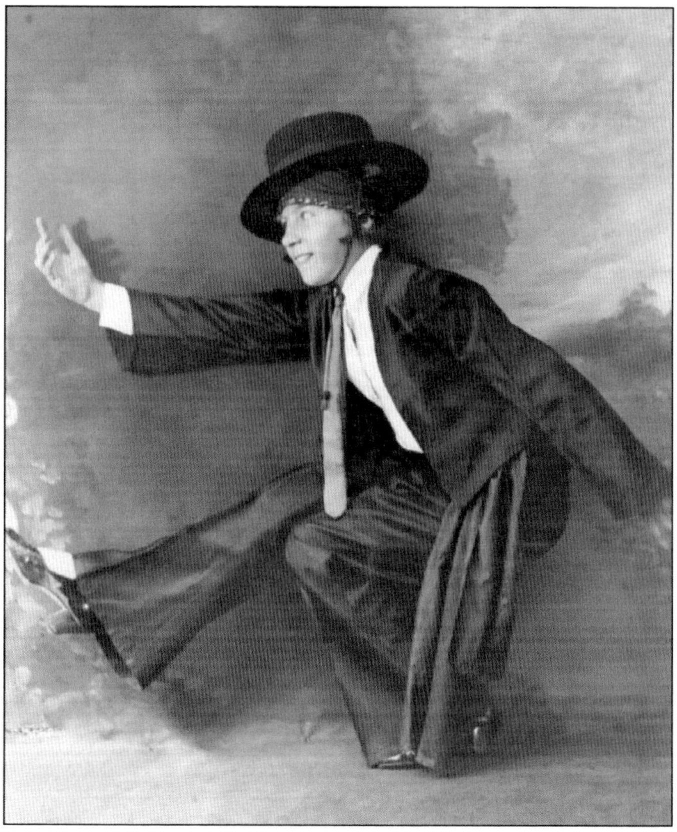

Seen here in Spanish costume, Catherine Voit (later Cinski), age 13, was a dancer at the Opera House, where Millvale's citizens came to be entertained. The second floor auditorium was used for plays, dances, operas, and meetings, including church services and high school commencement ceremonies. The Masonic lodge held meetings there until 1910. (Vincent Cinski.)

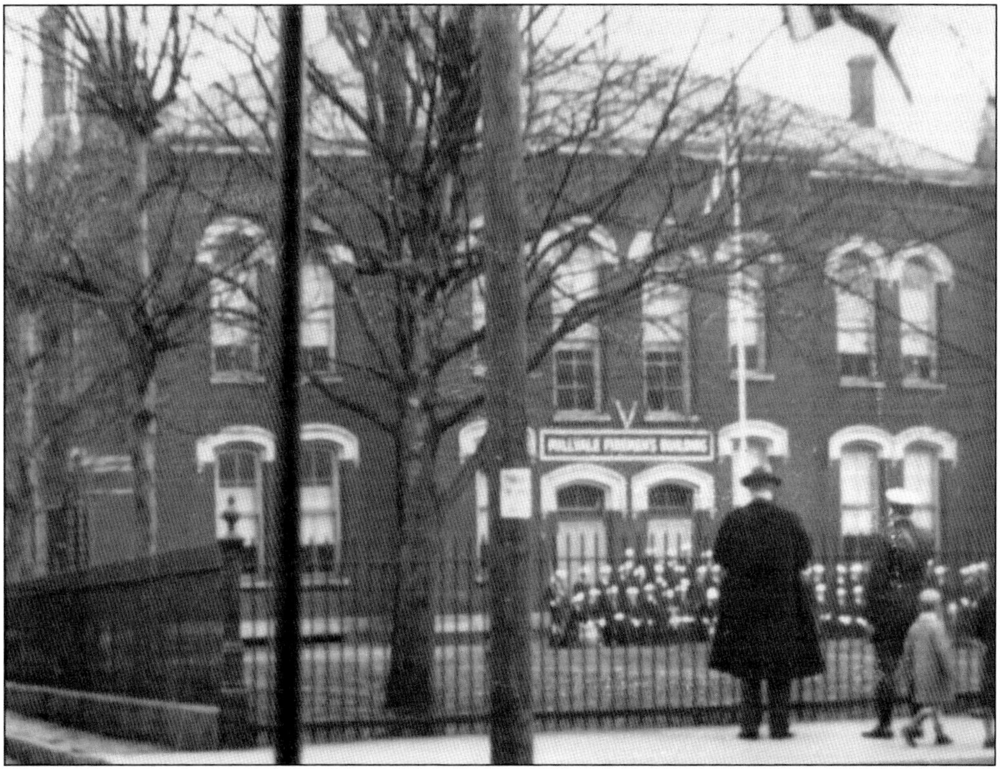

In 1873, Graff, Bennett & Company organized the first fire department, with a horse-drawn fire engine and hose carriage. The service was named the Franklin Fire Company. Records show that its members disbanded in November 1875 and reorganized only in January 1888. The engine house was located on Lincoln Avenue, next to the First Ward School, which was taken over by the Millvale Fire Company in 1938. (Richard Mikus.)

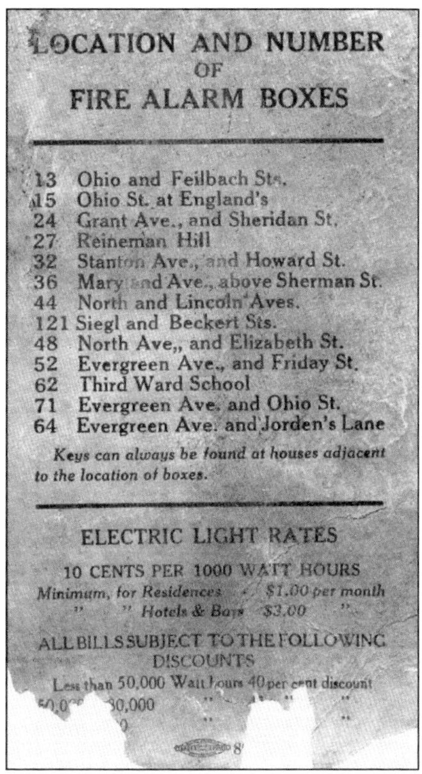

LOCATION AND NUMBER
OF
FIRE ALARM BOXES

13 Ohio and Feilbach Sts.
15 Ohio St. at England's
24 Grant Ave., and Sheridan St.
27 Reineman Hill
32 Stanton Ave., and Howard St.
36 Maryland Ave., above Sherman St.
44 North and Lincoln Aves.
121 Siegl and Beckert Sts.
48 North Ave,, and Elizabeth St.
52 Evergreen Ave., and Friday St.
62 Third Ward School
71 Evergreen Ave. and Ohio St.
64 Evergreen Ave. and Jorden's Lane

Keys can always be found at houses adjacent to the location of boxes.

ELECTRIC LIGHT RATES

10 CENTS PER 1000 WATT HOURS
Minimum, for Residences $1.00 *per month*
" " *Hotels & Bars* $3.00 "

ALL BILLS SUBJECT TO THE FOLLOWING DISCOUNTS
Less than 50,000 Watt hours 40 per cent discount
50,0[illegible] 80,000 " " "

In 1906, the fire department finally became the Millvale Volunteer Fire Department. This notice lists the location and number of Millvale's fire alarm boxes. Interestingly enough, the boxes were locked, but keys were available at the houses adjacent to the boxes. At this time, Millvale had its own electric light company, whose rate of 10¢ per 1,000 watt-hours is also included on the notice. (Millvale Borough.)

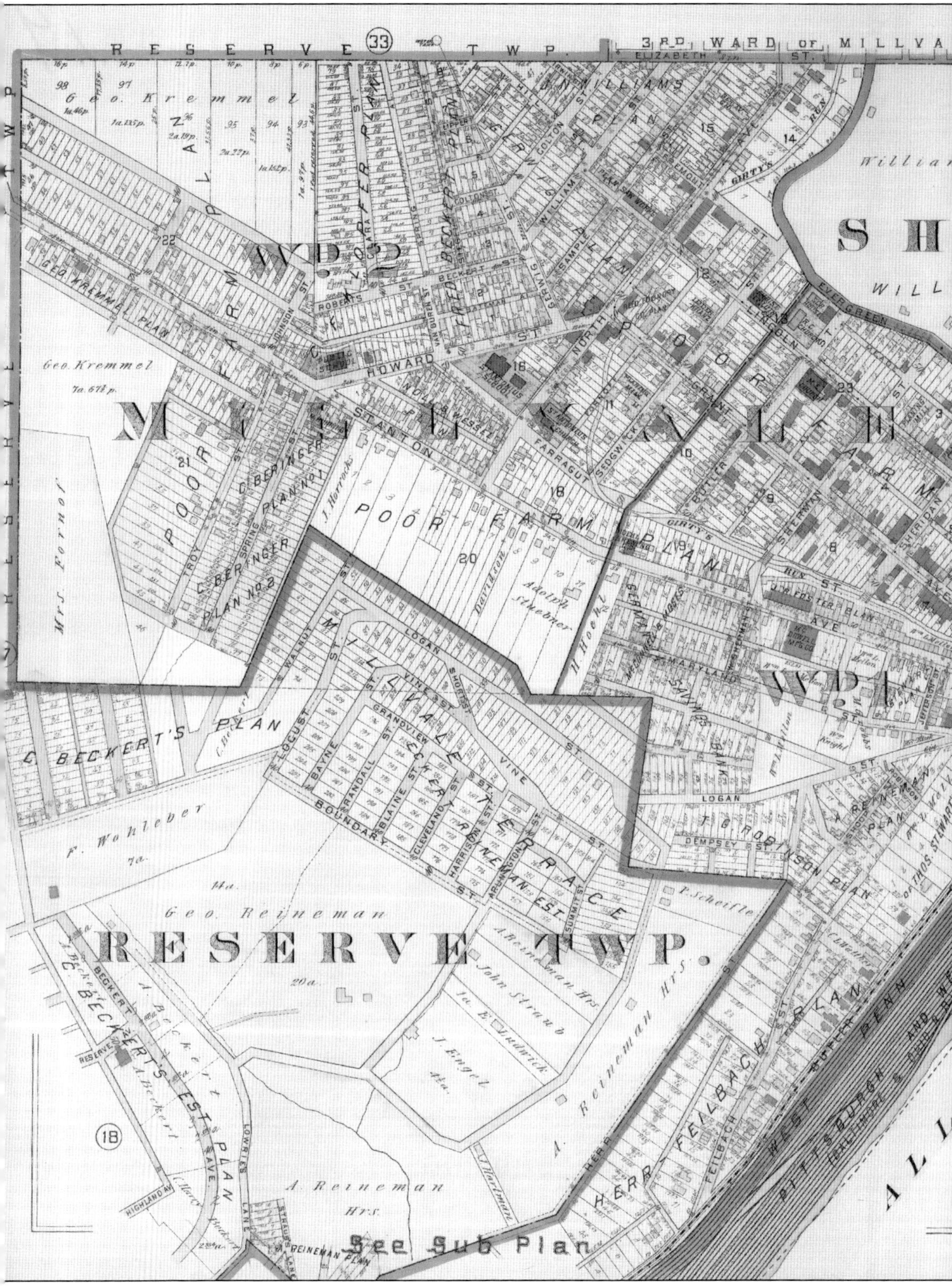
RESERVE TWP.
3RD WARD OF MILLVALE
WD. 2
POOR FARM PLAN
RESERVE TWP.
See Sub Plan
MILLVALE TERRACE
C. BECKERT'S PLAN
ROBINSON PLAN
FELBACH PLAN
HERR
C. BECKERT'S EST. PLAN
Geo. Kremmel
Geo. Reineman
A. Reineman Hrs.
John Straub
P. Wohleber
HOWARD
STANTON
LOGAN
VINE ST.
BOUNDARY ST.
EVERGREEN
LINCOLN
GRANT
FARRAGUT
SHERIDAN
MARYLAND
DEMPSEY ST.
LOWRIES LANE
PITTSBURGH BALTIMORE & OHIO

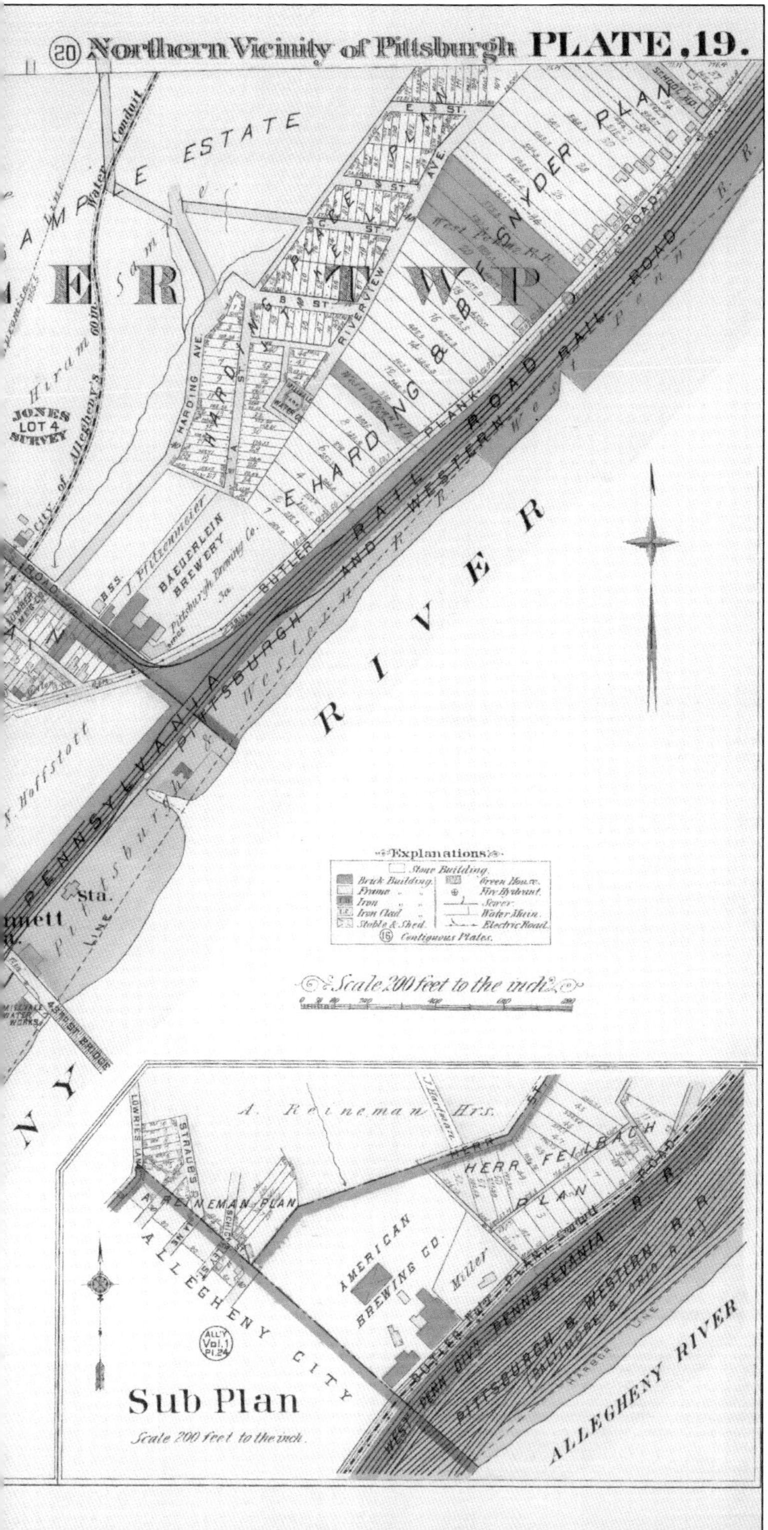

This 1906 G.M. Hopkins map shows housing growth in the First and Second Wards. Though most of the houses are timber, more brick buildings are visible along North Avenue (previously Race and Hooker Streets). There are significant housing plans, such as the Poor Farm Plan, T.G. Robinson Plan, and F. Klopfer Plan. Most obvious, the Graff, Bennett & Company mill is gone, sold to "General" Jacob S. Coxey and moved to Massillon, Ohio. The open space owned by F.N. Hoffstott would later be sold to the Pittsburgh Railways Company and become the site of its carbarn. Besides new businesses, two social organizations, Militar Verein, a Prussian veterans organization, and Franz Abt Leiderkranz, a German singing society, part of the Nord-Amerikanischer Sangerbund, can be seen on the map. (G.M. Hopkins Company Maps, 1872–1940, Archives Service Center, University of Pittsburgh.)

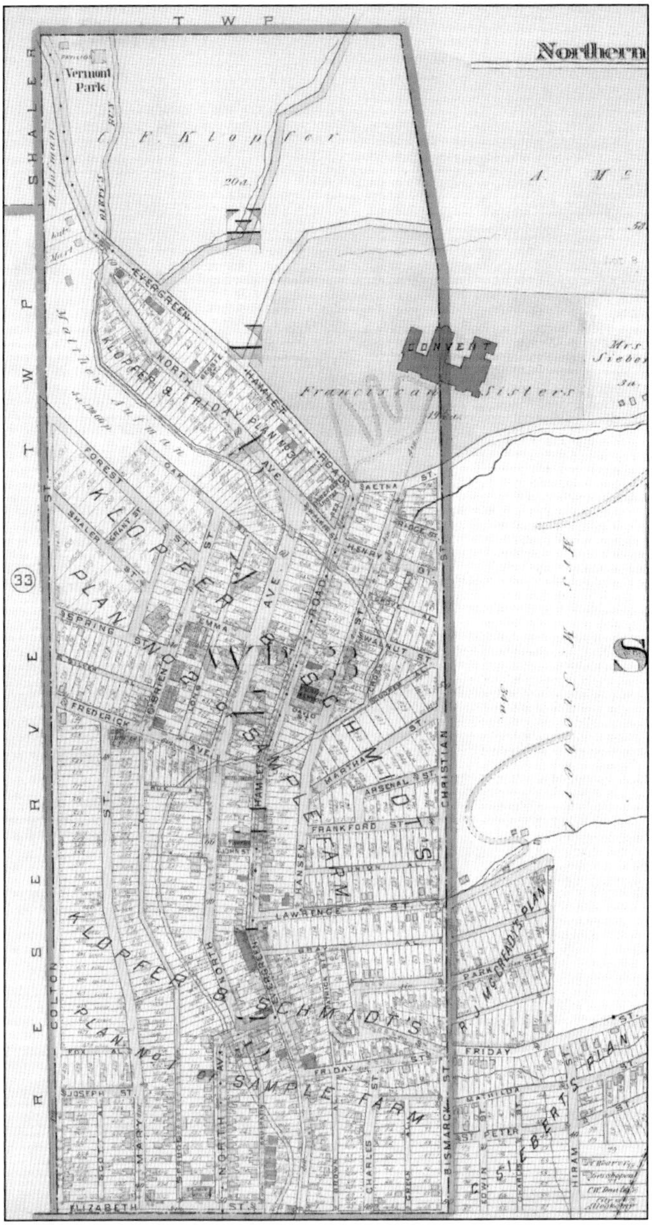

In 1893, the Third Ward was added to the borough from portions of the Sample farm and Shaler Township. It was a thin strip of land, as shown by this 1906 G.M. Hopkins map. Beginning at Elizabeth Street and ending in what today is Bauerstown, the land was developed into residential areas by Klopfer, Friday, and Schmitt. With the addition of the Third Ward, Millvale acquired at least four more hotels, including the Evergreen Hotel, across from Mount Alvernia, and the Hotel Haser, on Evergreen Avenue at Frederick Street. Millvale also gained another church, the German Lutheran Church on Frederick Street, and the public school on Evergreen Avenue. Farming was still a substantial business in the Third Ward, as illustrated by the greenhouses on O'Brien and Long Streets. Way out on North Avenue, there is Vermont Park with its pavilion. Millvale residents could enjoy traveling by trolley through town. (G.M. Hopkins Company Maps, 1872–1940, Archives Service Center, University of Pittsburgh.)

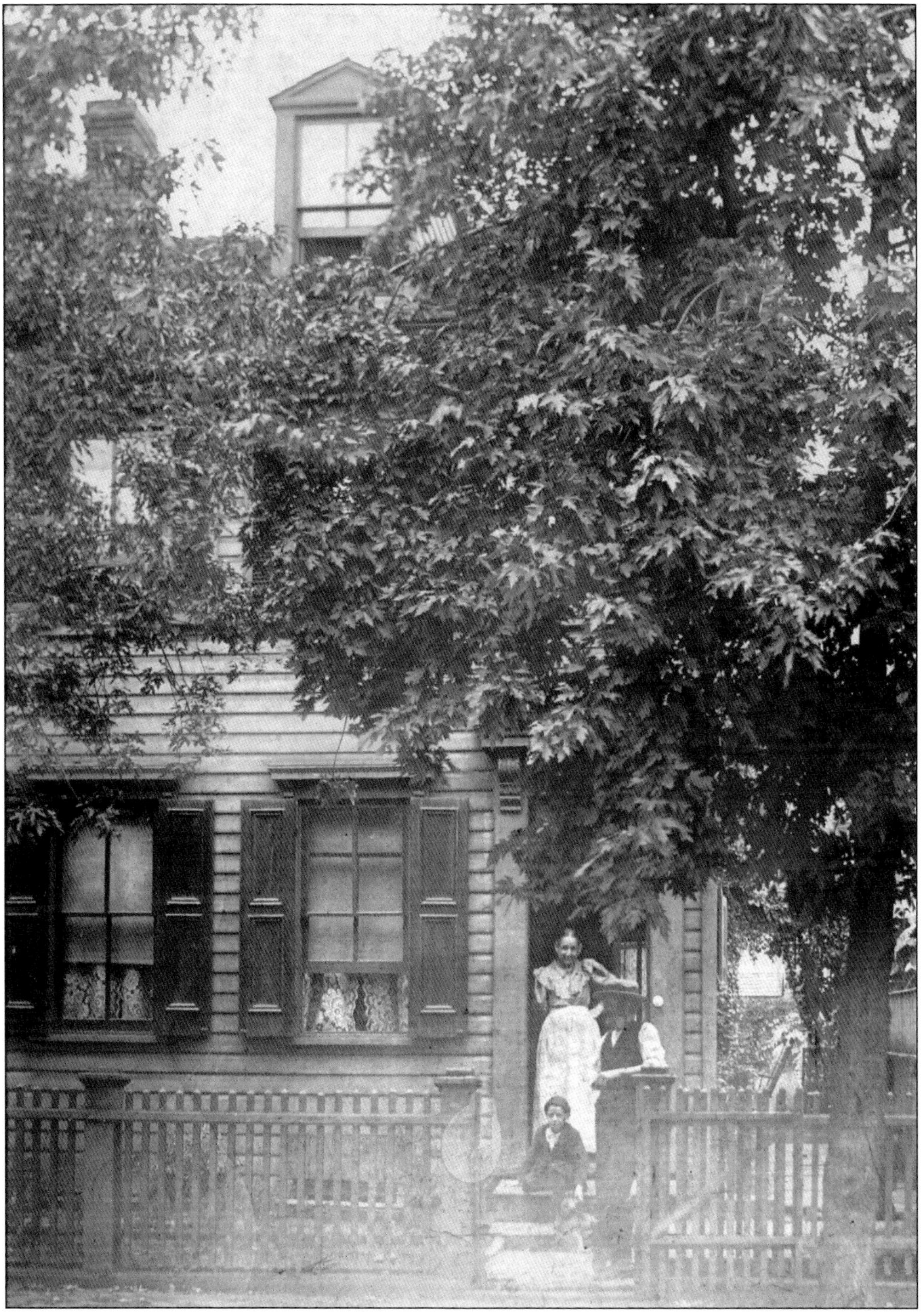

This residence at 120 Lincoln Avenue is a typical two-story frame house with an attic dormer. The lady of the house poses in its open doorway with her child at her feet. The man of the house in his straw hat leans against the front fence post. Shades and lace curtains are visible through the front windows, and huge trees line the walkway. (Jennifer Cohen.)

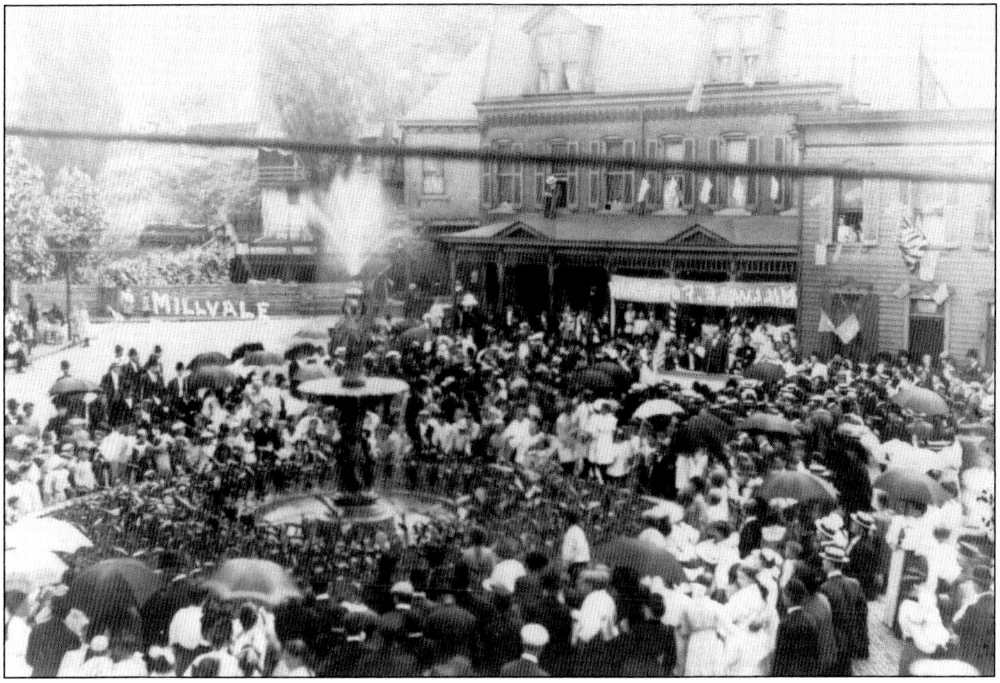

A crowd gathers in the early 1900s for the dedication of Millvale's fountain, which was located near the intersection of North Avenue and Elizabeth Streets. The fountain was later replaced by the soldier monument, known as "the Doughboy," which stood until 1931, when it was moved to Millvale Soldier Memorial Park in front of the VFW. (Heinz History Center.)

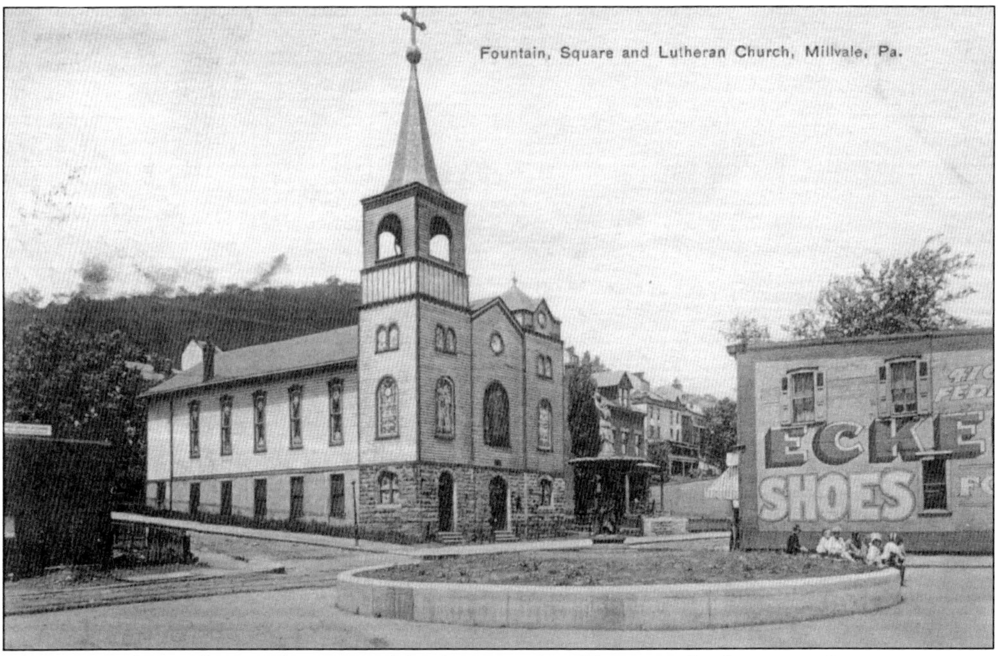

This postcard provides another view of the fountain. In addition to the fountain, there was a water trough for horses. After 1931, a Christmas tree was annually lighted at this spot during the holidays. Also prominent in this picture is the first St. John's Lutheran Church. (Carol Szwedko.)

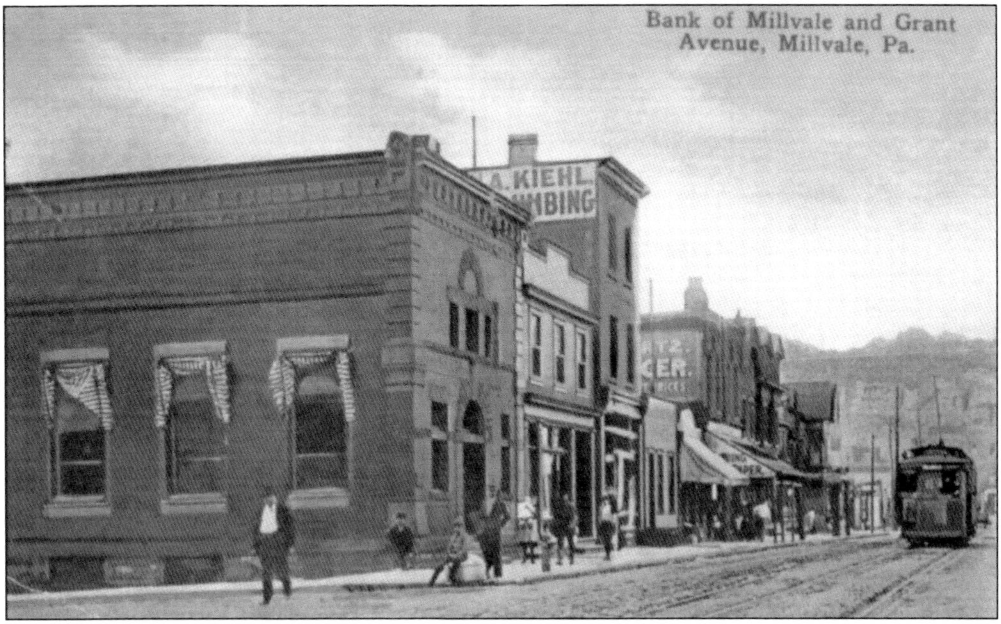

According to the *Pittsburg Leader*, by 1904, the Bank of Millvale, established in 1900, had deposits of about $300,000 and 1,000 accounts. Millvale's population was 11,000, so one out of every eleven people in the neighborhood had savings there. Given an average of five to a family, it meant that every other family in the borough was saving money. (Mary Ann Knochel.)

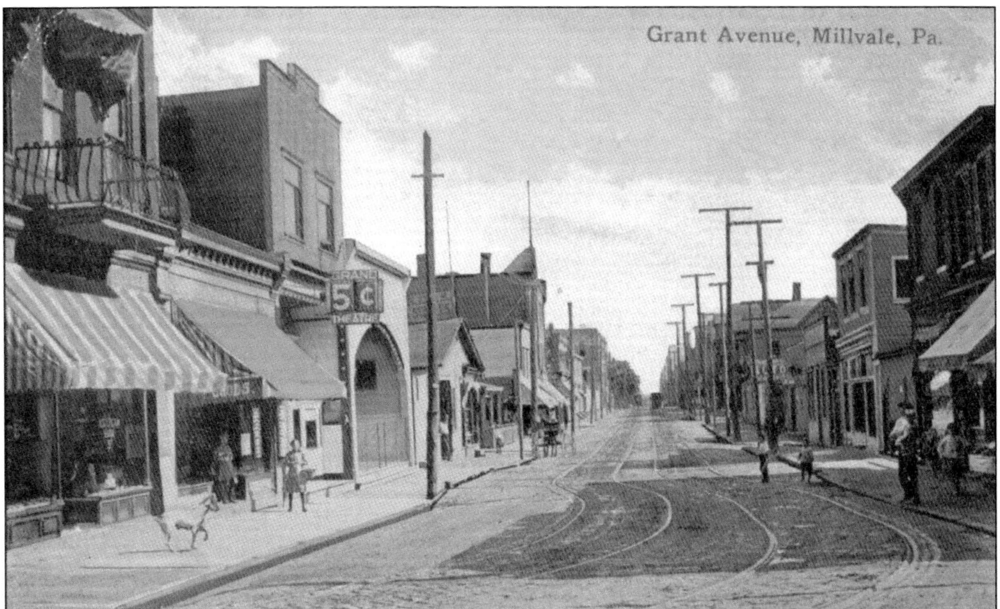

Millvale had four nickelodeons, early movie theaters. All four were on Grant Avenue: the Family Theater at 516 Grant, the Grand Theater at 518 Grant, the Lincoln at 139 Grant, and the Reliable at 515 Grant. Admission was 5¢. If a group of boys had only one nickel to share, the person paying would leave the back door open for his friends to sneak in. (Jean Domico.)

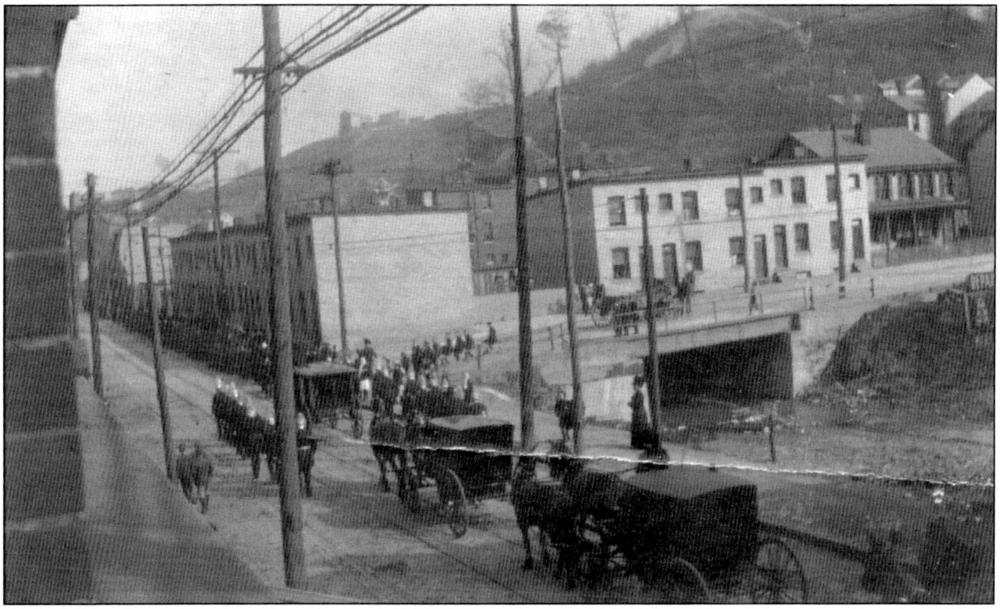

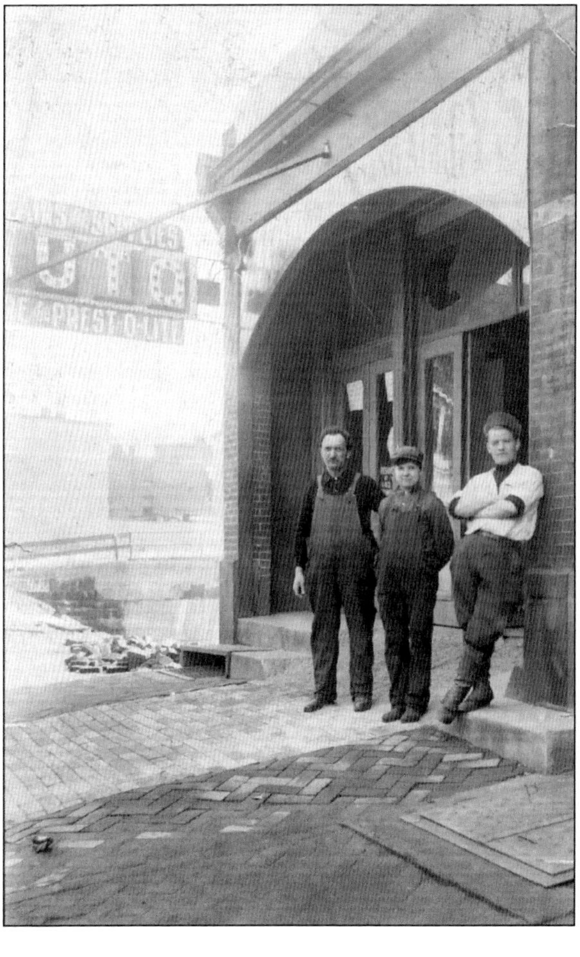

Horse-drawn carriages are part of a funeral procession from St. Anthony's Church, proceeding across one of the culverts spanning Girty's Run. This is the corner of Lincoln and North Avenues, where Lincoln Pharmacy now stands. Millvale is built atop many such culverts, as Girty's Run meanders through town. Many streets are in reality bridges over the culverts. (Jennifer Cohen.)

This photograph was taken in 1908, when Al Sirlin owned the first automobile garage in Millvale. It was located near the corner of North and Lincoln Avenues, where Lincoln Pharmacy is now located. (Jennifer Cohen.)

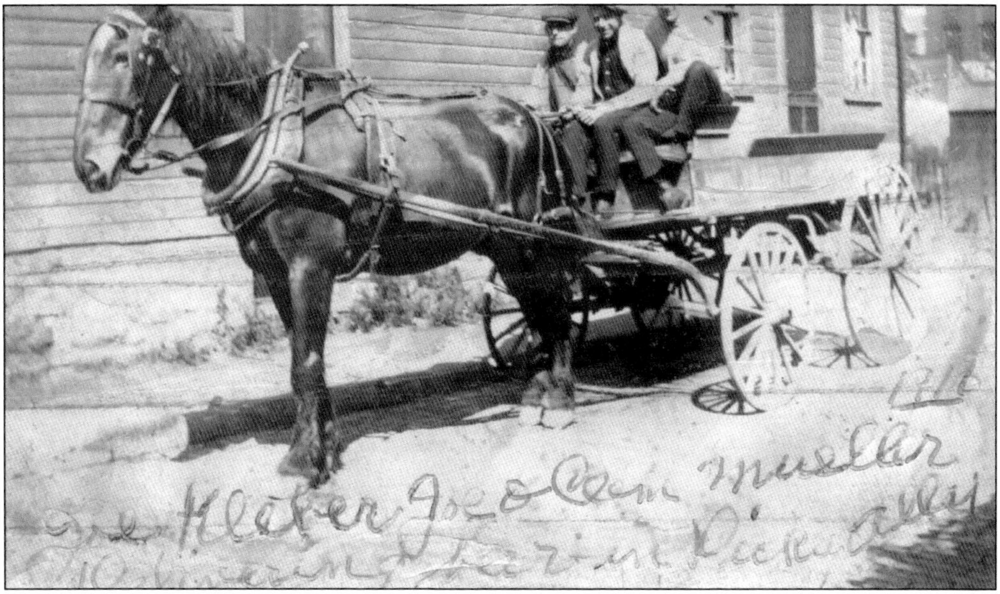

In the above photograph, as written, Joseph Kleber, Clem Mueller, and an unidentified friend deliver beer from their wagon in Dickey Alley in 1916. Many of Millvale's merchants, including Hebron and Bonshire Grocers and Ed Vero, relied on horse-drawn wagons for deliveries. In the below photograph, taken on May 6, 1905, Baeuerlein's deliveryman and his horse stand before the brewery. Baeuerlein ensured the prompt distribution of its products to customers and establishments. (Above, Jennifer Cohen; below, Janine Vecenie.)

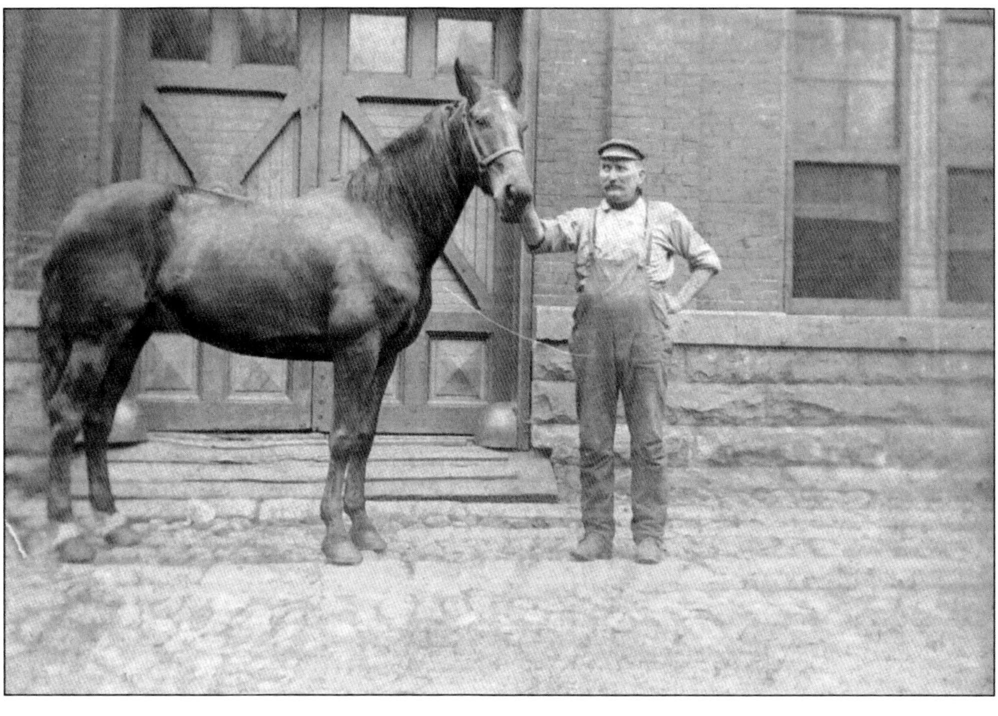

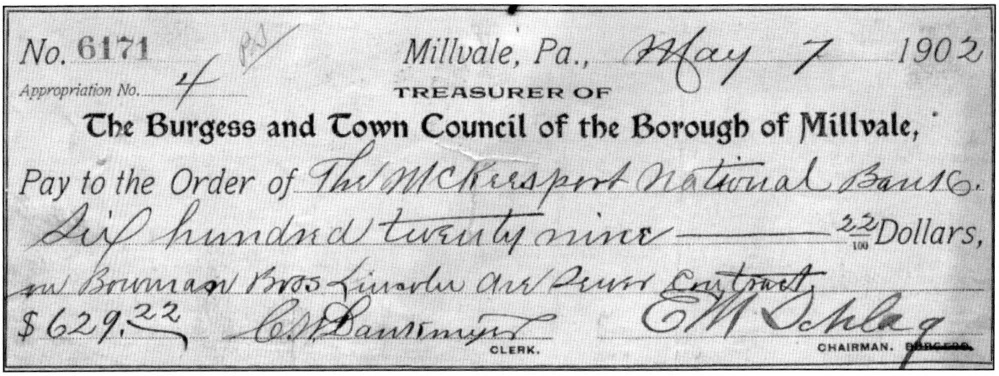

No. 6171 Millvale, Pa., May 7 1902

Appropriation No. 4

TREASURER OF

The Burgess and Town Council of the Borough of Millvale,

Pay to the Order of The McKeesport National Bank

Six hundred twenty nine 22/100 Dollars,

on Bowman Bros Lincoln Ave Sewer Contract

$629.22 CLERK. CHAIRMAN.

When Millvale incorporated as a borough in 1868, its governing structure consisted of a burgess (now mayor) and a town council, as illustrated by this 1902 borough check. Over the years, two leaders have served significant tenures: Burgess E.B.W. Pfischner (31 years) and Mayor Regis J. McCarthy (41 years). (Millvale Borough.)

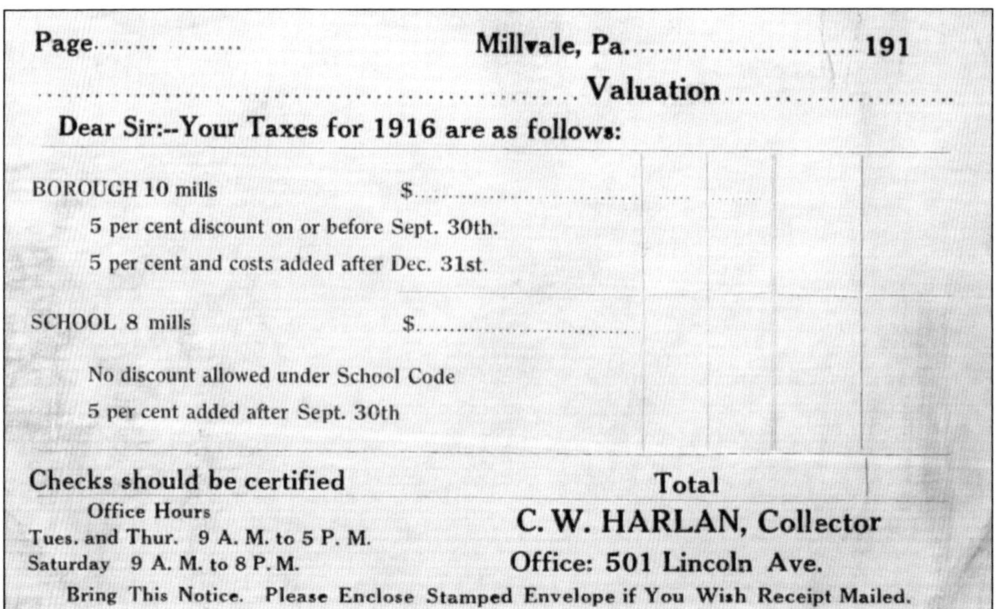

Page........ .... Millvale, Pa................. 191

.... Valuation......................

Dear Sir:--Your Taxes for 1916 are as follows:

BOROUGH 10 mills $..............................

5 per cent discount on or before Sept. 30th.

5 per cent and costs added after Dec. 31st.

SCHOOL 8 mills $..............................

No discount allowed under School Code

5 per cent added after Sept. 30th

Checks should be certified Total

Office Hours

Tues. and Thur. 9 A. M. to 5 P. M.

Saturday 9 A. M. to 8 P. M.

C. W. HARLAN, Collector

Office: 501 Lincoln Ave.

Bring This Notice. Please Enclose Stamped Envelope if You Wish Receipt Mailed.

As this card illustrates, in 1916, Millvale's residents paid both a borough tax of 110 mills and a school tax of 8 mills. The millage rate for 2012 was 8.5 mills, or $8.50 per $100 valuation on real estate, whether undeveloped (vacant) or improved. (Millvale Borough.)

Captioned "Mr. Golden and his pet," this photograph depicts the type of engines that were used for the narrow-gauge railroad that ran from Butler Plank Road, out Grant and Hooker Streets, to Evergreen Hamlet. (Jennifer Cohen.)

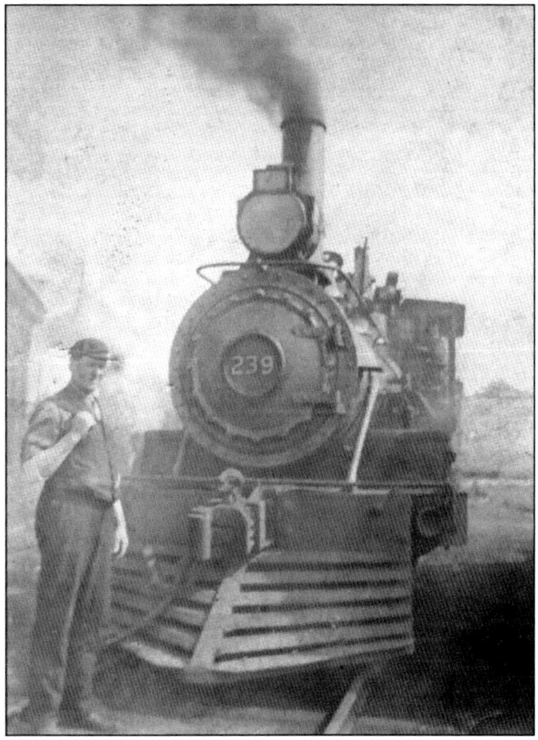

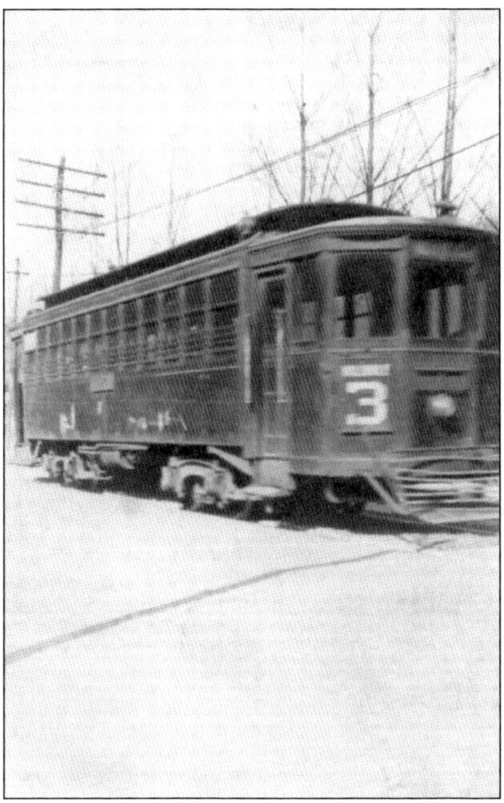

Pittsburgh Railways was formed in 1902, and electric cars (trolleys) would soon become the standard means of transportation within Pittsburgh and beyond. A streetcar accident injuring 30 passengers occurred when a car left the tracks near Bennett and went over an 18-foot embankment on February 24, 1906. Frost on the ground caused by warming weather was the reason for the accident. (Flo Silbach.)

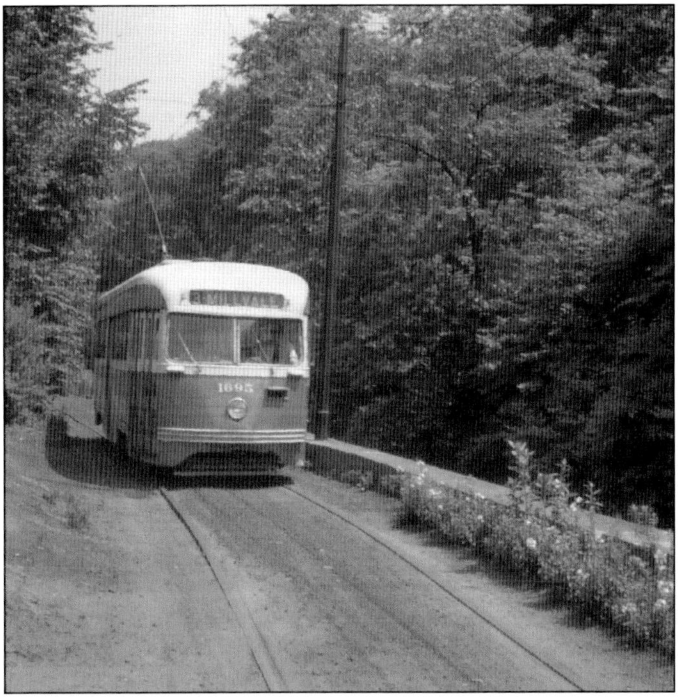

The No. 3 line ran from downtown, through the North Side, along East Ohio Street, up Grant, North, and Evergreen Avenues, and out to Bauerstown, which was the end of the line. In the 1930s, the cost to ride was a 10¢ token, or three tokens for a quarter. (Frank B. Fairbanks Rail Transportation Archives, 1948–1993, Pittsburgh History and Landmarks Foundation, Archives Service Center, University of Pittsburgh.)

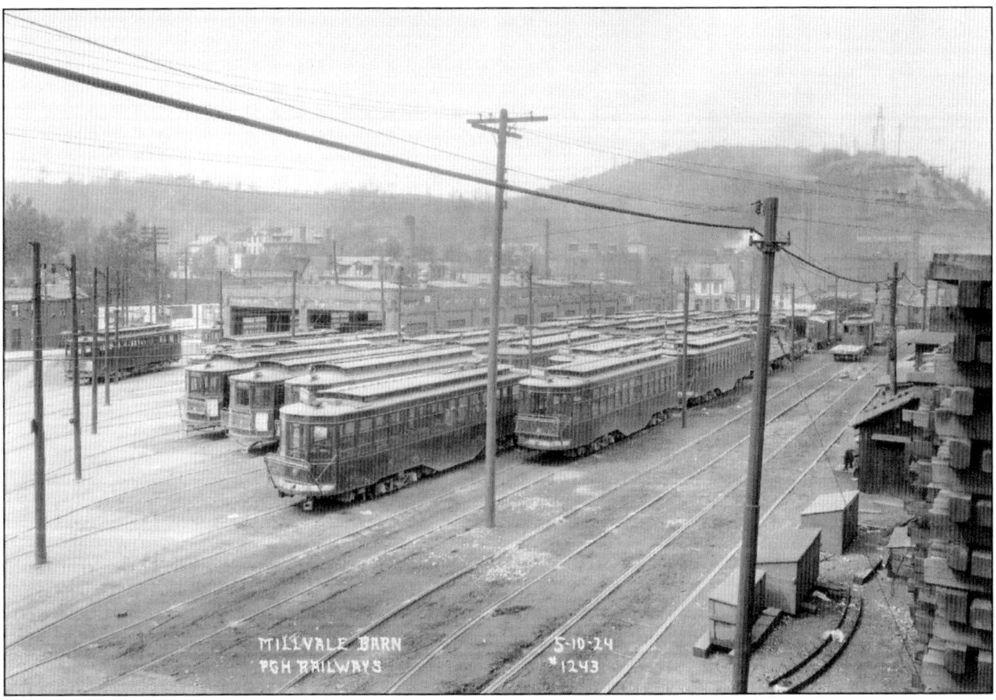

The empty property that once was the site of the Graff, Bennett & Company mill at the end of Millvale was sold by F.N. Hoffstott, president of the Pressed Steel Car Company, to Pittsburgh Railways, the predecessor of the Port Authority of Allegheny County. The carbarn served lines 1, 2, 3, 4, and 5. (Pittsburgh Railways Company Records 1872–1924, Archives Service Center, University of Pittsburgh.)

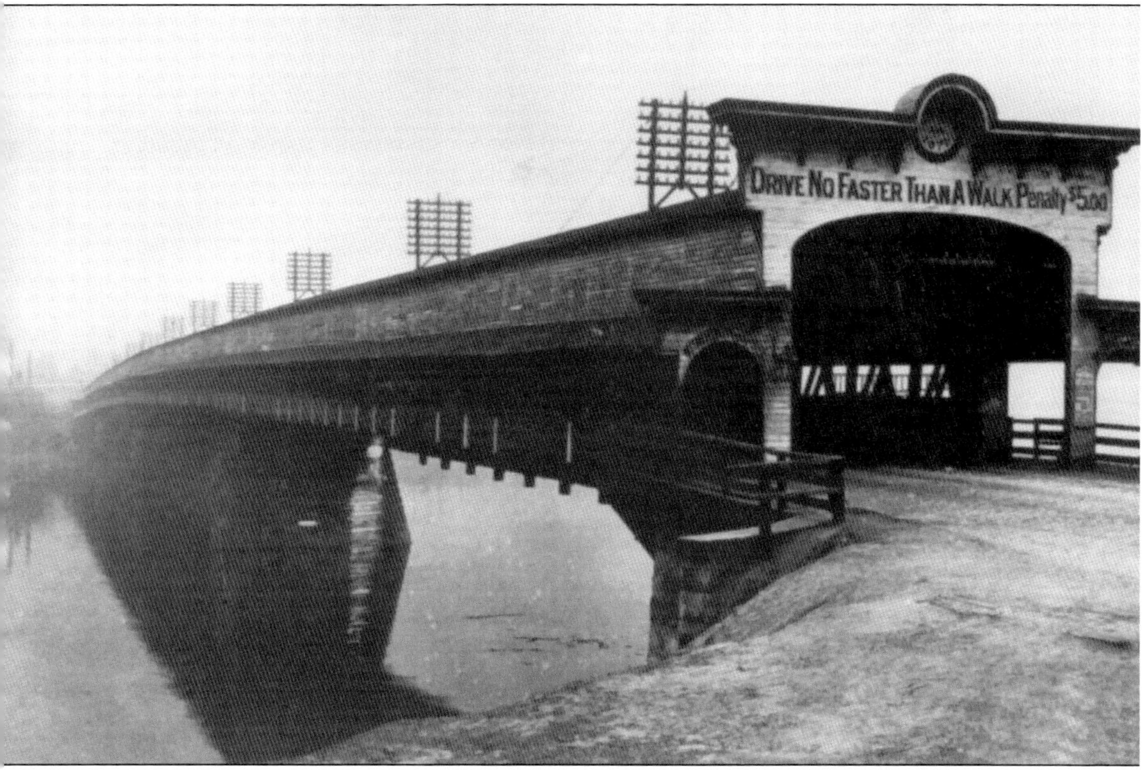

A historically prominent bridge that no longer stands was the Ewalt Bridge, or Forty-third Street Bridge, which was erected in 1870 and served the river communities of Millvale and Lawrenceville until the opening of the Washington Crossing Bridge in December 1924. The wooden covered bridge, designed by Felician Slataper, connected Butler Plank Road to Ewalt Street. This bridge brought tremendous growth in both population and business to Millvale. Huge timbers and planks spanned the stone piers, and the bridge had a cobblestone approach. On the Millvale side was a walk with a handrail for pedestrians so they could look down the river. The Ewalt Bridge Company was formed on March 22, 1869, with capital of $100,000, raised by selling 2,000 shares of stock at a par value of $50. Originally, the bridge toll was 1¢, later 2¢. In 1889, a petition was circulated in Millvale and Lawrenceville requesting the bridge company reduce the toll to 1¢ again. The petition was declined. (Bill Stout.)

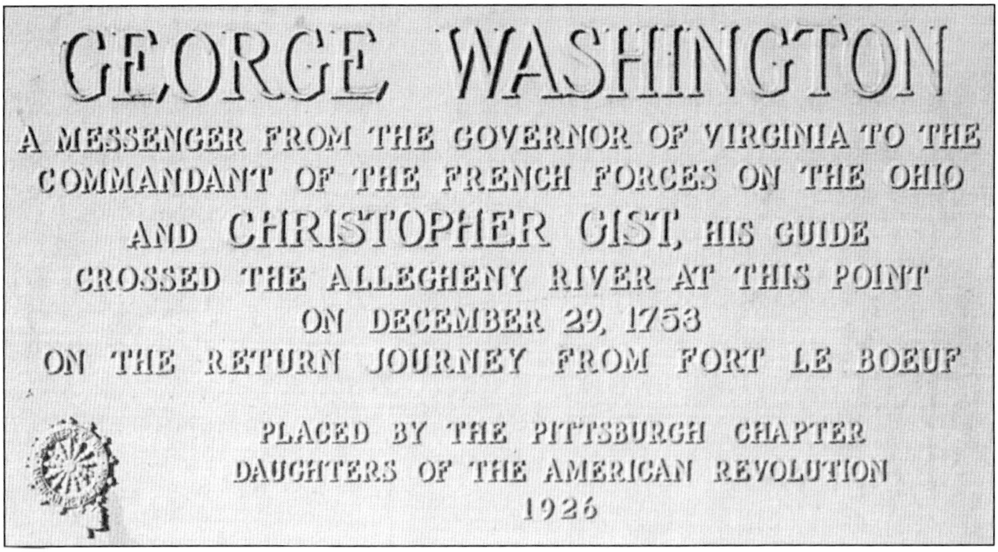

Returning from delivering Virginia's ultimatum to the French to leave the forks of the Ohio River, George Washington and his guide, Christopher Gist, crossed the Allegheny River on a raft near Girty's Run in Millvale. Washington was thrown into the icy stream, but he managed to escape to an island later known as Wainwright's Island (now Lawrenceville). This plaque on the Washington Crossing Bridge commemorates that event. (Bill Stout.)

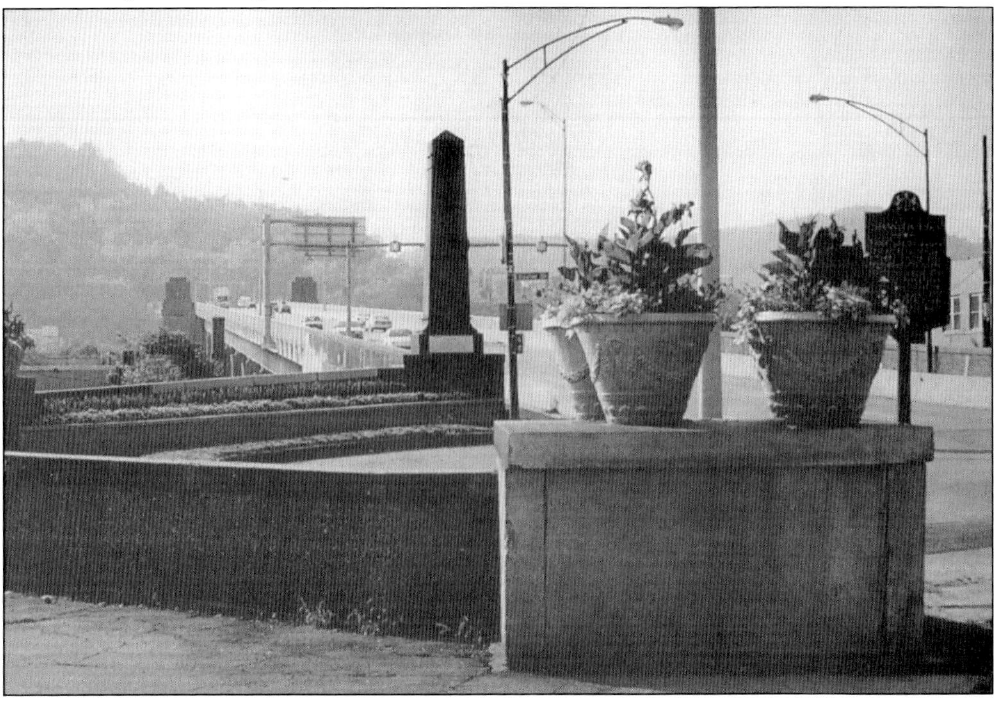

The Fortieth Street Bridge, considered the most artistic bridge over the Allegheny, was designed and erected by Benno Janssen, architect, and Charles Stratton Davis, associate engineer. To accommodate the expansion of Route 28, this grand entrance was destroyed, but the Lawrenceville side remains. The bridge cost Allegheny County over $2 million, which at the time was $1 million more than any other memorial to Washington. (Bill Stout.)

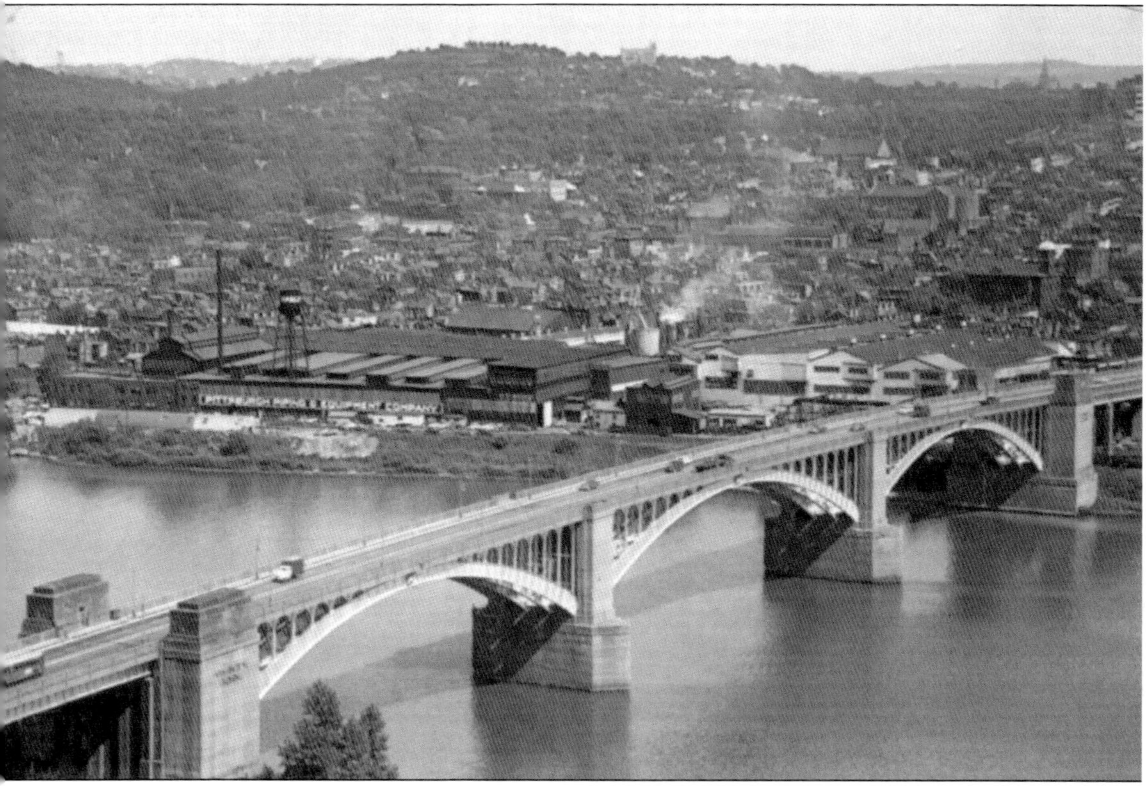

In 1922, the last remaining wooden river crossing, the Forty-third Street Bridge, was sold to the Diamond Match Company. Two years later, on the anniversary of George Washington's crossing the Allegheny River, a new Washington Crossing Bridge (Fortieth Street) was dedicated on Monday, December 29. Although it was a bitterly cold day, and a tremendously strong wind blew over the center of the bridge where the ceremonies were held, more than 6,000 persons witnessed the events. Preceding the dedication, a parade, including floats of civic and patriotic organizations and businesses, formed in the borough of Millvale. The bridge combines simple but carefully placed piers and solid-web steel arches that act like curved plate girders. The seals of the original 13 states adorn the railings. The bridge, originally designed for two lanes of traffic and one streetcar line, was re-decked in 1982 to enable a third automobile lane. (Bill Stout.)

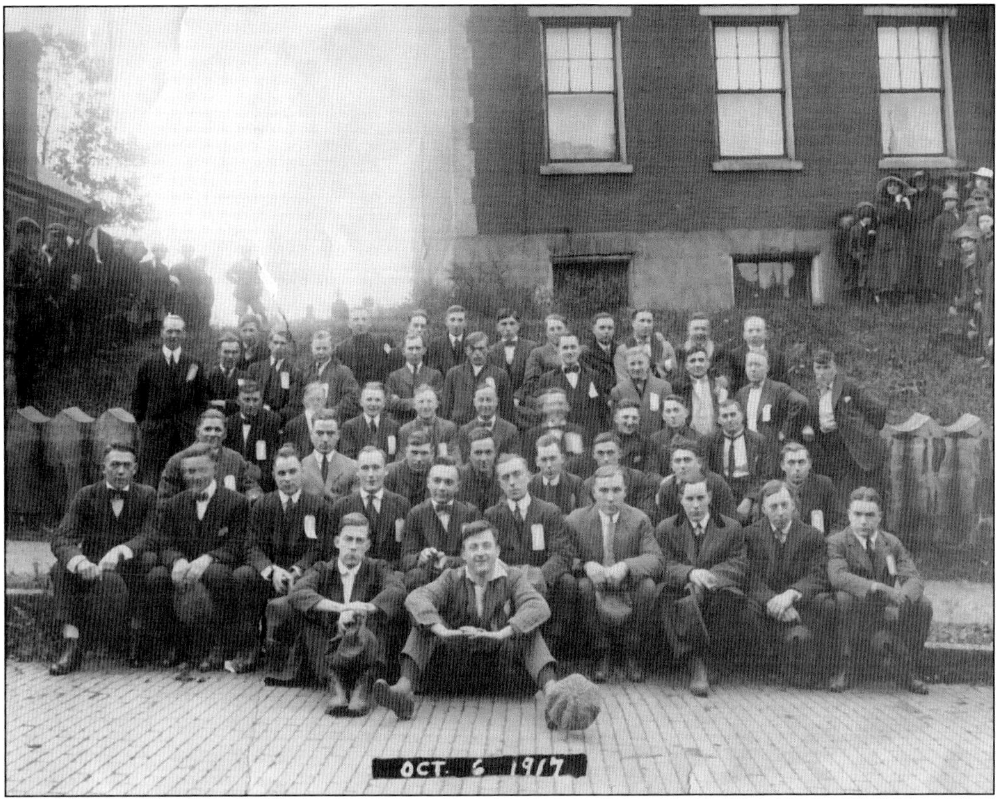

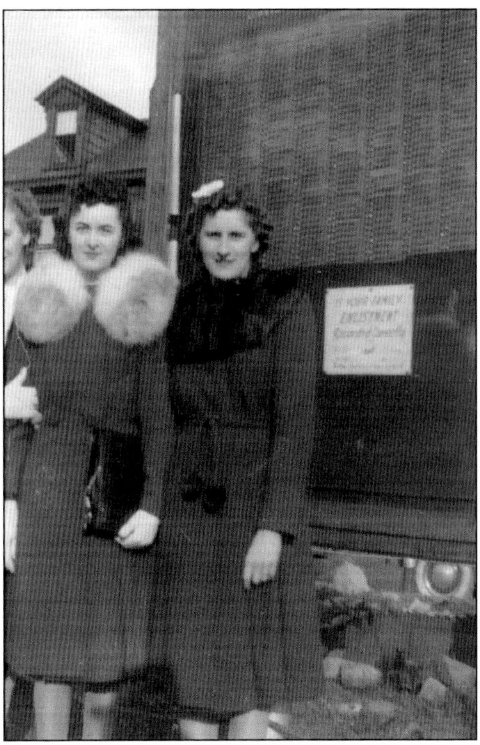

Seated before the building erected for Allegheny City's poor farm in 1845, young men drafted to fight the Germans proudly pose on October 6, 1917. (Jennifer Cohen.)

Mary Marlovits (right) and her sister Helen flank an unidentified friend before the list of enrollees posted in front of the VFW building during World War II. Checking the list for friends and family who have enlisted, the women ensured that the names are spelled properly, as instructed by the sign. A World War I field piece stood near this sign until 1943, when it was used for scrap metal. (Bill Stout.)

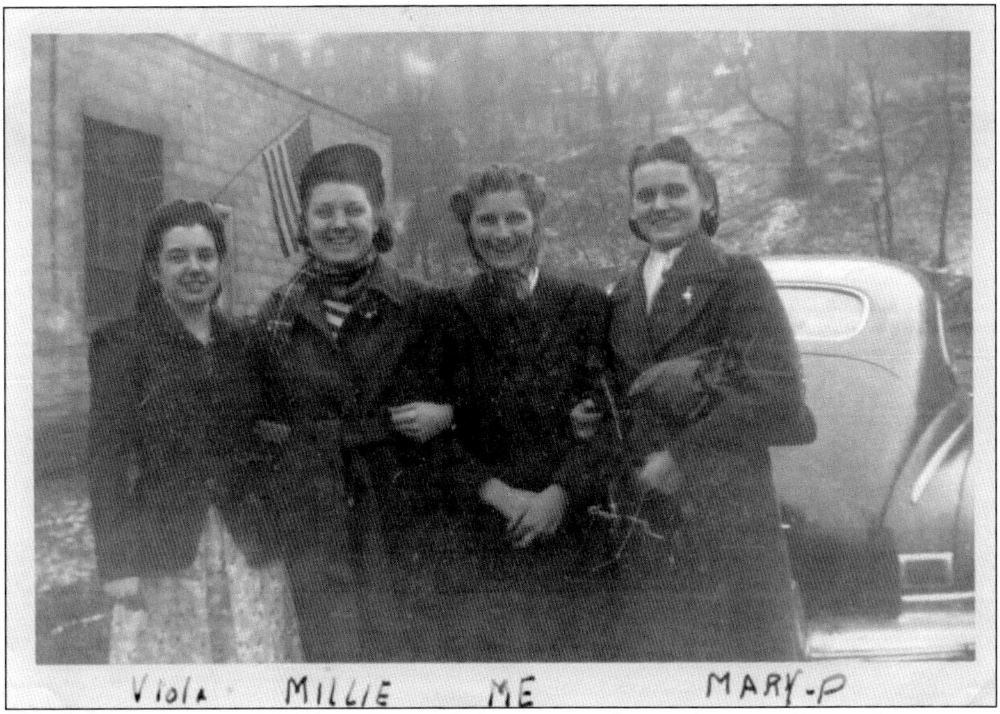

During World War II, Millvale's factories, including McDowell Manufacturing, Victory Engineering, Duquesne Mine, Standard Box, and E.T. Lippert, worked around the clock to help the war effort. Haser Trucking transported most of the material. Here, Millvale's "Rosie the Riveters" stand before the Victory Engineering Company after spending a day working to "beat the Nazis and the Japanese." The women still have smiles on their faces. (Bill Stout.)

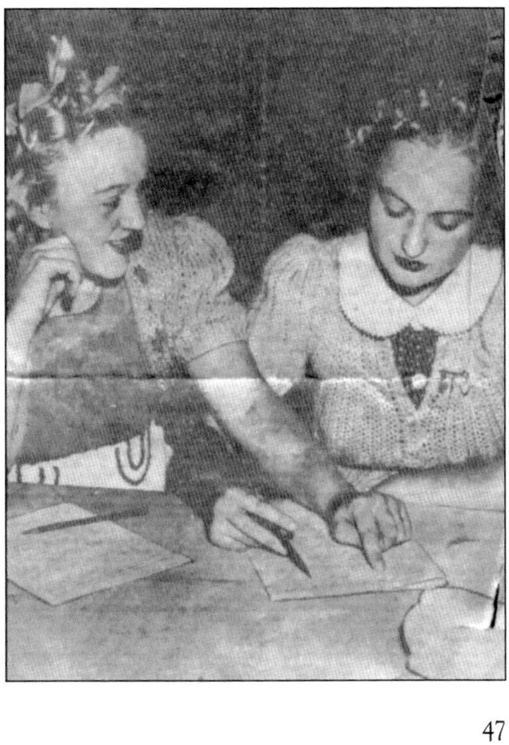

Caroline (left), age 18, and Anna Funovitz, 16, were among the first to register as aliens at the Millvale Post Office, as required by the Alien Registration Act of 1940 (the Smith Act). They immigrated to America with their parents as young children. Though their parents were naturalized citizens, the girls were considered aliens. (Bill Stout.)

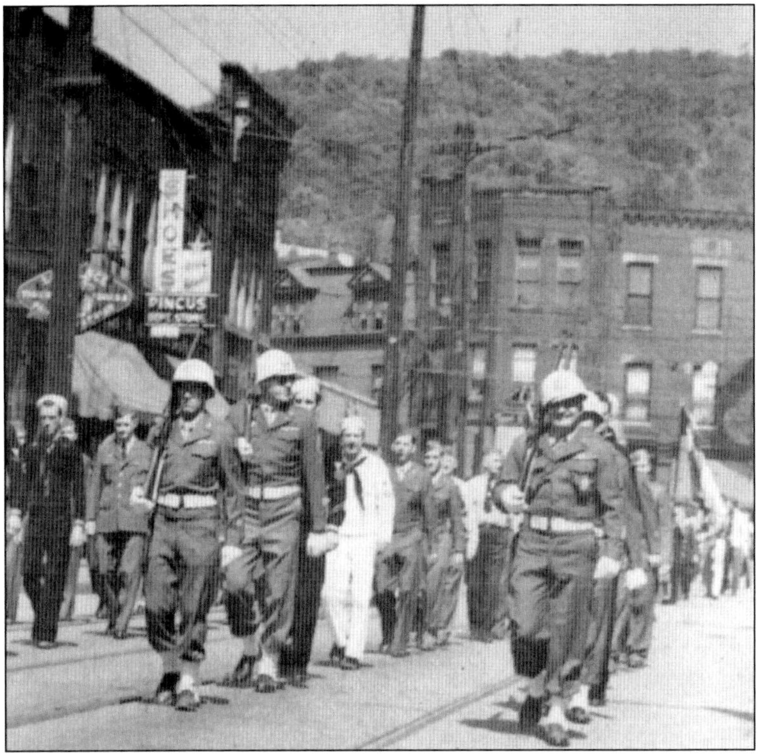

These soldiers, sailors, and Marines are celebrating the end to the war and their safe return home in a parade down Grant Avenue. The sign for Pincus Shoe Store, owned and operated by Abe and Herman Pincus from 1923 until 1961 at 511 Grant Avenue, is visible above the parade. Pincus occupied two-thirds of the current Attic Records store. (Jean Domico.)

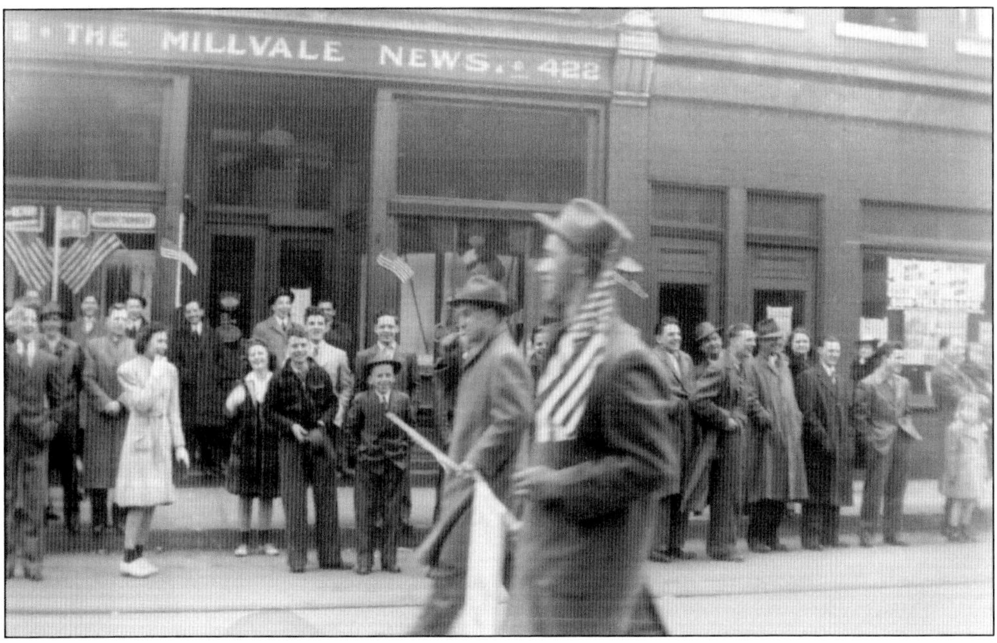

Millvale's first newspaper was the *Bennett Star*, with offices at 43 Grant Avenue. W.S. Scott and G.R. Dorman were the editors and proprietors. It was a six-column quarto, published weekly starting around 1886 and continued for over 20 years. The *Bennett Star* was succeeded by the *Valley Journal*, then the *Millvale News*, whose offices are seen in this photograph. The *Green Sheet*, a weekly newspaper of advertisements, is still printed locally. (Jennifer Cohen.)

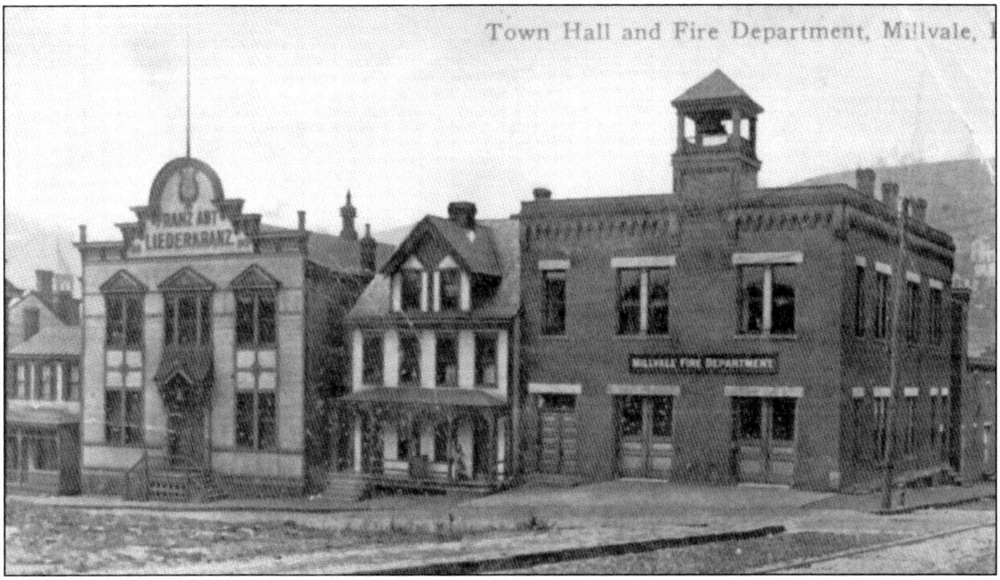

It was in 1906 that the Millvale Volunteer Fire Department finally received its name. On May, 31, 1907, the first meeting was held in the present engine house on Sedgwick Street, with F.C. Klussman as president and J.L. Gardner as fire chief. In 1920, the fire department became motorized with a Brockway pumper. The old horse was retired to pasture on the Baeuerlein farm. (Panza Gallery.)

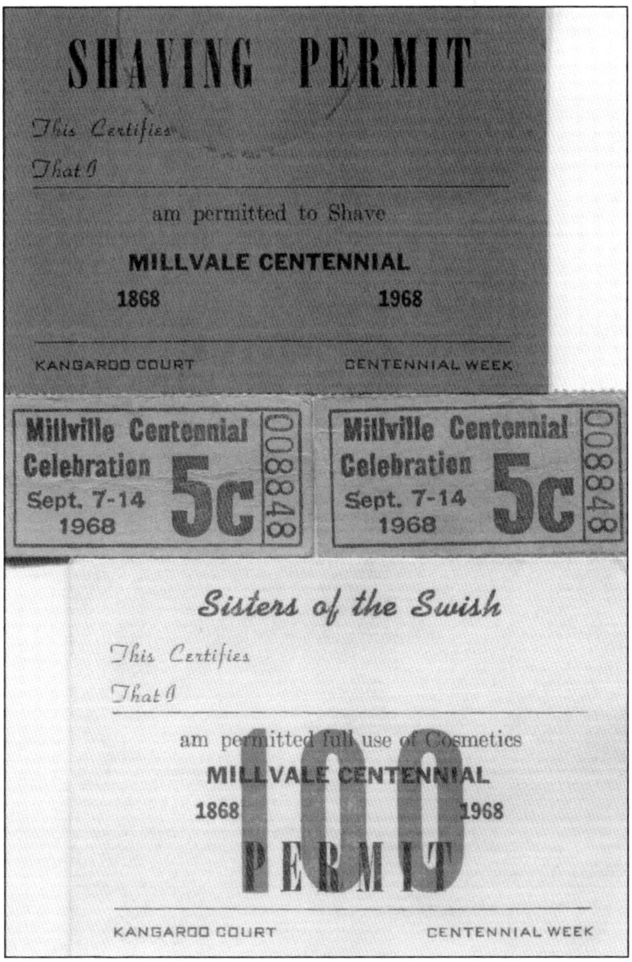

From September 7–14, 1968, the community of Millvale celebrated its 100th anniversary with church services, parades, amusements, and outdoor refreshments. As part of the festivities, men were not permitted to shave, and women were not permitted to wear makeup, unless they paid for the privilege and carried one of these cards attesting to the fact. (Al Atkinson.)

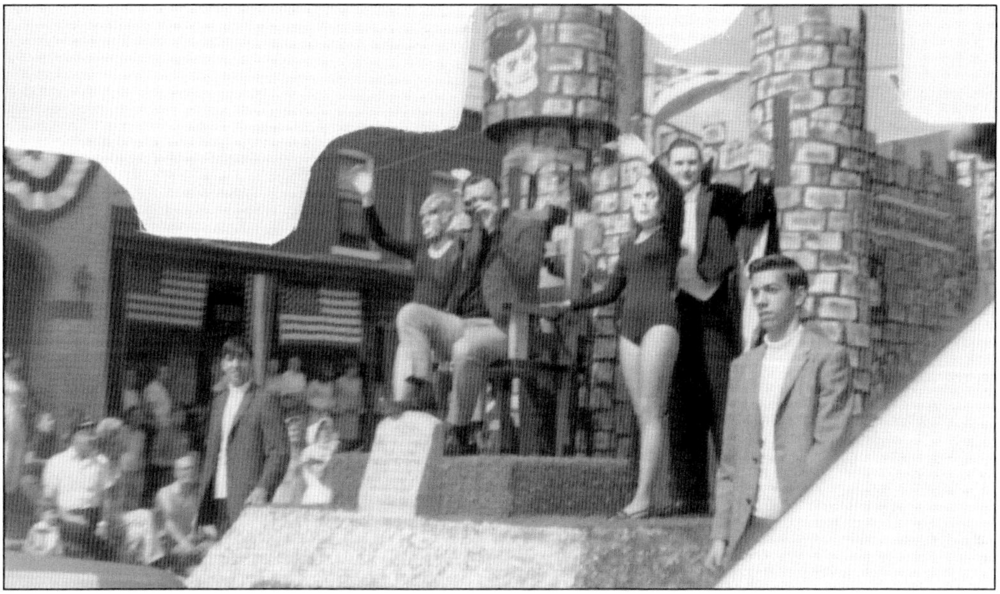

Bill Cardille, a local television celebrity, was the first voice heard when WIIC, channel 11, went on the air on September 1, 1957. He was best known as "Chilly Billy," the host of *Chiller Theater*, a late-night Saturday program that showcased horror and science fiction films. He is seen here (seated at center) joining in Millvale's centennial celebrations. (Vincent Cinski.)

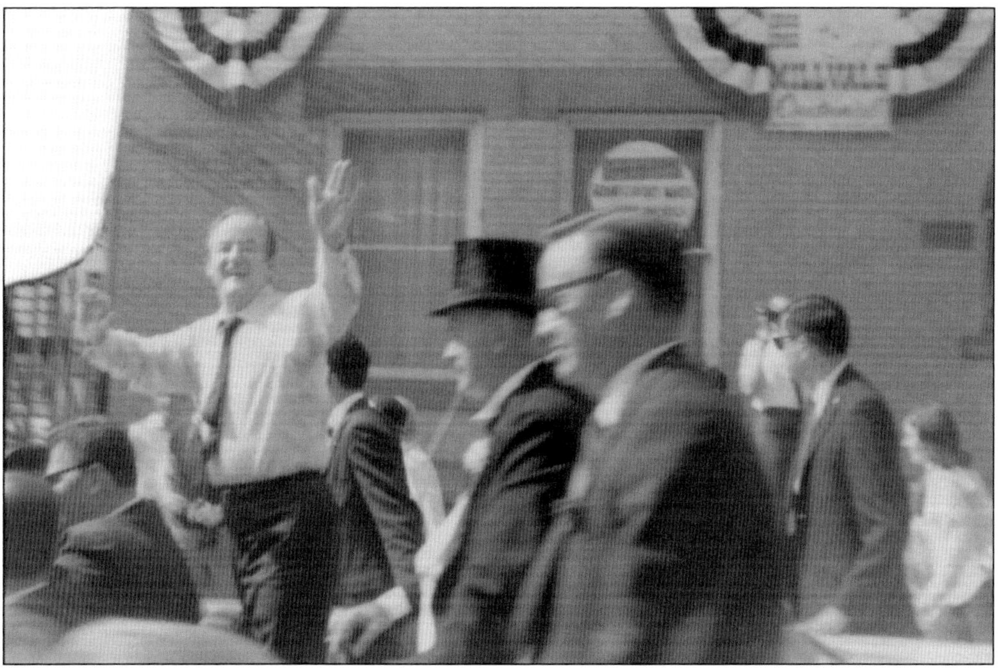

Vice Pres. Hubert Humphrey (waving) was the most nationally known participant in Millvale's centennial celebration. He is seen here with Mayor Regis J. McCarthy (in top hat). Humphrey, who decided to run for president after Lyndon Johnson declared his intention not to seek a second term, combined politicking with centennial activities during his visit. (Vincent Cinski.)

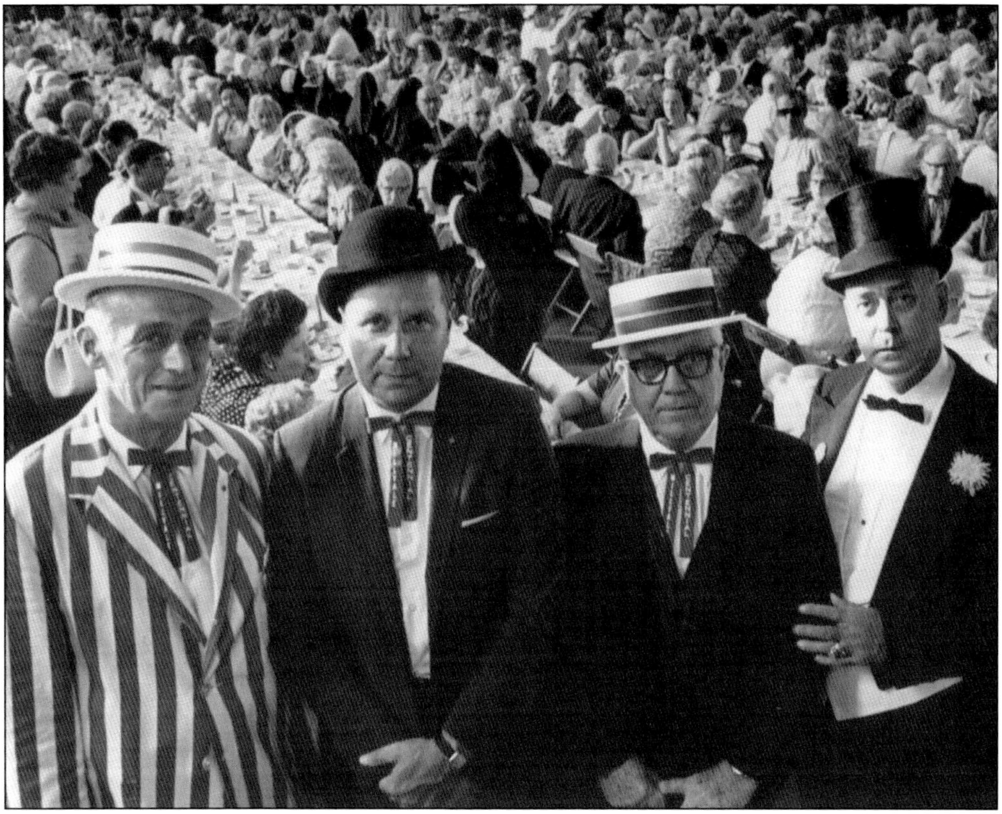

Shown here are, from left to right, John F. Lhota (centennial executive committee member), Walter Sperling Sr., James P. Swain (teacher and town historian), and Mayor Regis J. McCarthy. They are seen with hundreds of Millvale residents and guests at one of the recognition dinners during the town's centennial in 1968. (Jennifer Cohen.)

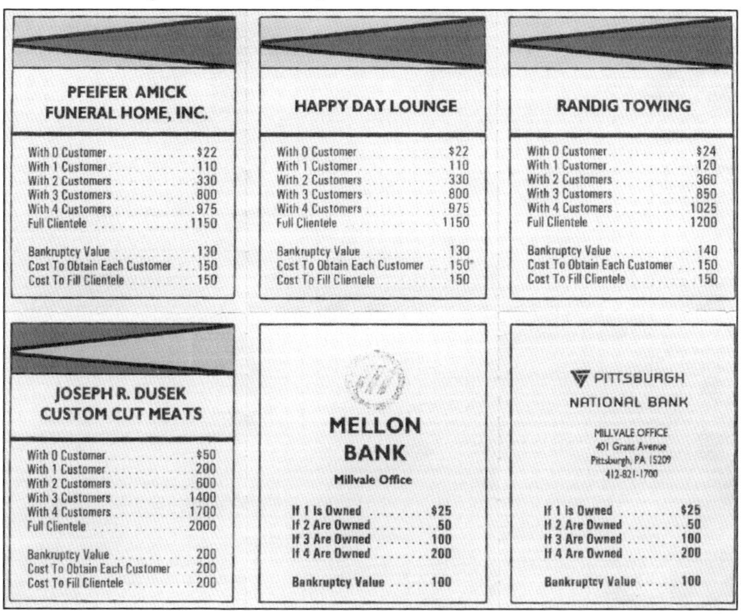

As a fundraiser for Millvale's 125th anniversary, Ed Carr and his committee developed the Millvale-opoly game, based on the popular Monopoly board game. It even included a "Get Out of Millvale Court Free" card, just in case a participant was caught speeding and had to appear in court before Richard K. McCarthy, district justice. (Bill Stout.)

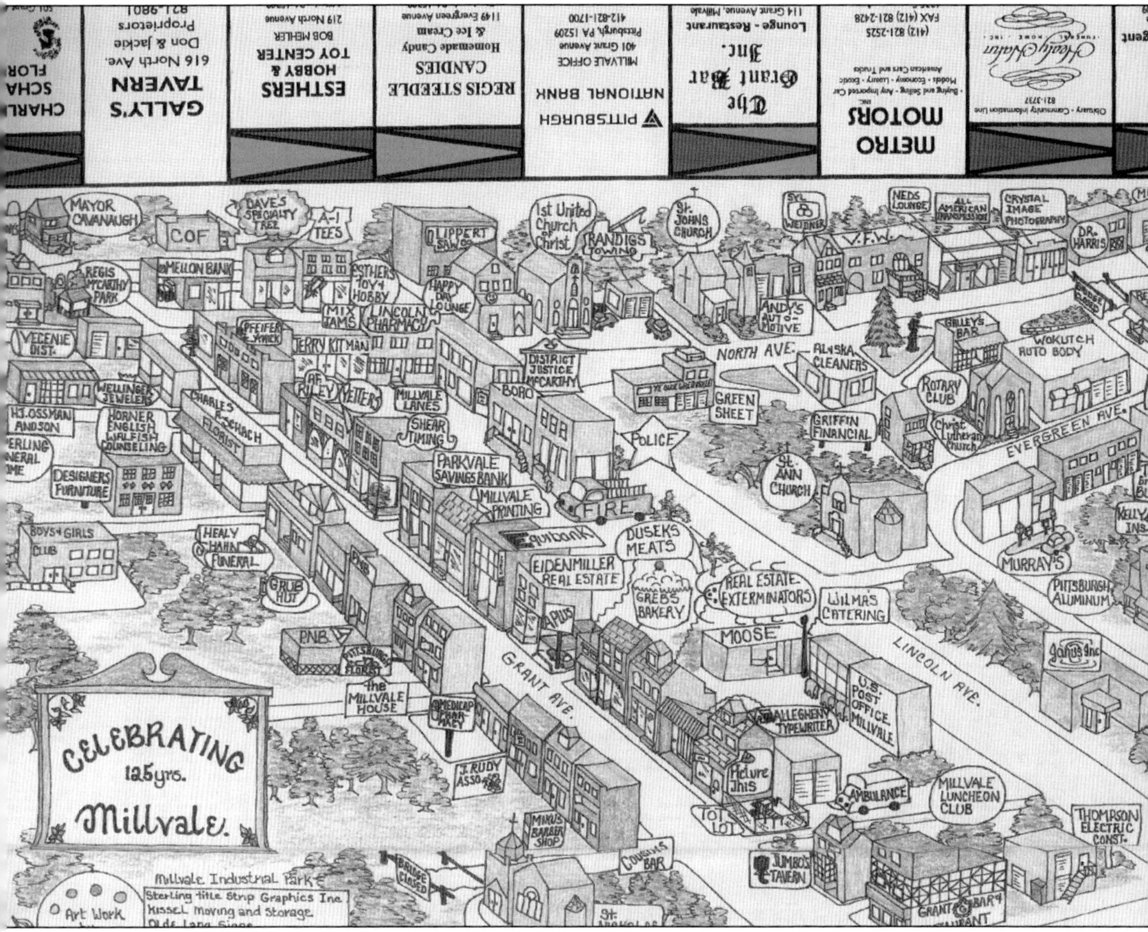

Millvale-opoly's board, designed by Carol Reihart, depicted Millvale's main business district along Grant and North Avenues. Among the properties on the board are businesses, including Rich Mikus Barber Shop, Greb's Bakery, Charles A. Schach Florist, Joseph S. Wellinger Jewelry Store, and Syl Weidner's Insurance Agency. These establishments are all now gone. (Bill Stout.)

Three

From Steeple to Steeple

While they might not have immigrated to America for religious freedom, Millvale's German, Croatian, Irish, and English citizens were very religious and insistent on the celebration of their faiths with their own traditions. Millvale's German Catholics split from the English-speaking members of St. Ann's in 1886 and built their own frame church, where mass was celebrated in German, in 1887. When their grand new church, designed by John T. Comes, was dedicated in 1915, the dedication booklet was printed only in German. Unable to reconcile a difference in faith, and also wanting to worship in their own language, the First German Evangelical Church (later First United Church of Christ) organized.

An unusual incident occurred in St. Nicholas Parish after the Diocese of Pittsburgh named Father Michael Tuzek, a German, not a Croatian, as pastor. Armed policemen escorted the priest from his rectory through an angry mob of 200 parishioners to the church, where he celebrated mass in his native German. In August 1906, a meeting was held among members of the parish to organize a Croatian Catholic Independent Church; this movement, however, was short-lived. After Father Tuzek was replaced with the Irish Father Walsh, Croatian priest Father Bekavac was named to restore order to the parish later in 1906. His stay was also short. Troubled times continued for several more years. What finally brought the parish together was the devastating fire in 1921 that destroyed everything but a statue of the Virgin Mary.

St. Nicholas, a landmark historic building, is now famous for its Maximilian "Maxo" Vanka murals, painted in 1937 and 1941 at the request of Father Albert Zagar. While most of the murals depict traditional Catholic scenes and topics, some of those painted in 1941 depict war-related themes, including figures wearing gas masks and a crucified Christ being stabbed by a soldier with a bayonet.

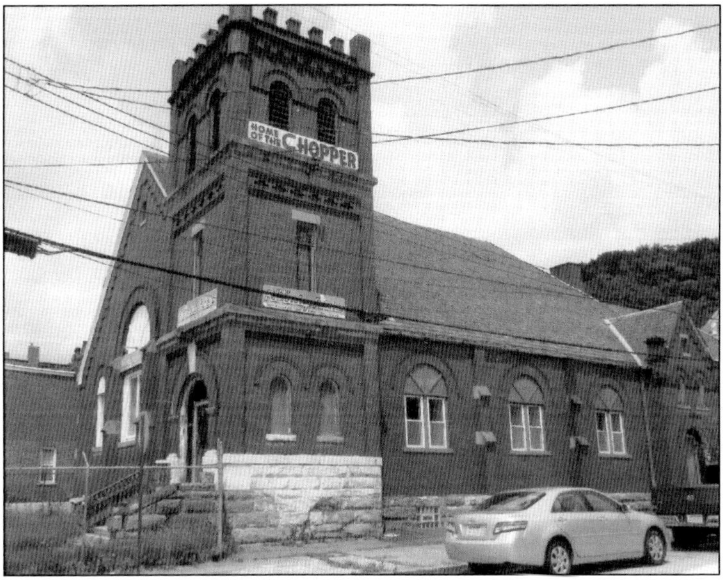

The Presbyterian church, located at the corner of Sheridan Street and Lincoln Avenue, was the first church to be built in Millvale. The cornerstone of this brick church was laid in 1869, one year after the borough's incorporation. Over the years, this building has been used as an antique store and a motorcycle shop. (Bill Stout.)

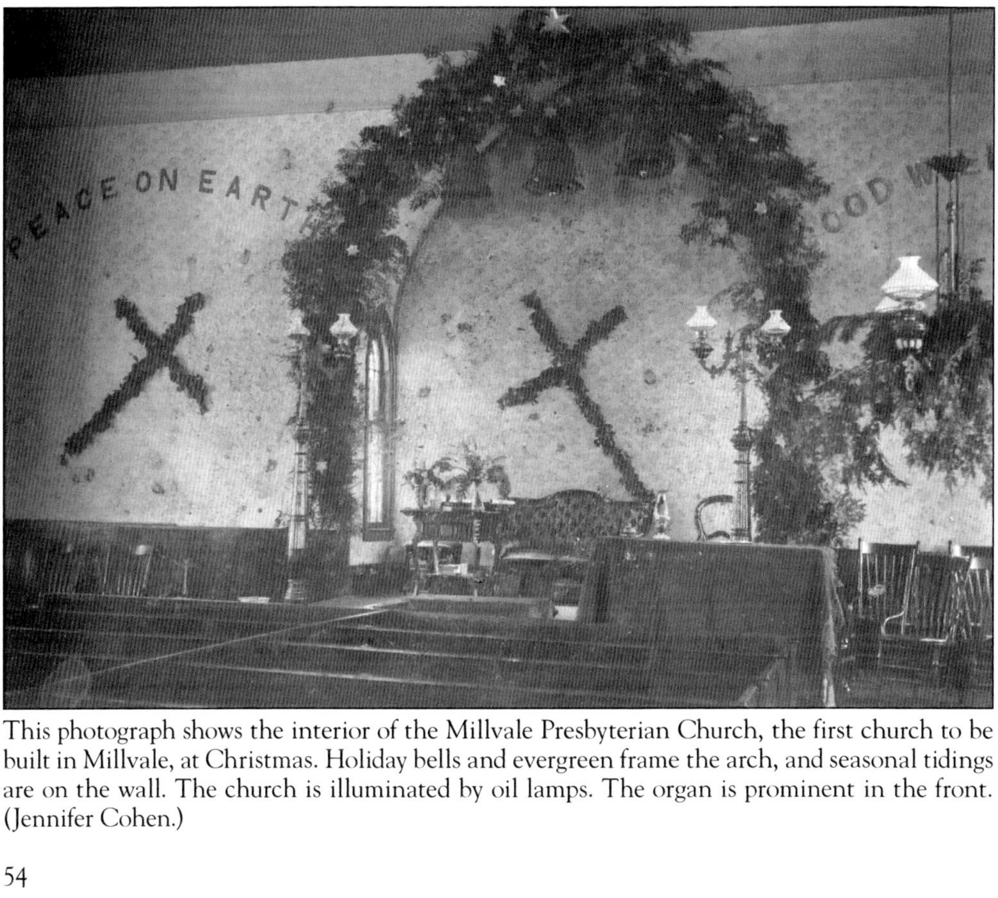

This photograph shows the interior of the Millvale Presbyterian Church, the first church to be built in Millvale, at Christmas. Holiday bells and evergreen frame the arch, and seasonal tidings are on the wall. The church is illuminated by oil lamps. The organ is prominent in the front. (Jennifer Cohen.)

By 1873, the number of Catholics in Millvale had grown to the point that building a church became practical. In 1875, St. Ann's became Millvale's first Catholic church. By the 1920s, the parish had grown so much that the present structure (seen here) was dedicated in March 1924. With Millvale's declining population, St. Ann's and St. Anthony's Parishes were combined into Holy Spirit in 1993. (Jean Domico.)

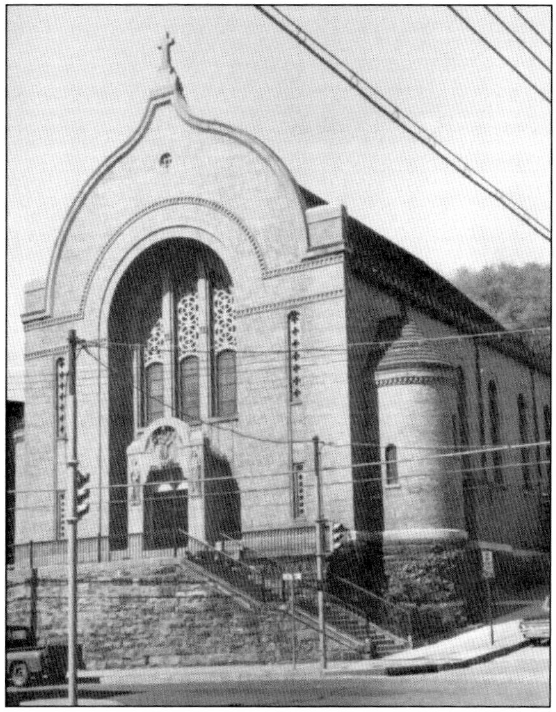

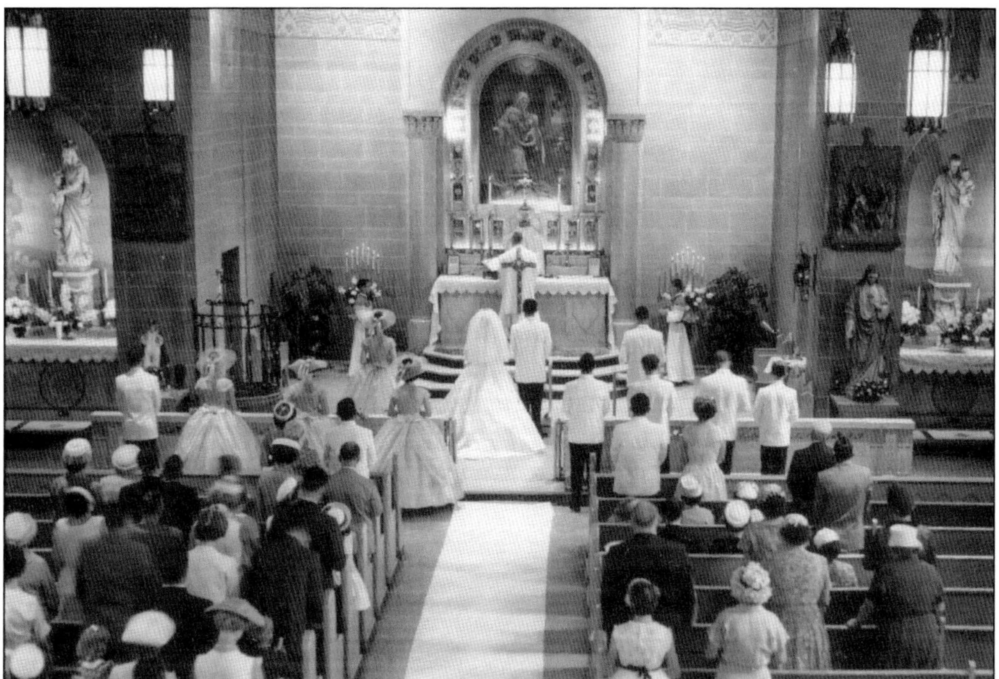

The beauty of the interior of St. Ann's Church is seen in this photograph of Nancy Orga and Ray Schaper's wedding, in August 1962. The bride's gown is lace over silk and covered with sequins and pearls, with a sweetheart neckline and three-quarters sheer lace sleeves. She wears a sequin and lace tiara with a short netting veil. The bride's ensemble cost $125. (Nancy Schaper.)

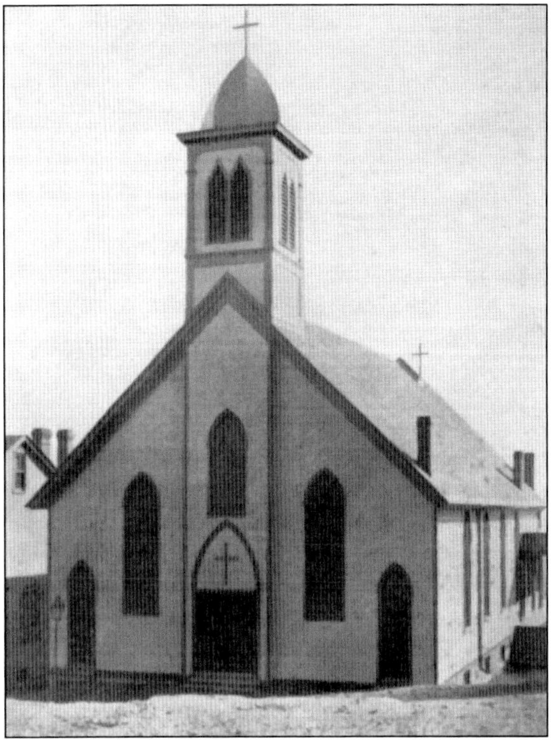

Wanting mass celebrated in their native language, Millvale's German Catholics split from the English-speaking St. Ann's in 1886 and built a frame church (shown here), dedicated on November 6, 1887. This church served the parish for over 20 years, but the congregation eventually outgrew it. After the new church was built, the old building was converted to a lyceum, which was destroyed by fire in 1923. (Mary Ann Knochel.)

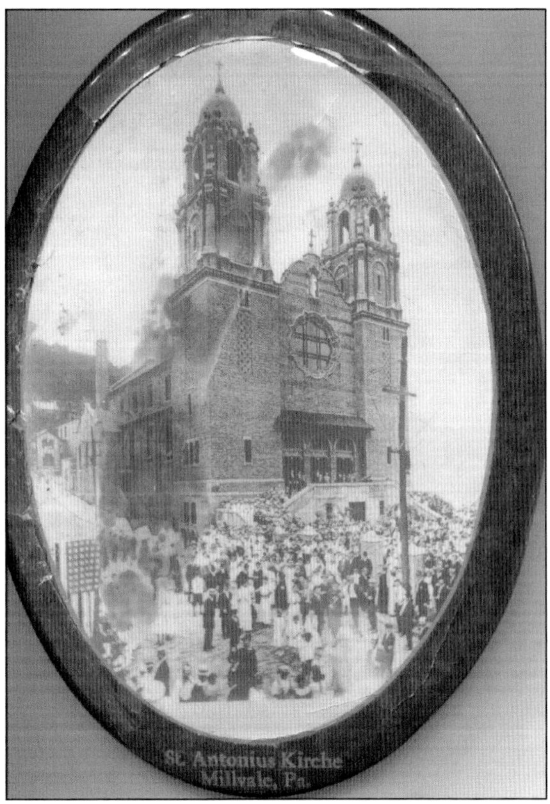

Though the vision of Father Dangelzer, it was Father Louis Spannagel who completed the new St. Anthony's Church. The dedication ceremony on August 1, 1915, drew hundreds of the faithful, who had donated generously to build and decorate the church. The three bells, costing $1,135.29, were donated by Company F, Knights of St. George. (Bill Stout.)

Eine kurze Geschichte

— der —

St. Antonius Gemeinde

Millvale, Pa.

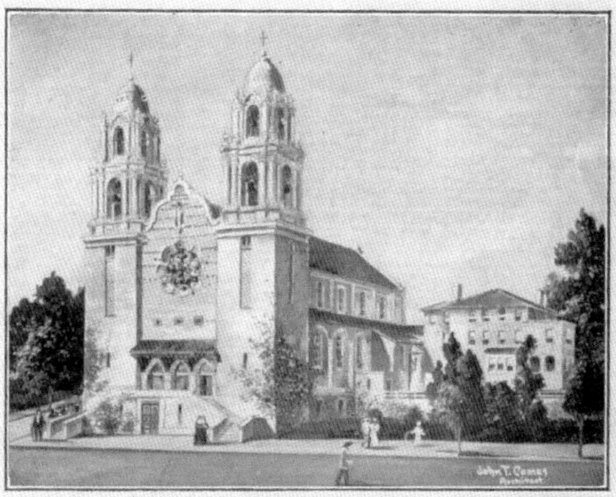

Zum Andenken

Der feierlichen Einweihung

der neuen Kirche

am 1. August, 1915

To accommodate the sevenfold increase in its congregation from the original 75 families, St. Anthony's sought to build a much grander church. John T. Comes, one of the finest architects practicing in Pittsburgh in the early 20th century, was commissioned to design the new building. St. Anthony's is one of his most interesting and unusual designs. The structure features bold, brown-brick towers dominating an exterior terminating in tiled domes. (Mary Ann Knochel.)

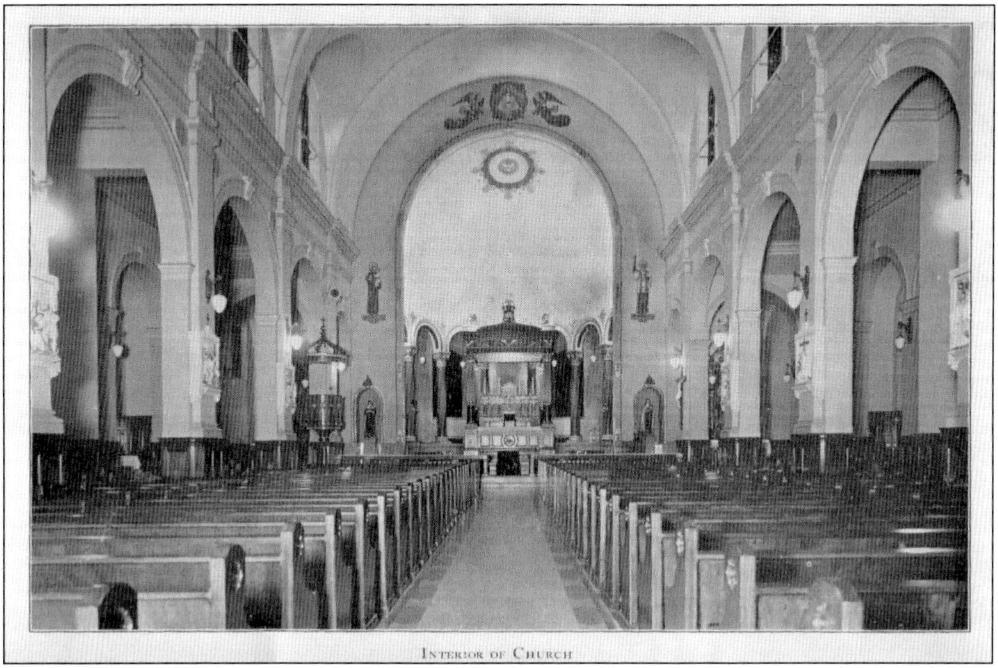

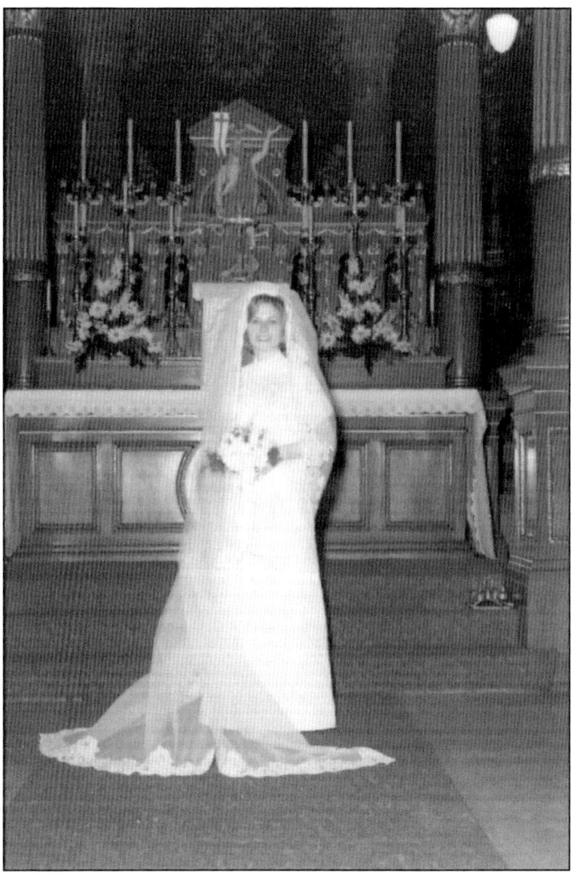

St. Anthony's, "the German church," was the largest of Millvale's three Catholic churches. It was built in 1914. Painted in intense, jewel-like colors, the church's original decorations made for an imposing interior, in striking contrast to the current color palette of cool, soft colors. (Bill Marlovits.)

Mary Ann Stout Alexander stands before the high altar, now gone, of St. Anthony's. The altar cost $1,147.50 when it was donated by the Christian Mothers in 1915. After the Second Vatican Council, during the papacy of Pope John XXIII, which significantly changed Catholic Church rituals, the priest celebrating mass faced his congregation at an altar placed directly behind the communion rail. (Bill Stout.)

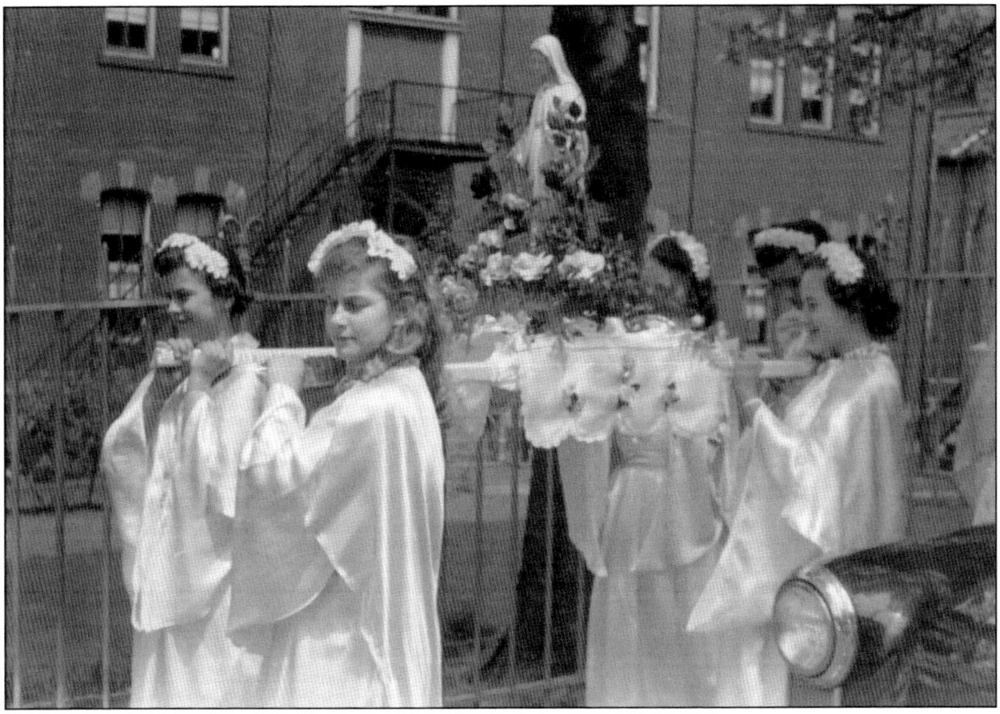

Religious events were an integral part of the lives of German and other European immigrants who populated Millvale. May Crowning is a Catholic ritual held in May to honor Mary, the mother of Christ. Here, four robed and floral-crowned elementary school students carry a statue of the Virgin Mary as part of a procession on the parish grounds. (Bill Stout.)

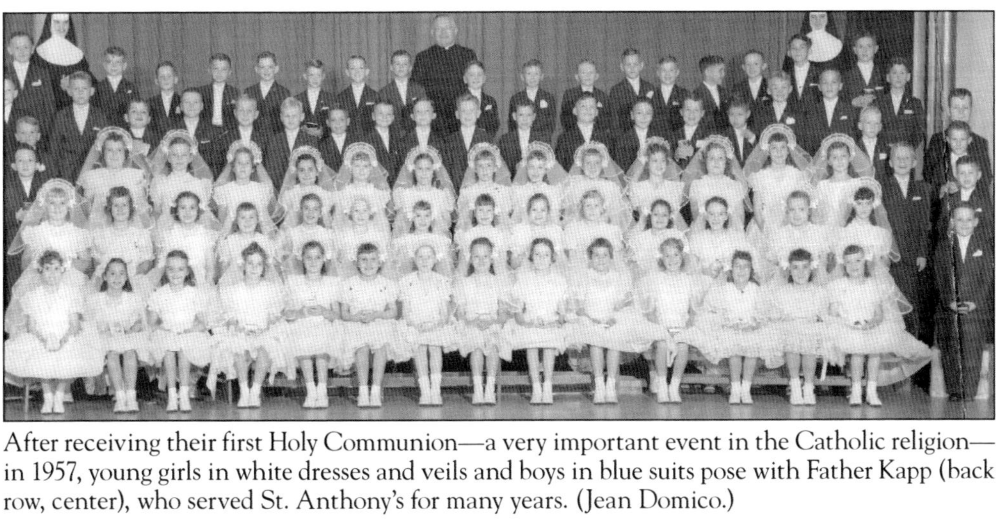

After receiving their first Holy Communion—a very important event in the Catholic religion—in 1957, young girls in white dresses and veils and boys in blue suits pose with Father Kapp (back row, center), who served St. Anthony's for many years. (Jean Domico.)

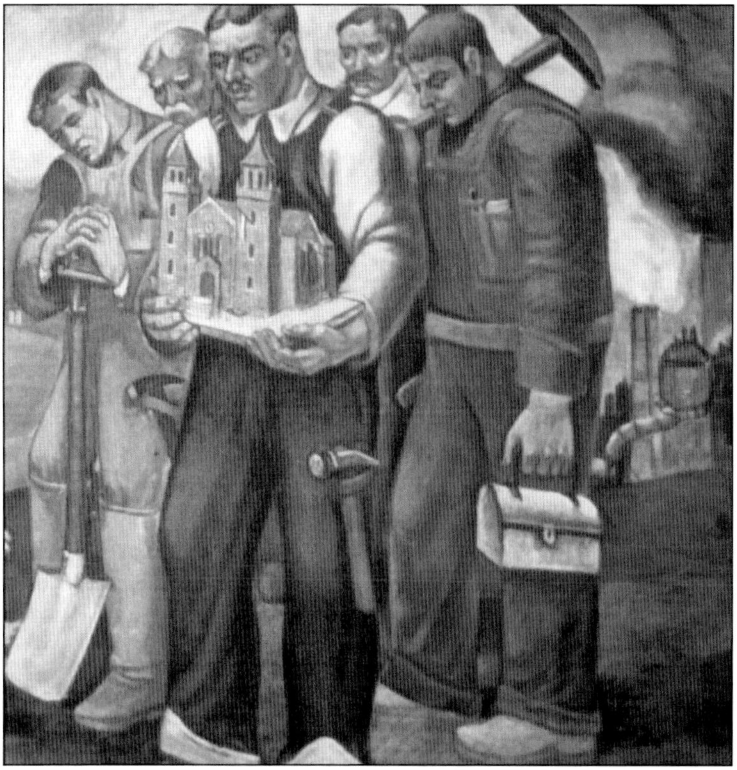

In rapid succession, a group of Croatian immigrants took out loans totaling about $30,000; purchased a hill in Millvale; hired an architect, Frederick Sauer; and dedicated the cornerstone for St. Nicholas Croatian Catholic Church on May 15, 1900. Maxo Vanka, following a 1937 invitation from Pastor Zagar, depicted these immigrants presenting the church to the Mother of God as industrial smoke covers the sky behind them. (Bill Stout.)

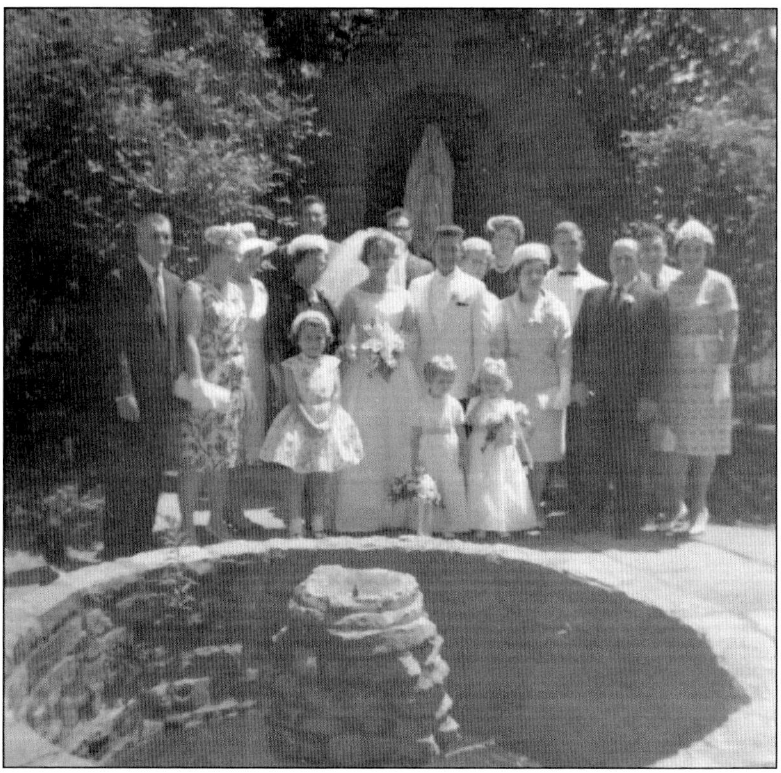

On its hill site, the parish built a grotto to Our Lady of Lourdes in the late 1940s. On June 26, 1965, newly married Nancy and Vince Jaksic stand before the grotto and its fountain. The structure has since been demolished and a smaller shrine created. (Nancy and Vince Jaksic.)

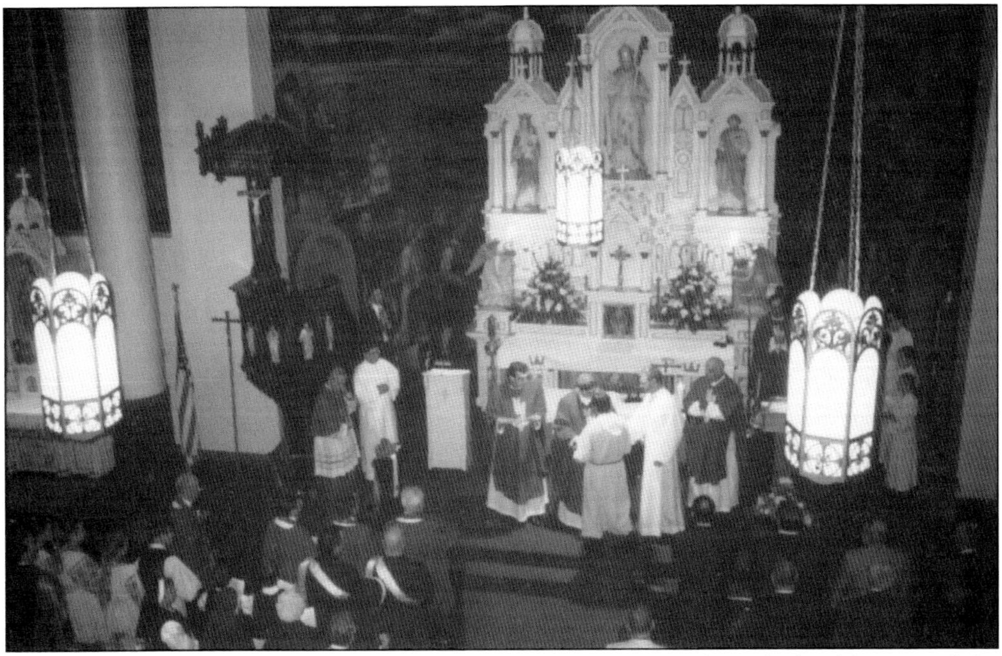

On March 26, 1921, a devastating fire gutted the church, but, through the diligence of the immigrant parishioners, a rebuilt church, designed by Sauer, was ready for dedication on May 30, 1922. As shown during a visit to the area, Cardinal Vinko Puljic of Sarajevo (at center, reading) and local Pittsburgh bishop David Wuerl (left center) celebrate Mass at the new altar on April 3, 1995. (Nancy and Vince Jaksic.)

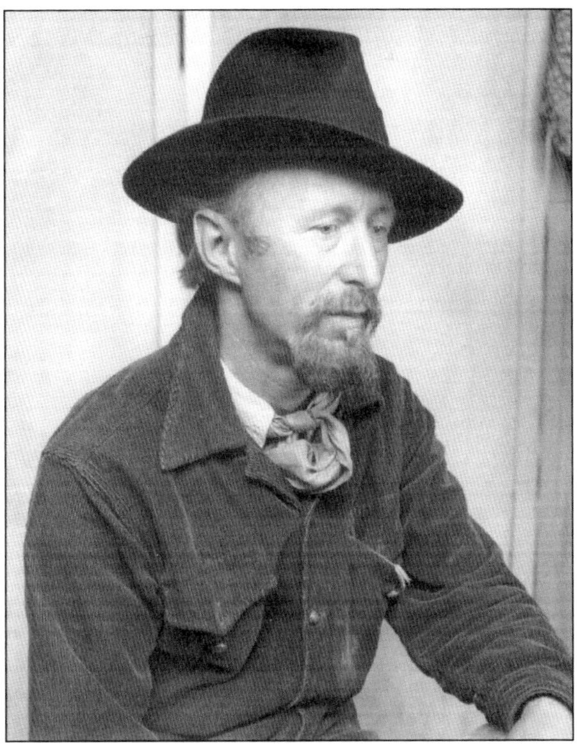

The well-known European artist Maximilian Vanka (1889–1963) immigrated here in 1934, but he always remained a Croatian at heart. He twice painted mural series at St. Nicholas. The first, composed of 11 images, was produced from April to June 1937. The second was a set of nine images, made from July to November 1941. He called these works his gift to America. Visitors have made the murals internationally famous. (Society to Preserve the Millvale Murals of Maxo Vanka.)

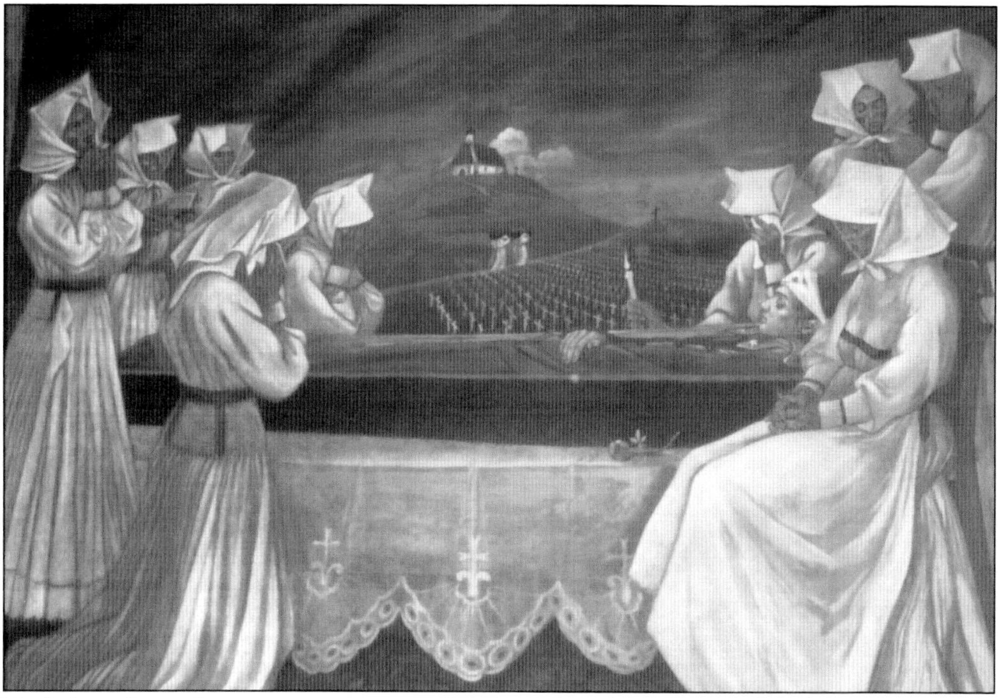

Vanka here forces the viewer to compare and contrast the calm and respectful *The Croatian Mother Raises Her Son for War* (above) to the uneasiness and bleakness of *The Immigrant Mother Raises Her Son for Industry* (below). In the above image, the quiet mourners of the Old World grieve in traditional white dresses around a coffined soldier. Below, dark emotion and rawness dominate the painting of a half-clothed corpse on newspaper in the New World. Using his talent for narrative themes, Vanka has breathed life into a story, recorded in the Johnstown Croatian newspaper, of a son having died in a mining accident, and the deaths of his three brothers during the rescue attempt. Millvale's immigrant population working in the area's mills and mines were well aware of the potential disasters, and of those that did occur, to relatives and friends. (Both, Bill Stout.)

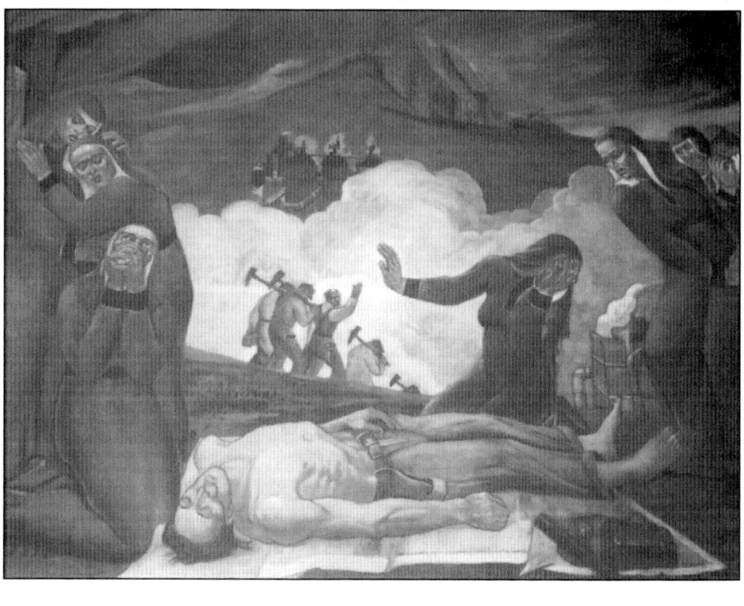

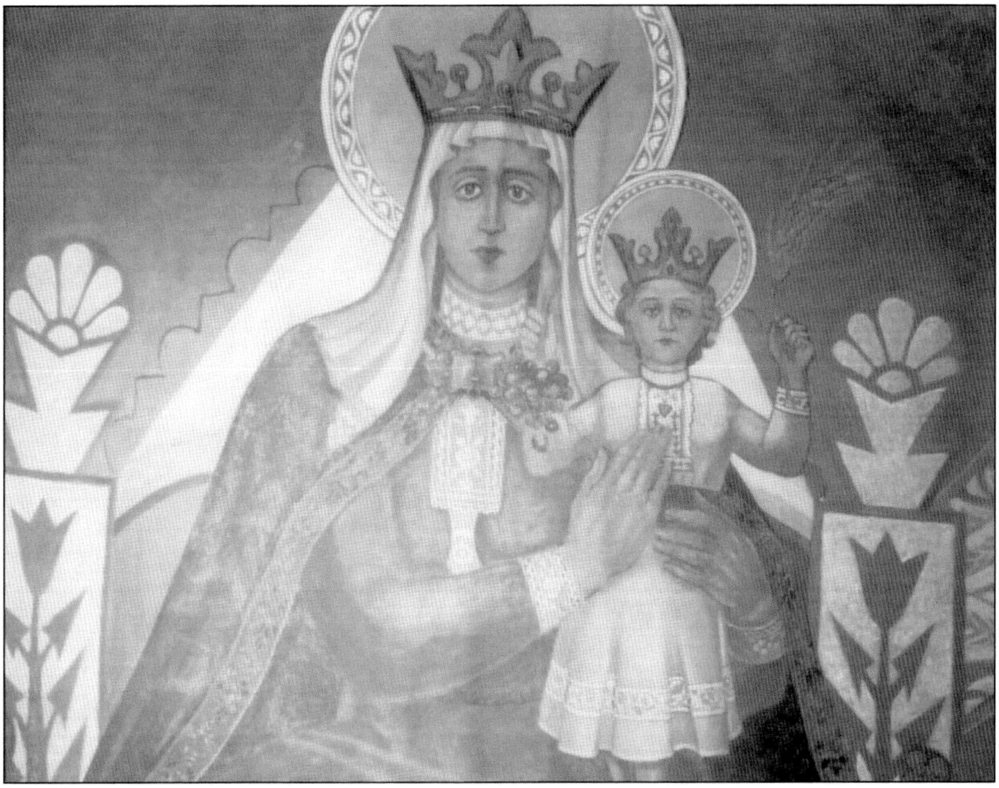

Mary, Queen of Croatia, dressed in royal colors, though clearly of peasant stock, holds the Christ child. Mary is shown here as the protectress of the high altar, as her image covers the sanctuary's ceiling. Vanka has created a memory link to the Byzantine church frescos remembered by the immigrant parishioners. Their church is a refuge from the shocks of the New World. (Bill Stout.)

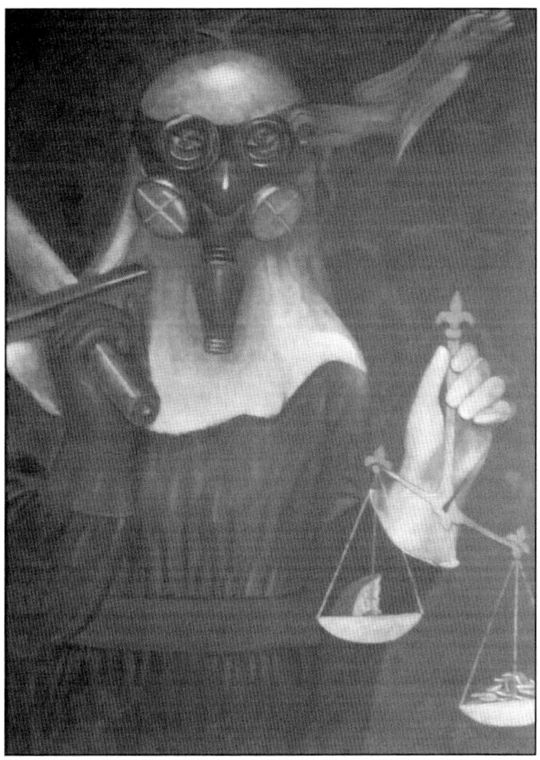

Remembering the horrors of World War I, when he volunteered as an ambulance driver for the Red Cross in Belgium, Vanka has created a most horrific image of *Injustice* wearing a gas mask, carrying a bloody sword, and displaying a scale on which gold outweighs bread. In this work, created in 1941, as a new world war engulfed the planet, the viewer is challenged to unmask this mysterious figure. (Bill Stout.)

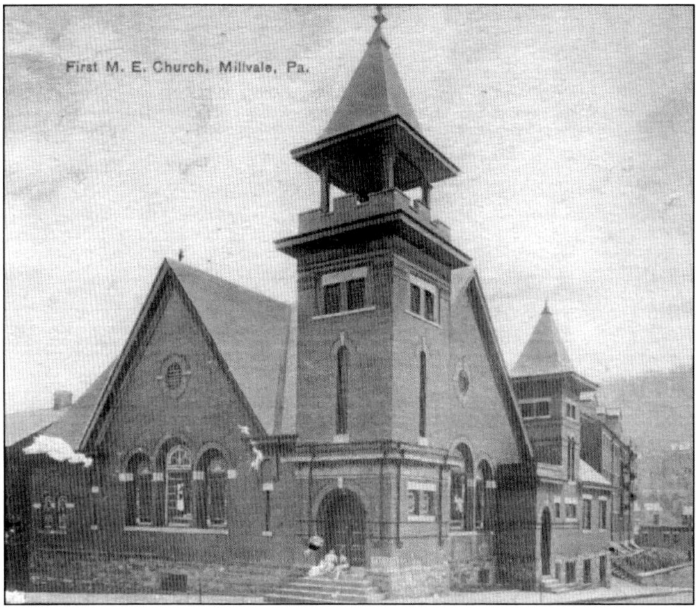

A one-story church known as the Hudson Episcopal Church, on the corner of Hooker (now North) and Elizabeth Streets, was built in 1878 to serve the Methodist congregation. In February 1904, the present structure on Lincoln Avenue and Butler Street (shown here) was dedicated as the First Methodist Church of Millvale. The old property was sold to E.T. Lippert for use by St. John's Evangelical Lutheran Church. (Mary Ann Knochel.)

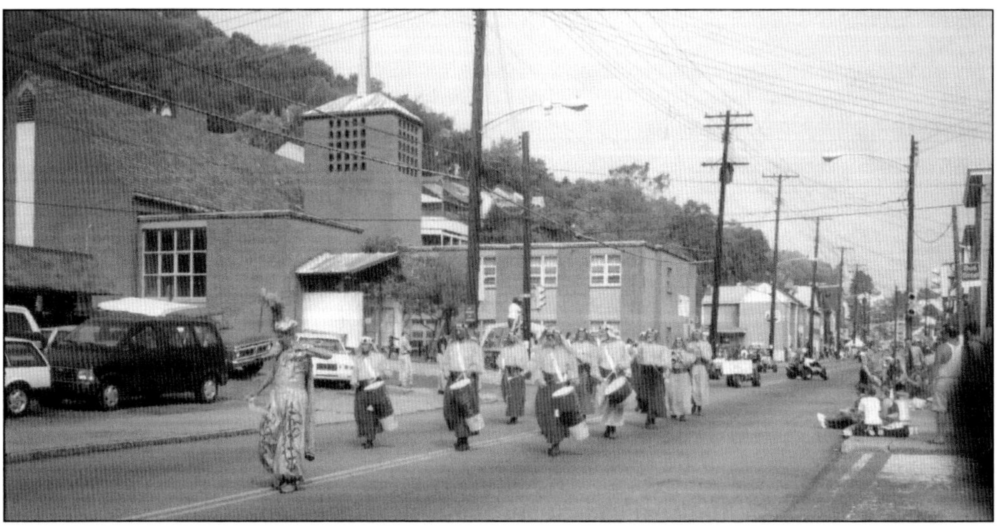

St. John's Lutheran Church, shown here, is the newest in Millvale. Dedicated in 1957, it replaced the church bought by E.T. Lippert in 1904 and donated to the congregation of the German Evangelical Lutheran St. John's Church. (Bill Stout.)

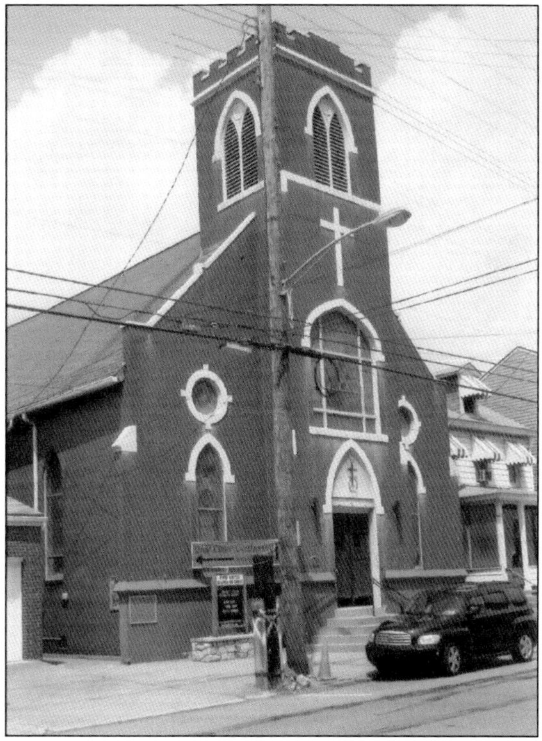

In 1930, the First Evangelical Church underwent renovation after it was decided to install a brick veneer to the building and add several memorial windows. The rededication of the church was held on October 12, 1930. On July 4, 1961, the Congregational Christian Churches and the Evangelical and Reformed Church united to form the new United Church of Christ. (Bill Stout.)

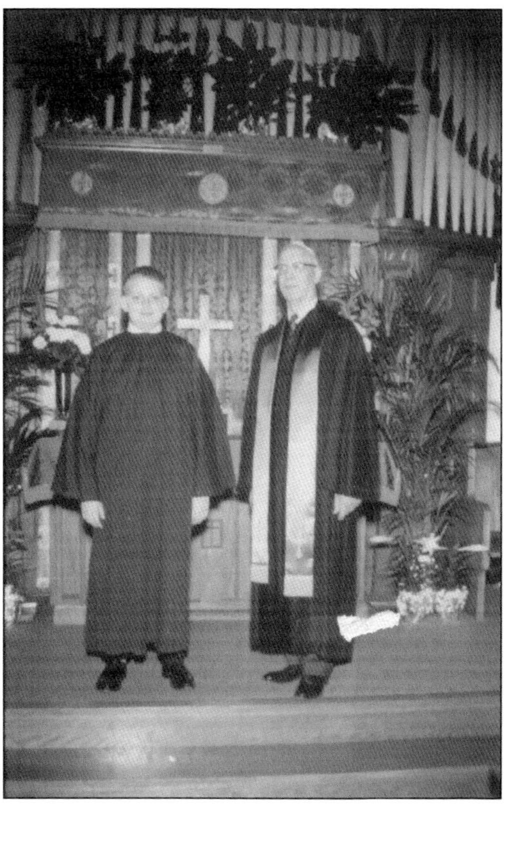

In September 1887, a difference of opinion among the members of the German Reformed Church of Girty's Run resulted in the creation of the First German Evangelical Church (now First United Church of Christ). On August 19, 1888, their new church on Hooker Street (now North Avenue) was dedicated. Robert Stoltenberg (left) poses following his confirmation. (Debra Stoltenberg.)

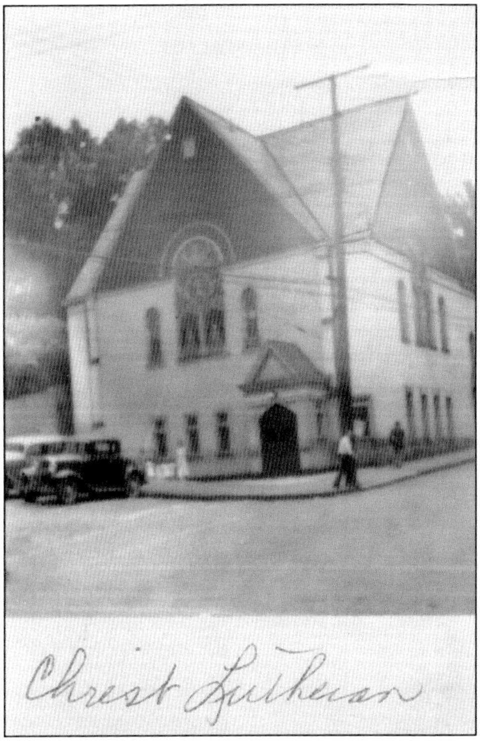

After conducting services in the Opera House and in the hall above Goodwin's Pharmacy for over two years, a new church for the Christ English Evangelical Lutheran community was built on the corner of Lincoln Avenue and Sedgwick Street. Services were first held in the new building on October 11, 1903. (Christ Lutheran Church.)

A massive landslide on January 14, 1914, sent tons of rock and earth through the rear wall of Christ Lutheran Church, damaging the altar, the organ, and furniture. Parishioners rallied and restored the church to its former glory, as depicted in this photograph. The altar is seen here at harvest time on Sunday, September 26, 1915. (Christ Lutheran Church.)

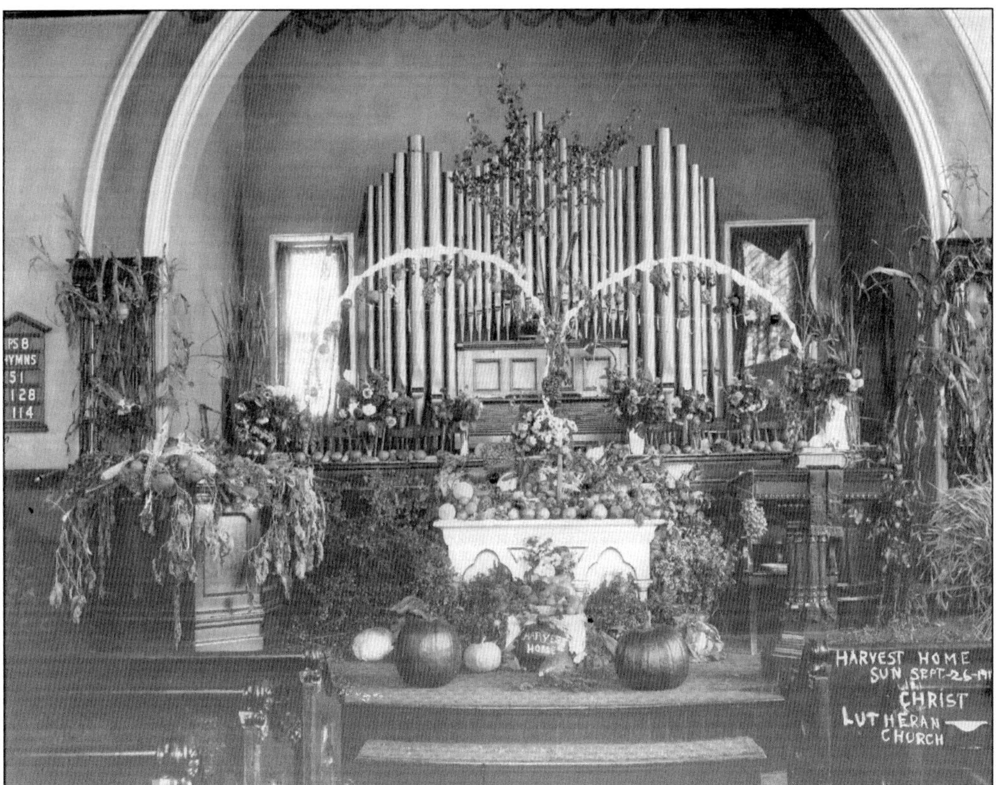

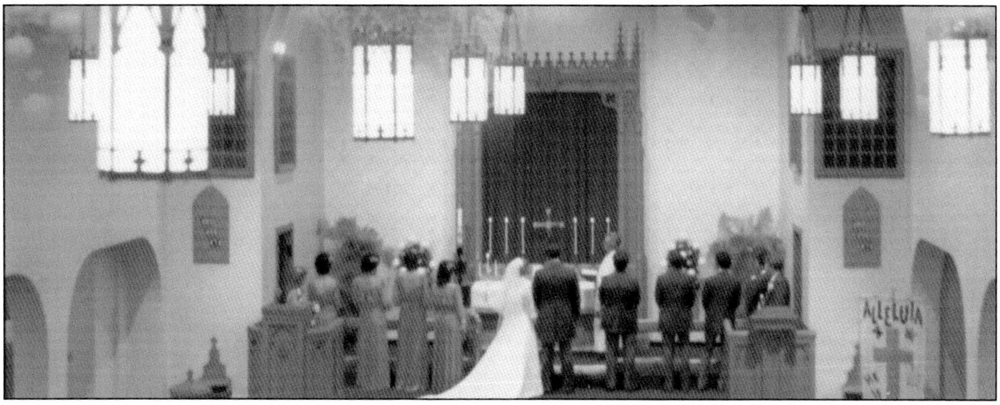

On April 23, 1983, Karen Tritinger and Dennis Wittmer say their wedding vows before the altar at Christ Lutheran Church. This photograph provides a good glimpse of the church's relatively unadorned interior. (Karen Wittmer.)

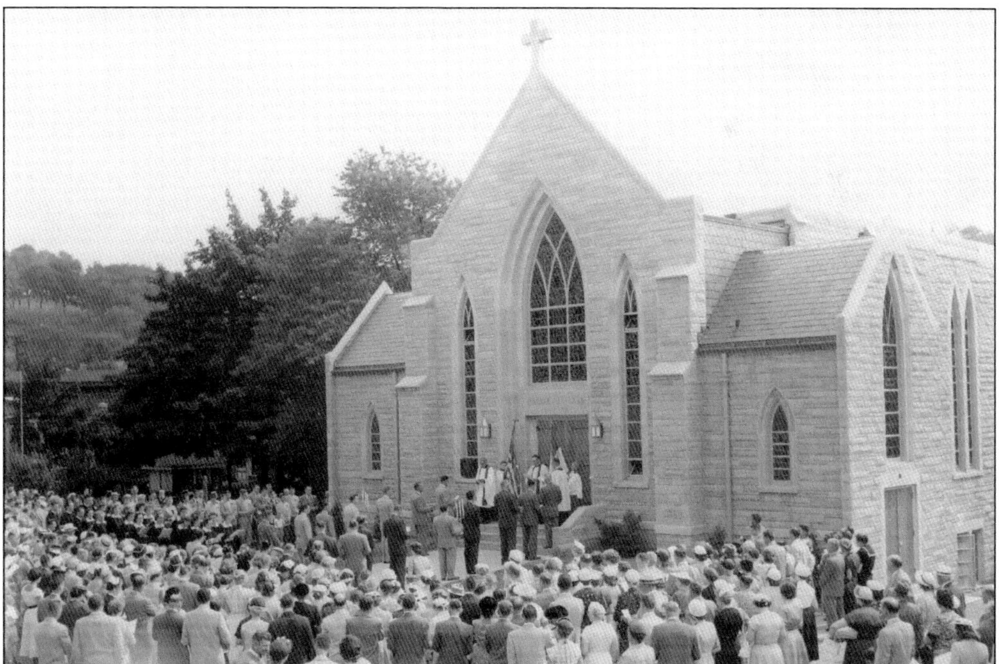

Population growth following World War II was the major factor in initiating plans for a new Christ Lutheran Church. Ground breaking for the new stone structure on North Avenue took place on September 27, 1953, and the new building was dedicated on August 22, 1954. (Christ Lutheran Church.)

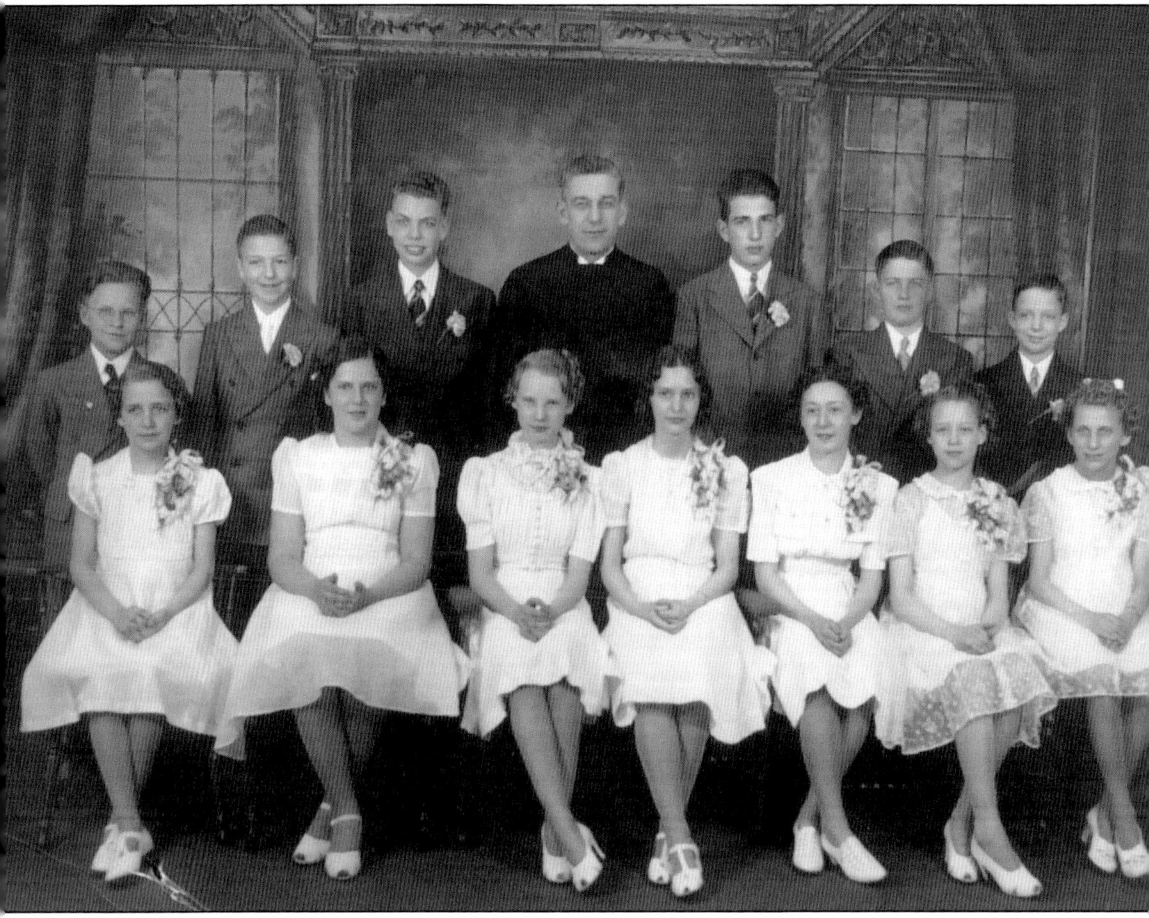

Pastor Clarence B. Daniels (second row, center) poses with the 1940 confirmation celebrants of Christ Lutheran Church. Shown here are, from left to right, (first row) Alvira Allerton, Terese Waddell, Ruth Ann Herbe, Edith Ann Bauer, Loretta Worst, Dorothy Niely, and Jean Zeilfelder; (second row) Ralph Thompson, Elmer Setzenfend, James Cooper, Pastor Daniels, William Wilkinson, Wade Bender, and Frank Ramendi. (Christ Lutheran Church.)

Four

The Teacher Says

Although the First Ward School is generally recognized as Millvale's first school, there were two, if not three, earlier schools in the area. The earliest school for which there is documentation was constructed in 1849 in the Borough of Duquesne on Bank Lane, along the old Pennsylvania Canal. While it would become part of the borough with its incorporation in 1868, this timber structure, finally razed in 1923 to make room for the Washington Crossing Bridge, is remembered more for being the office of Ed Vero, a businessman and burgess, than for being a schoolhouse. An old redbrick building, built around 1876, still standing on the corner of Frederick and O'Brien Streets, is believed to have been a school serving Shaler Township.

The history of Millvale's Catholic schools is intertwined with that of the Sisters of St. Francis. On January 7, 1885, two years before the church was built, the sisters took charge of St. Anthony's School. As there was no place for them to live, they traveled daily from St. Mary's Convent in Sharpsburg for three months during the harsh winter. In April 1886, a convent was opened in the town for the four sisters. In 1893, they began teaching at St. Anne's after accommodations were made to the school to include two classrooms. As a religious rule forbade a sister to walk alone through public streets, it was necessary for two sisters to travel from St. Anthony's convent to St. Ann's. Later, Mount Alvernia, the motherhouse of the sisters, would accommodate an all-girls high school until 2010.

In 1971, Millvale High School closed its doors for the last time. It grew from one teacher and 25 students in 1898 to 26 teachers and 450 students in 1971. The Shaler Area School District now serves Millvale and Etna Boroughs and Reserve and Shaler Townships.

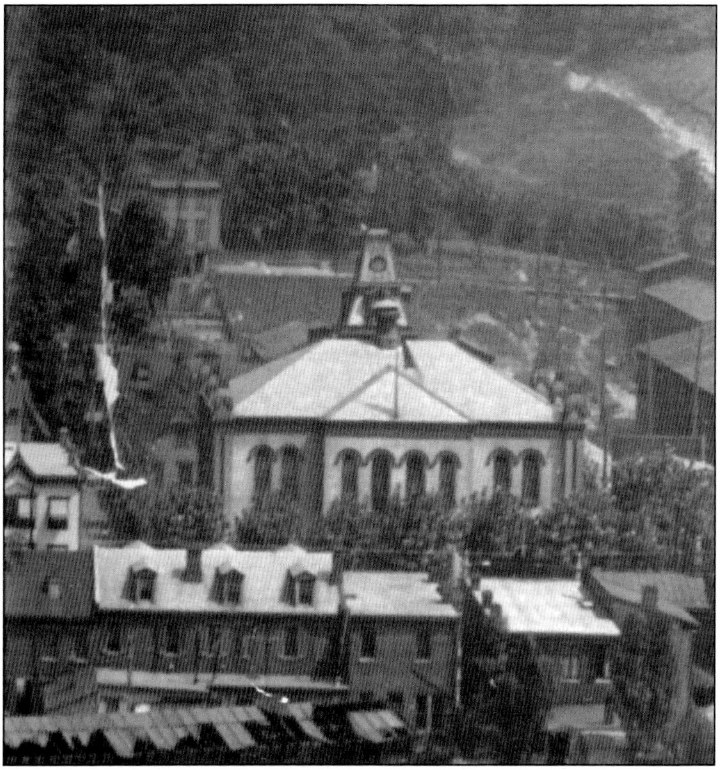

The First Ward School was built in 1874 on what was aptly named School Street. Classes were discontinued there after the 1936 flood. In 1938, the Millvale Fire Company took over the building. During World War II, it was used as a ration center for food and gasoline stamps. (Richard Mikus.)

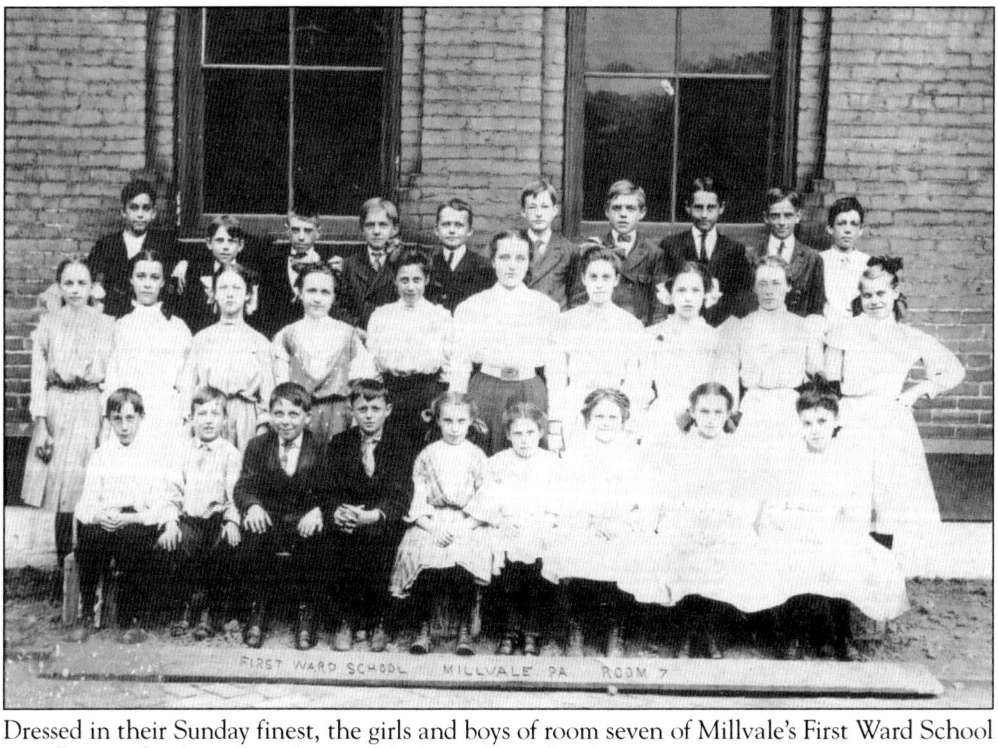

Dressed in their Sunday finest, the girls and boys of room seven of Millvale's First Ward School proudly pose for their class photograph. (Jennifer Cohen.)

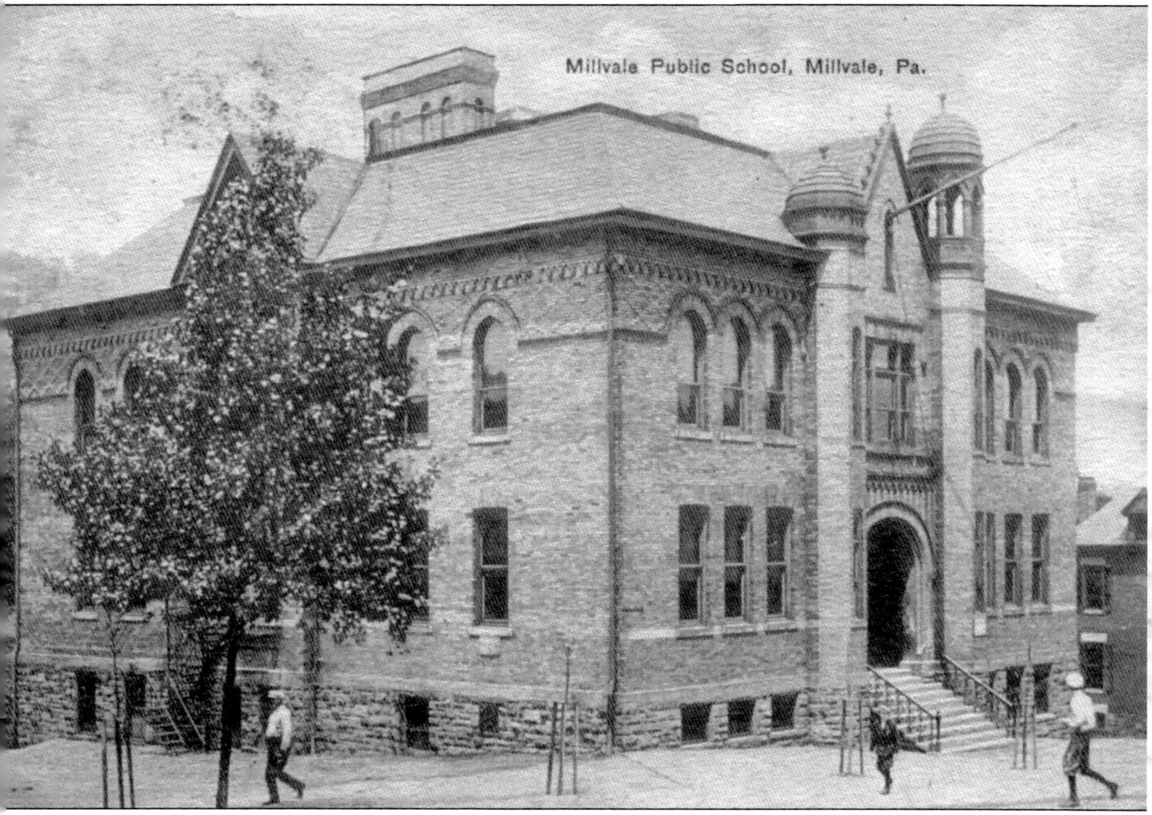

The Second Ward School on Howard Street and Stanton Avenue was dedicated on July 23, 1885, with a solemn ceremony and a parade by the Millvale Masonic Lodge. The redbrick school with red mortar was thought to be one of the finest school buildings in Allegheny County at the time. The size of the building was 71 feet by 81 feet. The roof was made of Vermont green slate. The concrete basement was divided into an election room, separate bathrooms for boys and girls, and a large room for the furnace and storage of coal. The first floor had four classrooms, a principal's office, and a broad flight of stairs to the second floor, which had five classrooms. The floors were laid in hard maple. The blackboards were four and a half feet high and composed of shaved slate. The building was wired for electric lighting, and speaking tubes ran from all classrooms to the principal's office. The building was razed and replaced with the Regency apartment complex. (Mary Ann Knochel.)

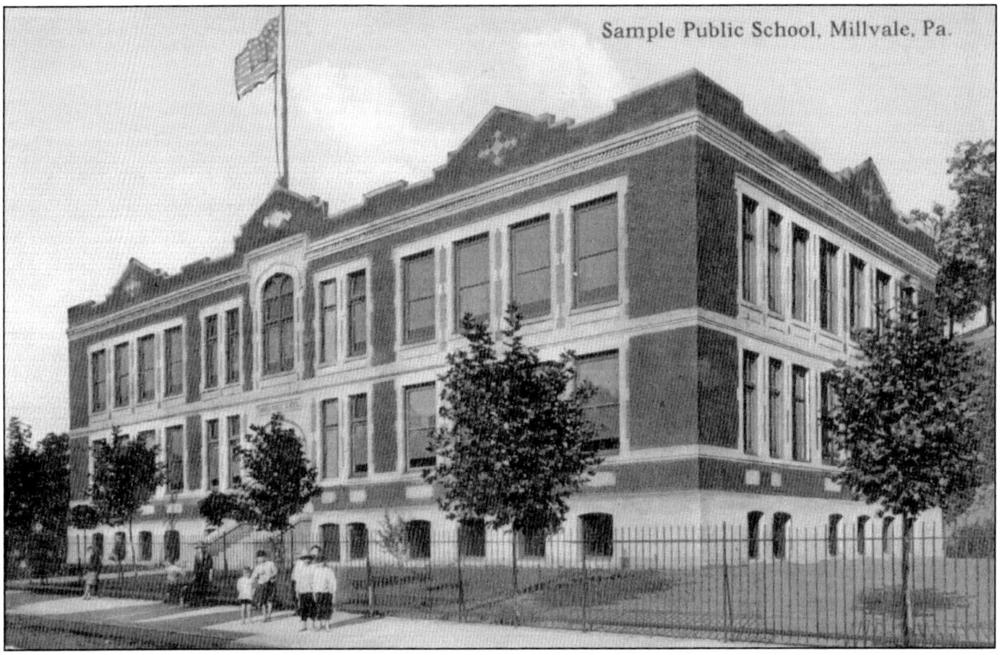

Built in 1908, the Sample School on Evergreen Avenue is the third in a series of schools serving Millvale's Third Ward. The original school still stands on Frederick Street and functions as a double dwelling. The second school, built on Evergreen and Davis Streets, was later torn down to erect the Sample School. (Carol Szwedko.)

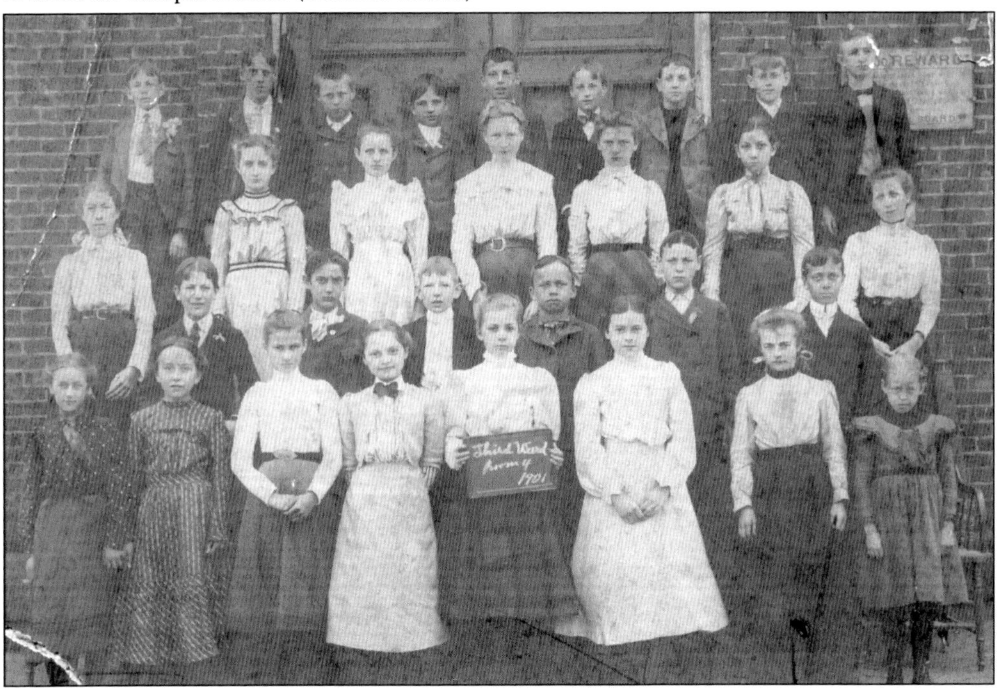

Standing on the steps of the old Third Ward School, located on Evergreen and Davis Streets, the students of room four pose for their class photograph. This is the second of three buildings that served as Millvale's Third Ward School. (Millvale Borough.)

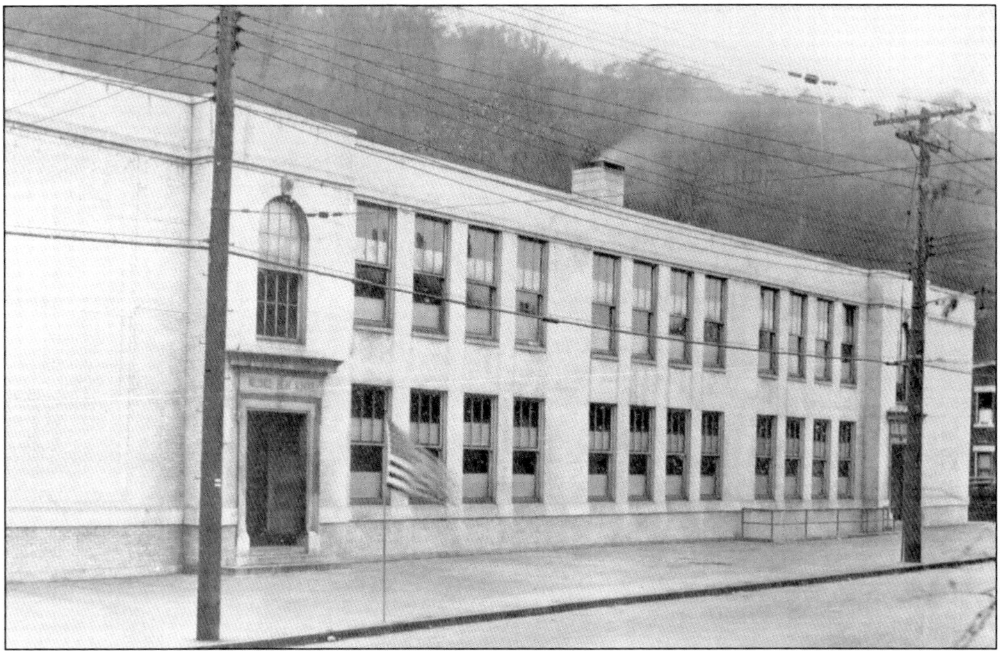

Millvale High School, which opened in January 1926, was the last public school to be built in Millvale. Prior to its erection, two-year high school classes were held on the upper floor of the Third Ward School until 1919, when the curriculum was extended to three years. High school studies were not extended to four years until 1923. (Mary Ann Knochel.)

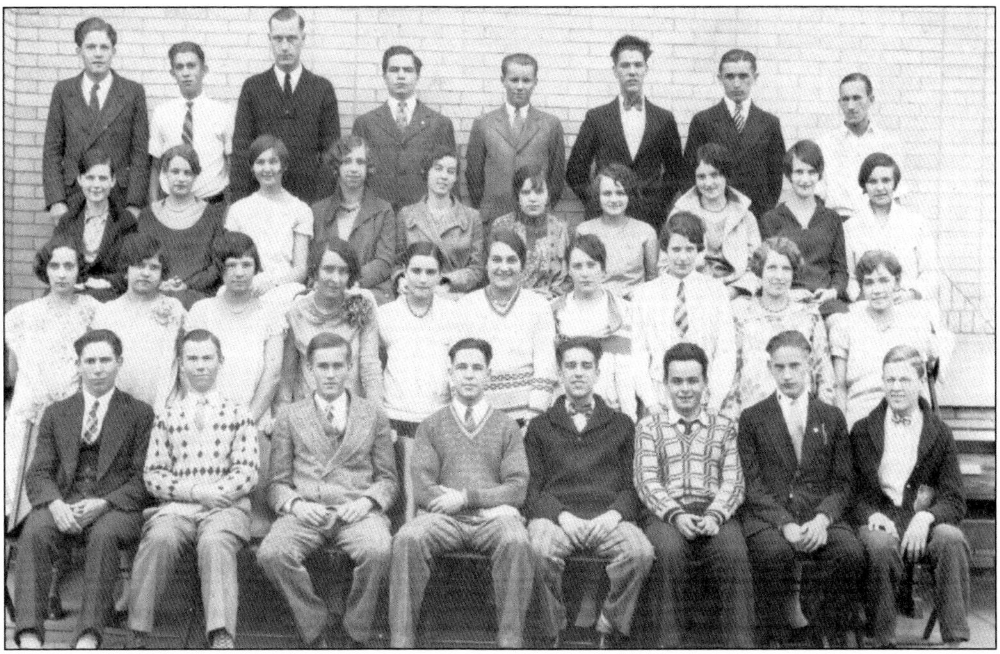

The graduating class of 1929 had originally, as freshmen, numbered 98. It was divided into one commercial and two academic groups. By junior year, the class numbered 44 and had academic, commercial, and vocational courses. Ultimately, 38 students graduated. It was the largest graduating class up to that time. (Mary Ann Knochel.)

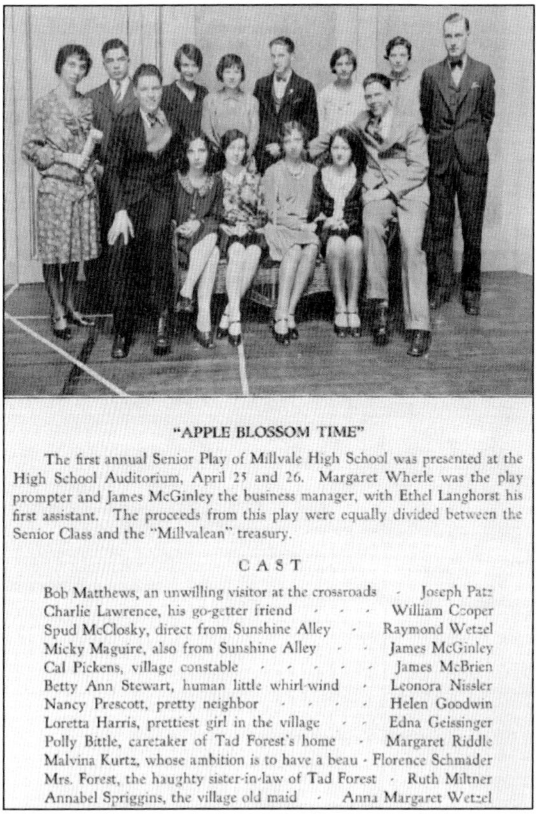

"APPLE BLOSSOM TIME"

The first annual Senior Play of Millvale High School was presented at the High School Auditorium, April 25 and 26. Margaret Wherle was the play prompter and James McGinley the business manager, with Ethel Langhorst his first assistant. The proceeds from this play were equally divided between the Senior Class and the "Millvalean" treasury.

CAST

Bob Matthews, an unwilling visitor at the crossroads - Joseph Patz
Charlie Lawrence, his go-getter friend - - - William Cooper
Spud McClosky, direct from Sunshine Alley - Raymond Wetzel
Micky Maguire, also from Sunshine Alley - - James McGinley
Cal Pickens, village constable - - - - - James McBrien
Betty Ann Stewart, human little whirl-wind - Leonora Nissler
Nancy Prescott, pretty neighbor - - - - Helen Goodwin
Loretta Harris, prettiest girl in the village - - Edna Geissinger
Polly Bittle, caretaker of Tad Forest's home - Margaret Riddle
Malvina Kurtz, whose ambition is to have a beau - Florence Schmader
Mrs. Forest, the haughty sister-in-law of Tad Forest - Ruth Miltner
Annabel Spriggins, the village old maid - Anna Margaret Wetzel

Apple Blossom Time was the first annual senior play at Millvale High School. It was performed in the high school auditorium on April 25–26, 1929. The proceeds from the play were divided equally between the senior class and the *Millvalean* yearbook treasury. (Mary Ann Knochel.)

This picture depicts the state-of-the-art auditorium of Millvale High School, where plays, activities, and commencement ceremonies took place. (Mary Ann Knochel.)

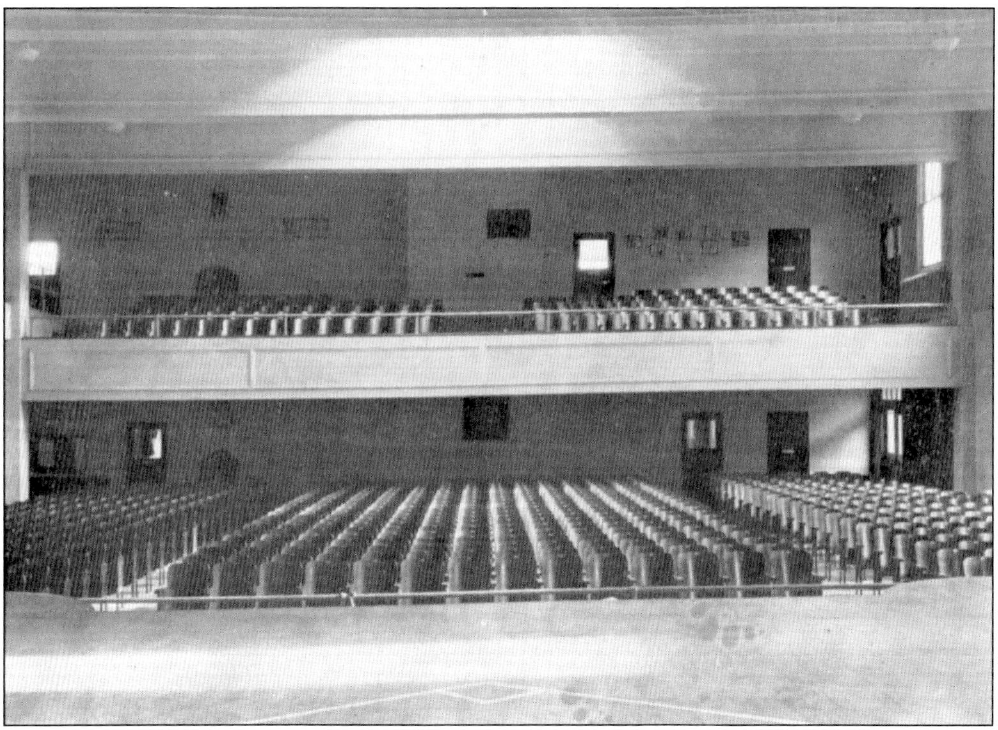

In addition to the academic and business classes listed here, the school offered athletics, including swimming (in the pool at the back of the school building), football, baseball, and basketball. (Mary Ann Knochel.)

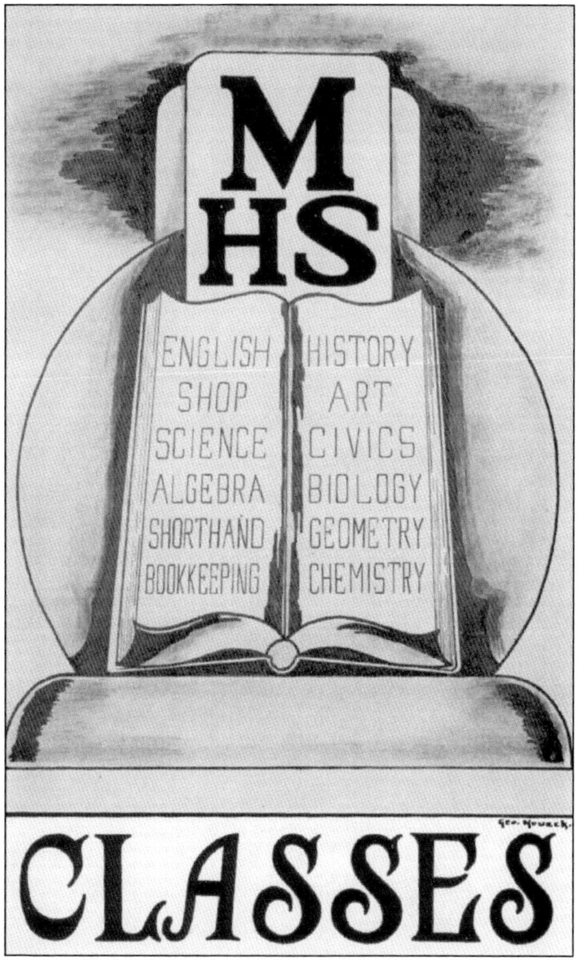

Proudly displaying the diplomas they were just awarded by Millvale High School on June 2, 1940, Dorothy Bertram (third from right) and this group of her friends pose for family pictures. (Dorothy Bertram Pfischner.)

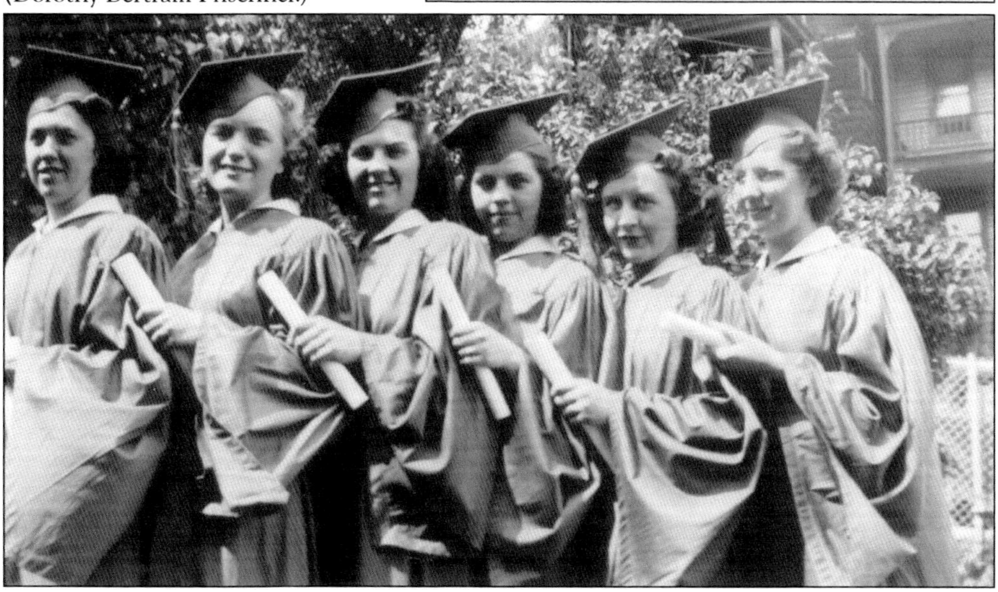

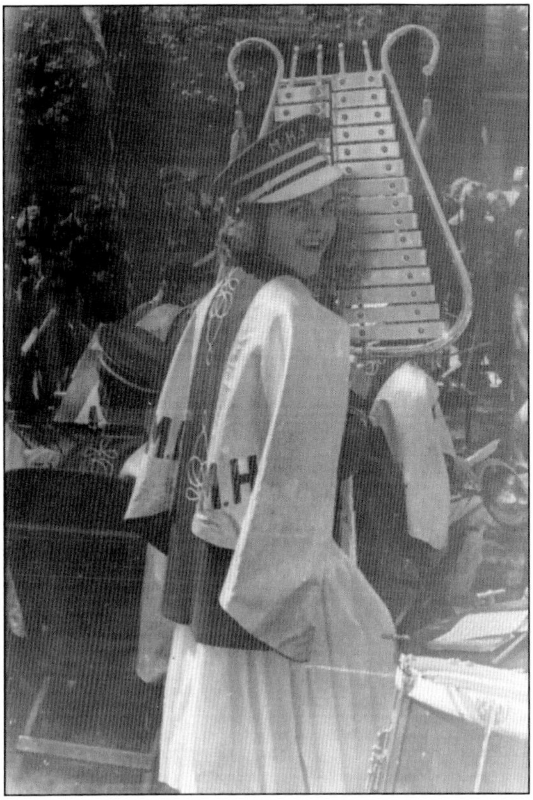

The marching band, an important part of Millvale High School's program, played at games, parades, and events. Here, Dorothy Bertram poses with her bell lyre before performing. The bell lyre is a glockenspiel mounted in a portable lyre-shaped frame and used especially in marching bands. (Dorothy Bertram Pfischner.)

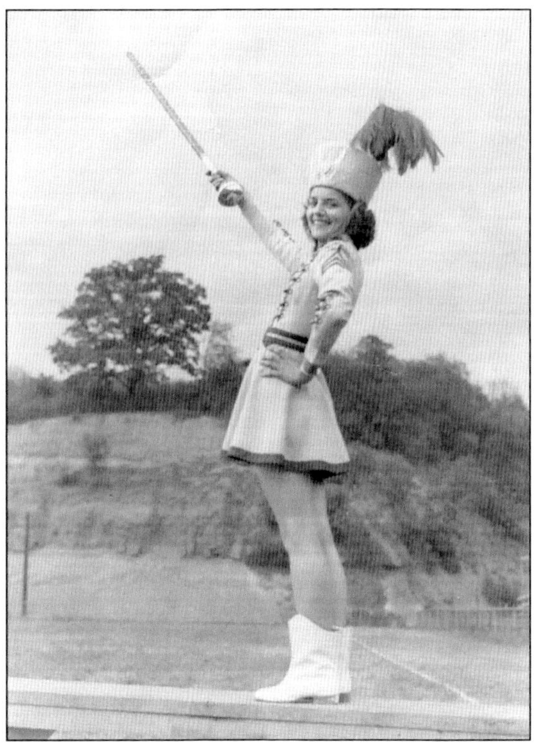

Getting ready to lead the Millvale High School band, Elsie Marlovits poses in her cream and red-trimmed uniform. Seen here in 1948, she was the band's drum major. (Elsie Marlovits Grubic.)

Under the coaching of Joseph T. McCarthy, a former Duquesne University fullback, Millvale High School's football squad became tri-borough champions for the first time in 1939. The following year, the team suffered only one loss and was acknowledged with a banquet at the Pittsburgh Athletic Association. In 1941, the team became the Class B champion and was inducted into the Shaler High School Hall of Fame in 2011. (Mary Ann Knochel.)

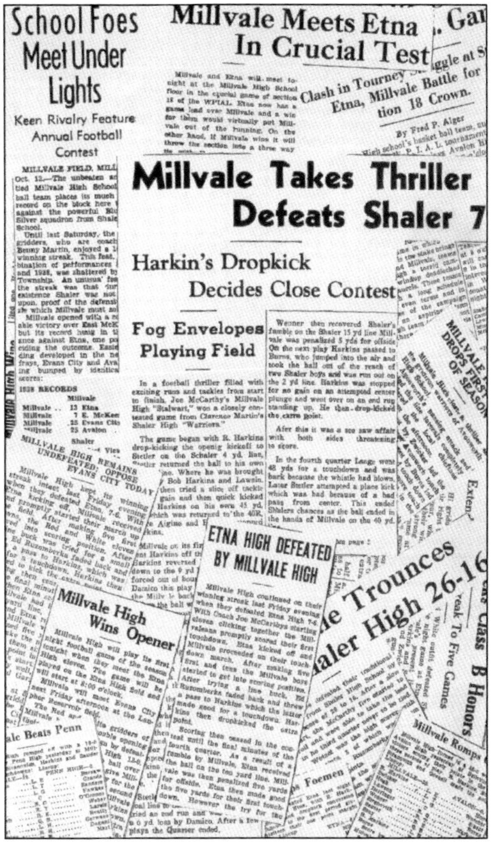

Each of Millvale's Catholic churches had elementary schools. This unusual photograph depicts the Sisters of St. Francis serving as the faculty of St. Ann's School in 1938. Shown here are, from left to right, (first row) Sisters Francis Clare Baumann, Clementine Battaglia, and Aelreda Hesidence; (second row) Sisters Mary Howard Kalchthaler, Audrey Sieger, Regina Mary Callaghan, and Teresa Rengers; (third row) Sisters Norma Sieger, Juliana Stein, Mary Paul Houser, Evanilde Heinrich, and Florence Sieber. (Mount Alvernia Archives.)

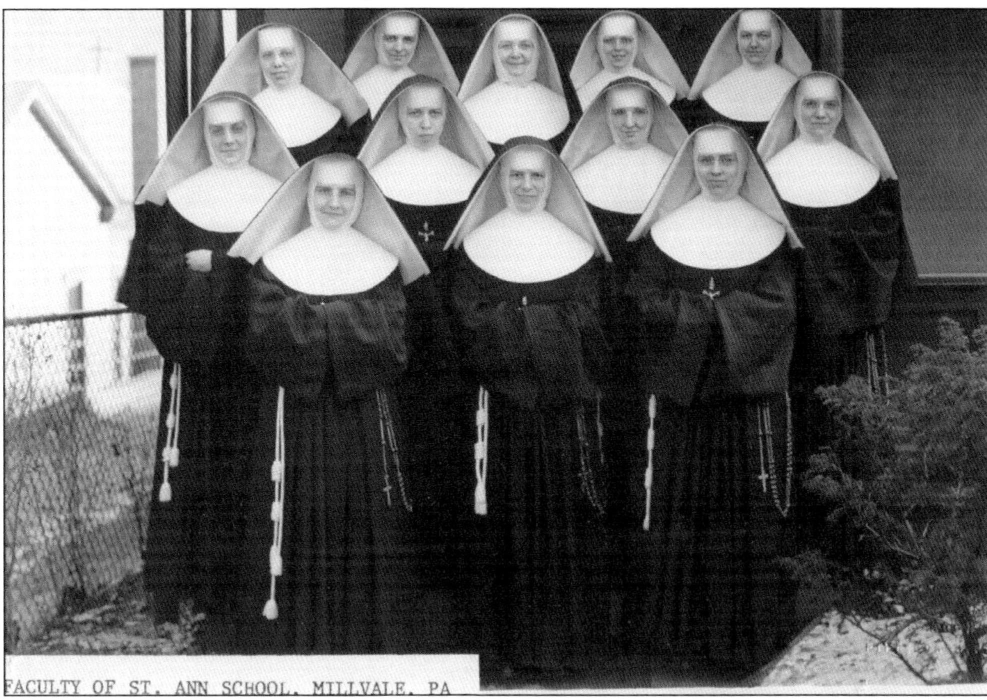

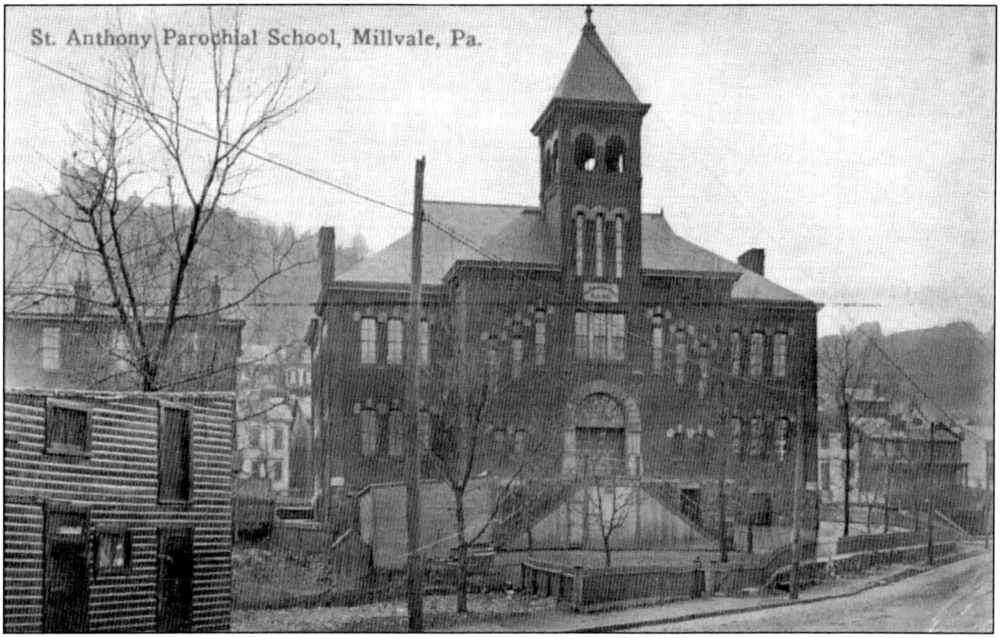

In 1876, the original German school built by the Holy Ghost Fathers was a two-room brick structure. In 1892, Pastor Zielenbach personally visited the 339 member families of St. Anthony's, impressing on them the need for a new school. The old structure could no longer accommodate the students. The new school was dedicated in 1893 and used until it was demolished in 1963. (Mary Ann Knochel.)

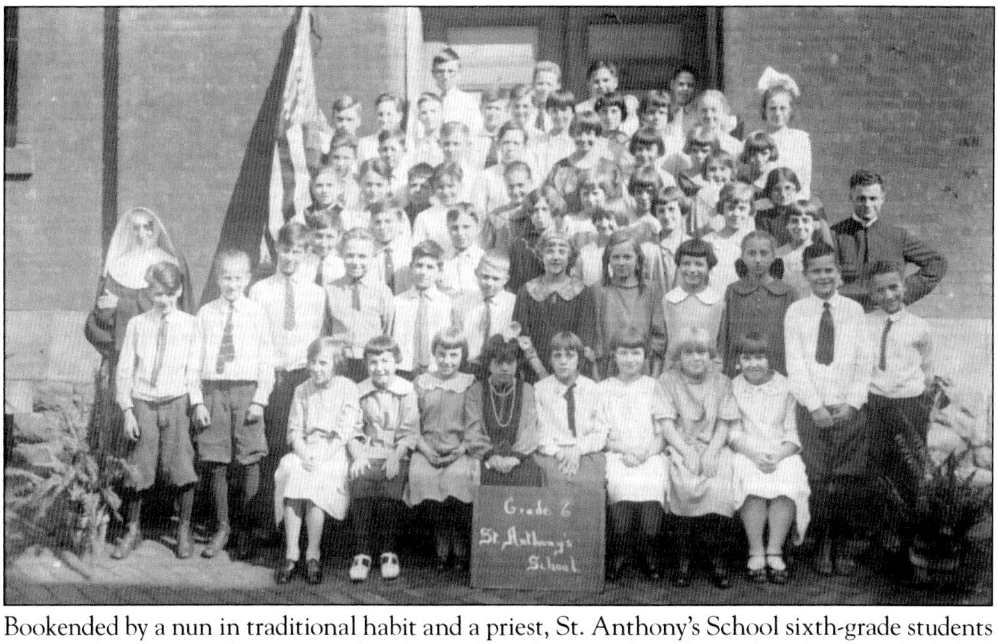

Bookended by a nun in traditional habit and a priest, St. Anthony's School sixth-grade students pose in their best outfits. Boys in knickers, white shirts, and ties have their hair neatly slicked down. The girls—some sporting ringlets, others bobbed haircuts, and even two with a bow—wear plain dresses accented with lace or cloth collars. One adds to her fashion by wearing pearls. (Sudie Schindler.)

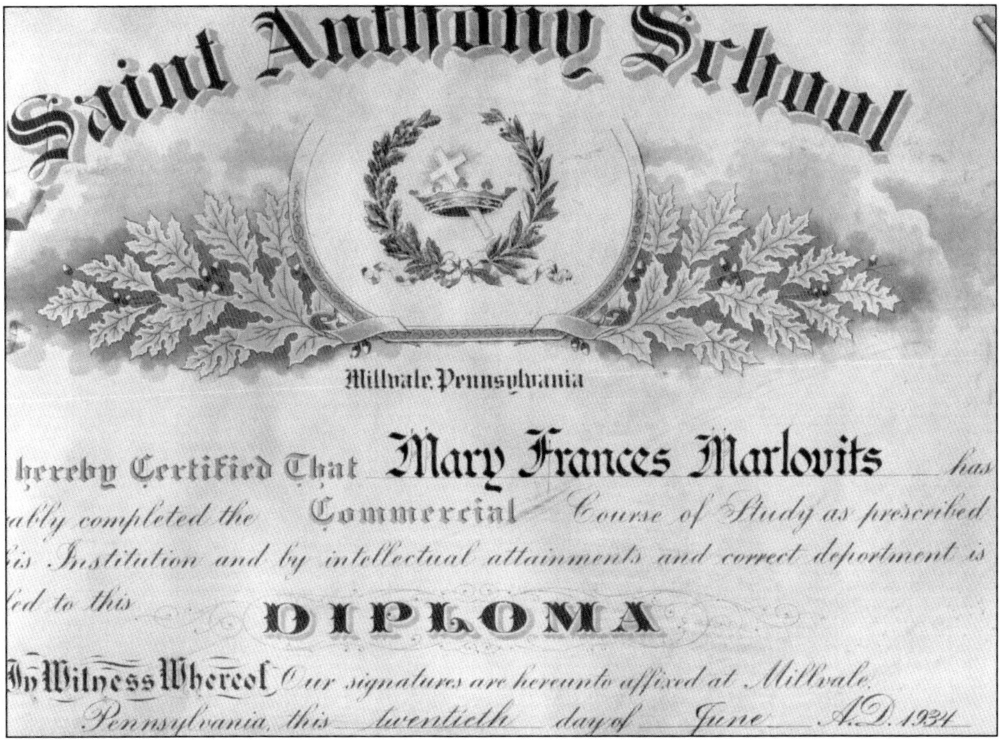

Saint Anthony School

Millvale, Pennsylvania

hereby Certified That Mary Frances Marlovits has
ably completed the Commercial Course of Study as prescribed
his Institution and by intellectual attainments and correct deportment is
led to this

DIPLOMA

In Witness Whereof Our signatures are hereunto affixed at Millvale,
Pennsylvania, this twentieth day of June A.D. 1934

Since attending high school was not an option available to many grade-school students, St. Anthony's Parochial School developed a commercial course of study in 1916 that enabled its graduates to successfully enter the workforce. During the Depression and the subsequent economic distress, the number of students decreased, and the class was discontinued. (Jean Domico.)

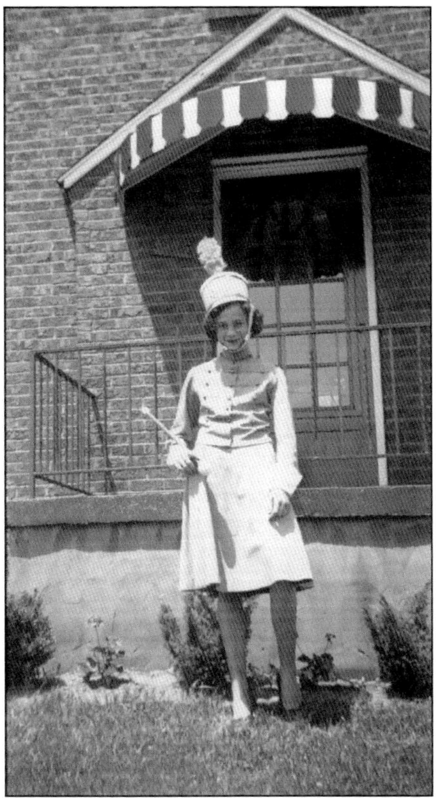

Majorette Jean Mikus proudly poses before her home in 1950. She is dressed in her uniform for St. Anthony's marching band. Every year, the band performed in the Christmas parade in East Liberty. (Jean Mikus Anson.)

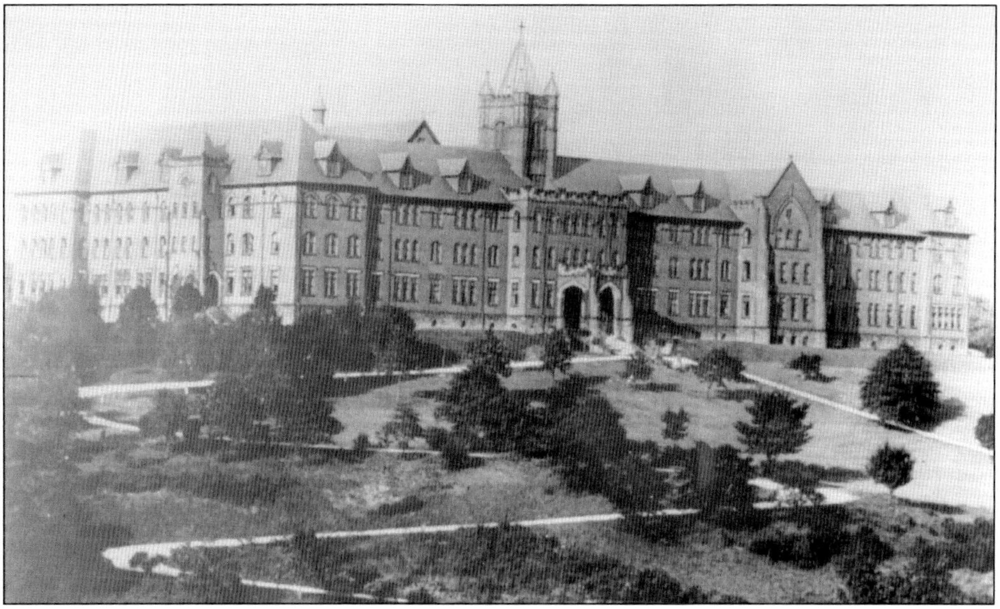

In 1891, a "convent school" was opened in the first motherhouse of the Sisters of St. Francis on Pittsburgh's South Side. When the motherhouse moved to Mount Alvernia, so did the "convent school." By 1931, the school became accredited by the Commonwealth of Pennsylvania. In 1936, it opened its doors to day students in addition to those boarders who desired to join its community of nuns. (Mount Alvernia Archives.)

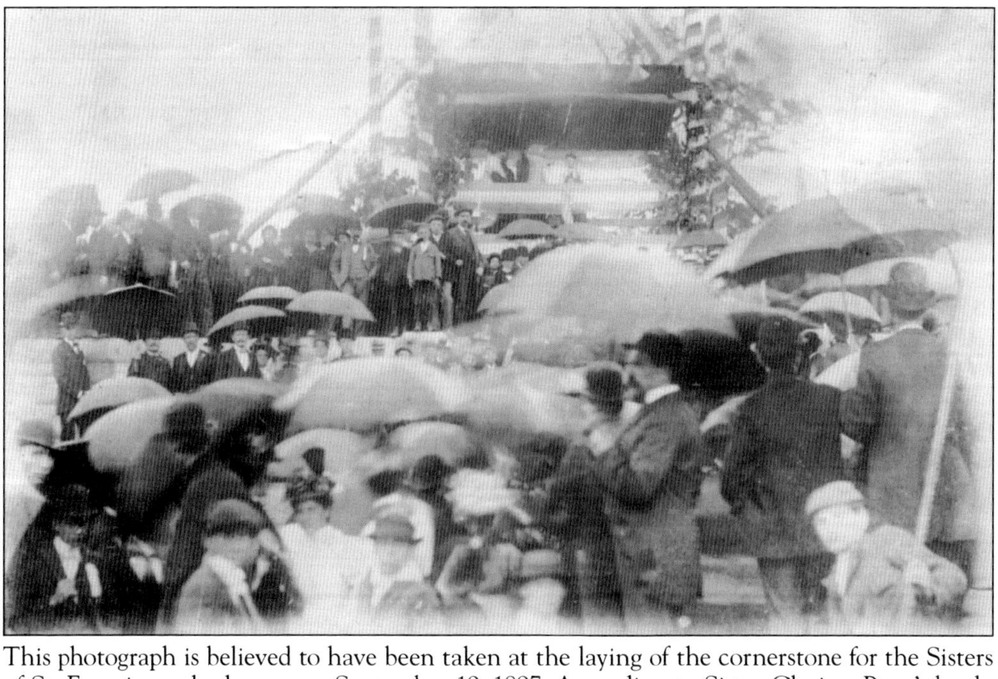

This photograph is believed to have been taken at the laying of the cornerstone for the Sisters of St. Francis motherhouse, on September 19, 1897. According to Sister Clarissa Popp's book, the day began bright and sunny, ideal for the thousands of dignitaries and people who attended. The unexpected rain seemed like a benediction from heaven, but exercises had to be performed hastily. (Mount Alvernia Archives.)

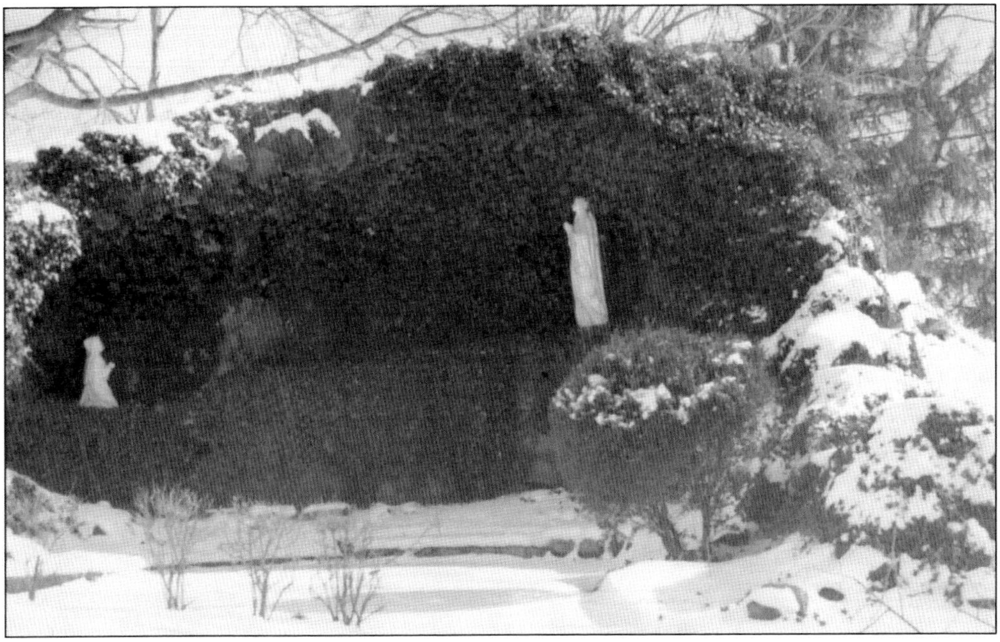

Halfway between the motherhouse on the hilltop and the entrance to the driveway on Evergreen Avenue is a replica of the famous shrine of Lourdes in France. In this natural rock grotto are statues of the Virgin Mary and a simple French peasant maiden kneeling in adoration. Thousands of people from Millvale and greater Pittsburgh would come and kneel in devotion in the early 1900s. (Mount Alvernia Archives.)

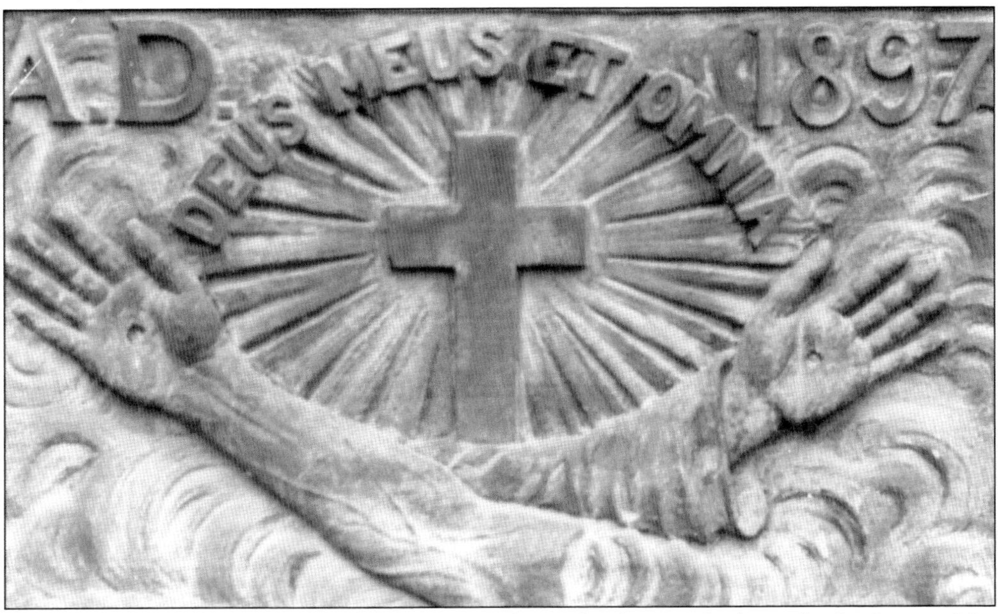

The spot on the hilltop overlooking Millvale was chosen for their motherhouse by the Sisters of the Third Order of St. Francis. It was named Mount Alvernia after the mount in Assisi, Italy, where a seraph imprinted the Sacred Stigmata upon St. Francis. The sisters have served as teachers and nurses around the world, but especially in Pittsburgh, where they established and ran St. Francis Hospital. (Mount Alvernia Archives.)

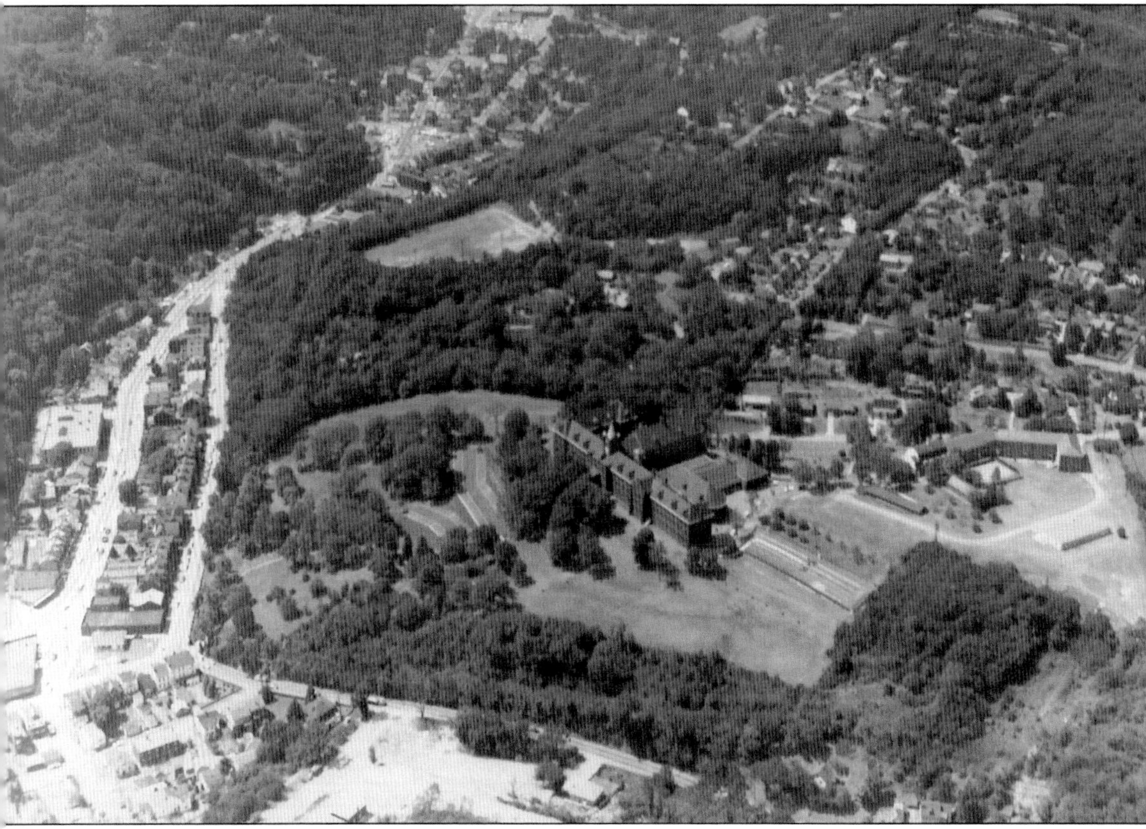

William Seibert emigrated from Germany in 1836 and eventually moved to Pittsburgh, where he opened a shoe store in what is now known as "the Strip." Later, he moved to Millvale and bought a farm on what is now Mount Alvernia. The motherhouse is situated on 22 acres in two adjoining tracts of land in Millvale and Shaler Township. The land was purchased in 1894. (Mount Alvernia Archives.)

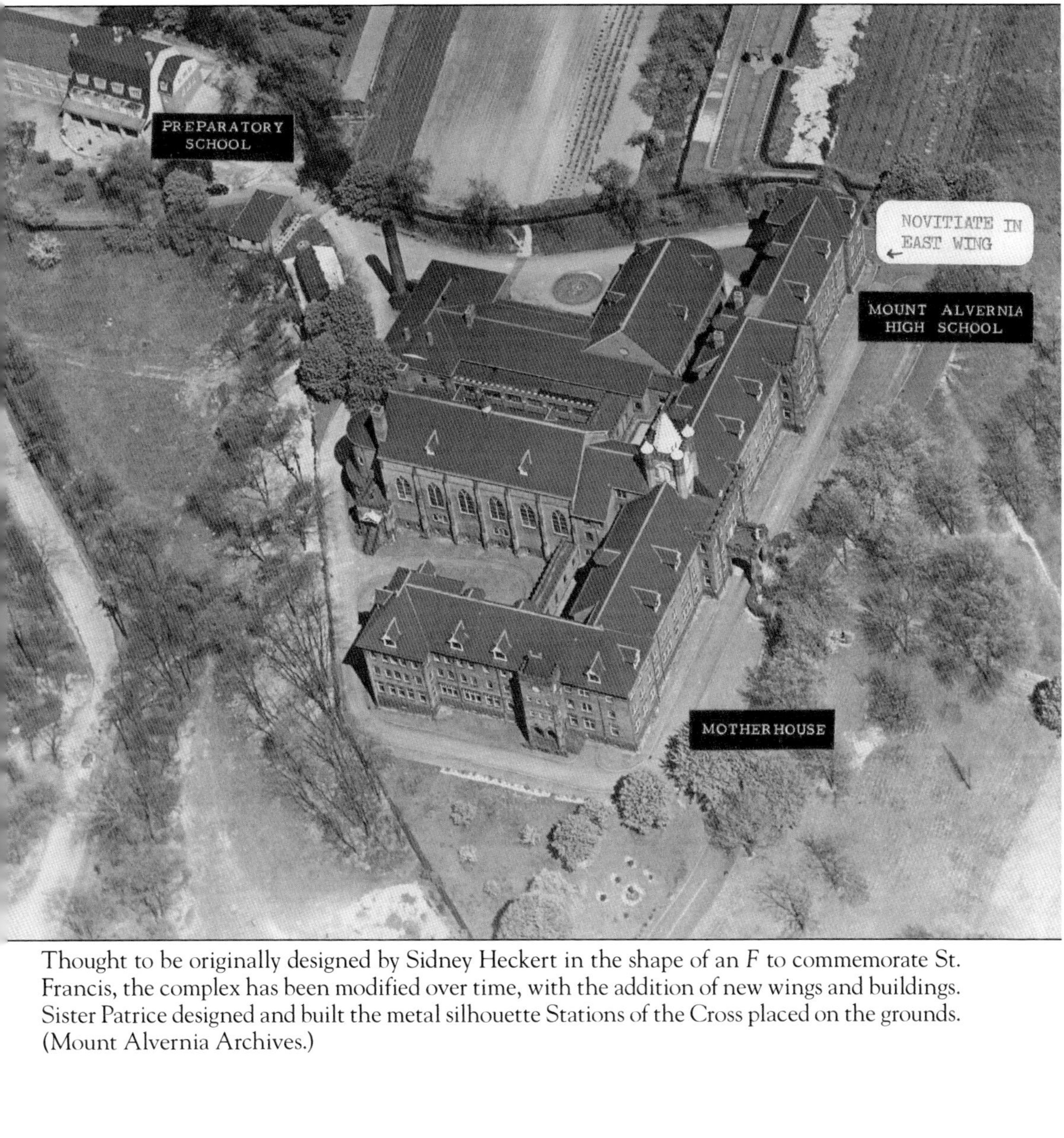

Thought to be originally designed by Sidney Heckert in the shape of an *F* to commemorate St. Francis, the complex has been modified over time, with the addition of new wings and buildings. Sister Patrice designed and built the metal silhouette Stations of the Cross placed on the grounds. (Mount Alvernia Archives.)

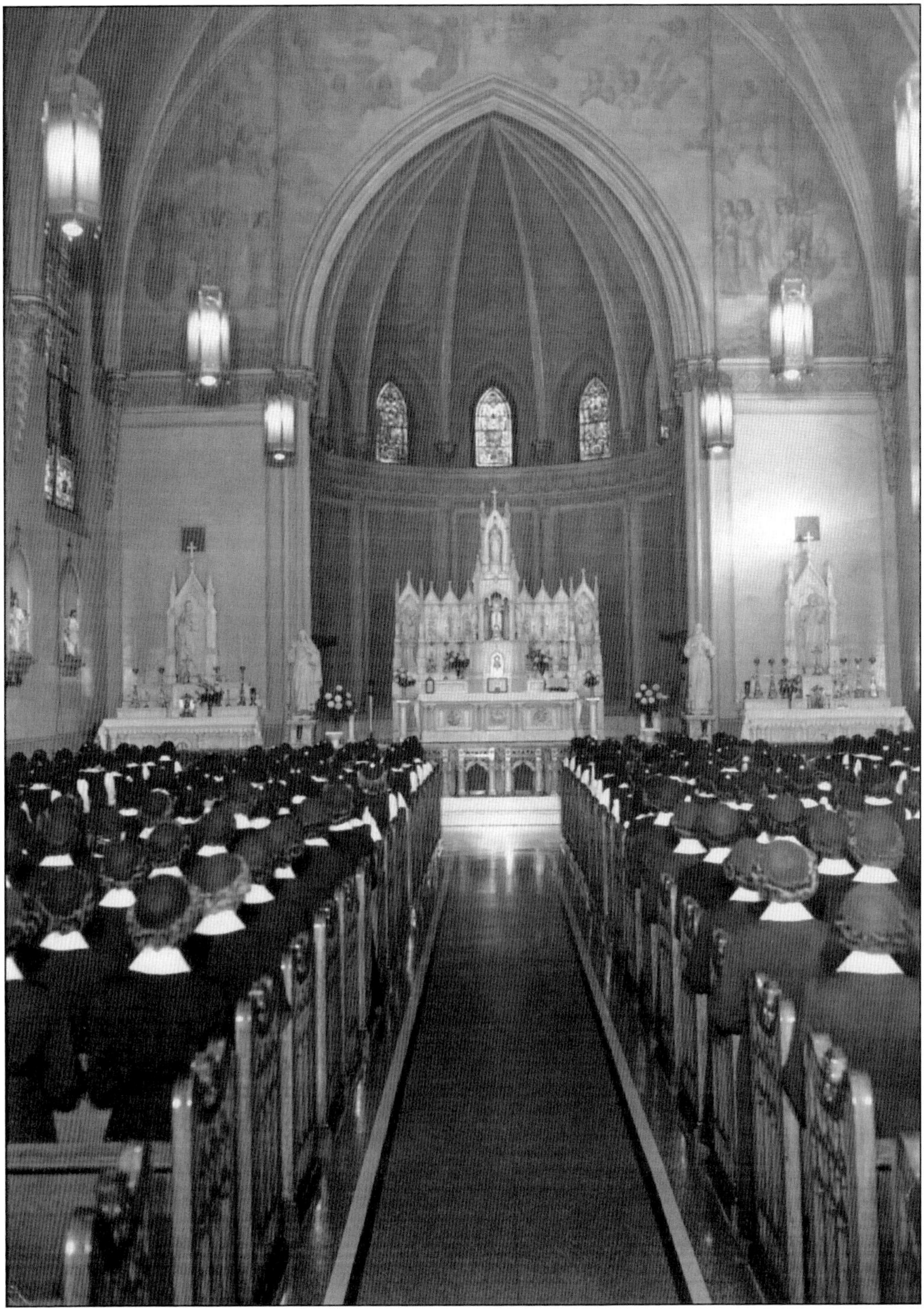

Clad in their navy blue uniforms, white blouses, and navy blue beanies, Mount Alvernia students attend services in the very beautiful chapel within the motherhouse of Mount Alvernia in 1940. Due to declining student enrollment, the school closed its doors in June 2010, after 74 years. (Mount Alvernia Archives.)

Five

FLOODS AND FIRES

Built along the Allegheny River, with Girty's Run coursing through the town, Millvale has weathered many floods and other tragedies, including fires. As early as August 28, 1879, flooding in Millvale made the newspapers, when 30 houses were flooded and Evergreen Railroad lost seven bridges and hundreds of feet of track. In August 1887, another storm with heavy winds and rain blew down the new mill at Graff, Bennett & Company, resulting in $4,000–$5,000 damage. In 1889, Girty's Run rose 10 feet in 30 minutes, causing culverts under the streets to be flooded. In September 1911, a storm hit Millvale, Etna, and Sharpsburg, causing $500,000 in damage.

But none of these events can match the St. Patrick's Day flood of 1936, when the Allegheny River crested at 46 feet, 21 feet over flood stage. A year later, on January 26, and again on April 27, 1937, Millvale was flooded again. After waters swept through Millvale three times in 1973 and 1974, the Army Corps of Engineers built a flood-control project on Girty's Run. However, Tropical Depression Ivan brought unprecedented rainfall in September 2004, and even the flood controls were of little help. Millvale got muddy and flooded again.

Millvale's first reported fire occurred in 1875, when lightning struck and destroyed the Riverside Oil Refinery. Doubtless, the town's most destructive fire occurred on Sunday, December 11, 1881, when the Graff, Bennett & Company mill was totally destroyed. Fire has claimed three church buildings: St. Nicholas in 1921, the old St. Anthony's in 1923, and Christ Lutheran in 1947. Madden Funeral Home, along with the Voit and Feidt Barber Shop and J.I. Herbert's restaurant, burned down in 1945. The corner building at Grant and North Avenues housing Vecenie Beer Distributors, Plut's Market, and Frank Mereci Shoe Repair was destroyed on December 19, 1950. Other fires claimed a portion of the Baeuerlein Brewery in 1973, the Green Sheet building in 1982, and groups of residences on lower Lincoln Avenue in 1992 and on Butler Street in 2002.

PITTSBURGH'S BIG FLOOD.

ALLEGHENY CITY FRONT, BETWEEN HAND STREET BRIDGE AND HERR'S ISLAND.

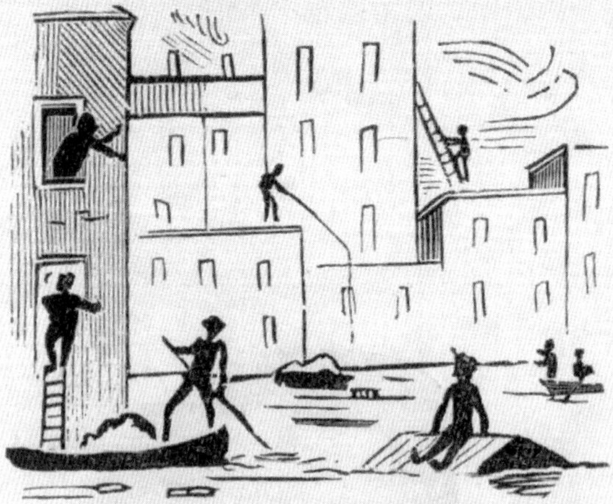

A COFFIN SCENE.

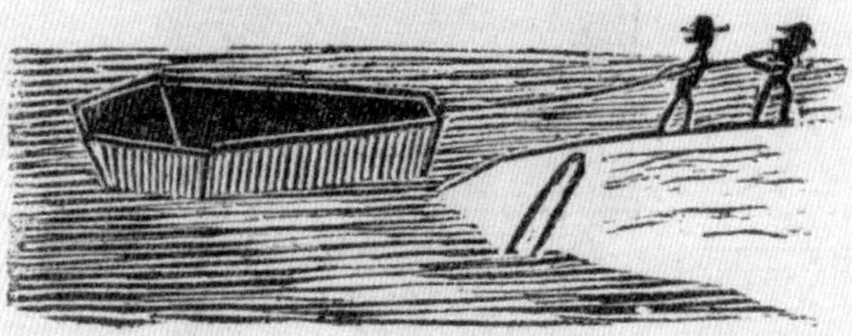

An incident of the flood, with a tonch of pathos in it, happened in Lawren ville. Leslie Bros., liverymen, had a funeral from Millvale, to take place at t o'clock. They started the horses and carriages off only to find they could get further than Willow street. What to do was a mystery. Mr. Leslie finally things through, but not without the greatest difficulty. The remains and the fam and friends were brought to this end of the Forty-third street bridge in expr wagons. Rafts were then procured. and the coffin with its following of sorrowing r atives and friends towed through the water to where the carriages were standi The funeral cortege then proceeded to the Allegheny cemetery. Hundreds of p ple gathered about them on the flats, lifted their hats and bowed their heads submission to the dead. The scene was one that recalled to mind the fune scenes of Venice.

Perhaps the most unusual reporting of the events of one of Pittsburgh's many floods, this account appears in the *Globe Illustrated Annual for 1886*. It is said that Pittsburgh has more bridges than Venice, but this is perhaps the first and only time a coffin was towed across the Allegheny River on its way to the Allegheny Cemetery in Lawrenceville. (Archives Service Center, University of Pittsburgh.)

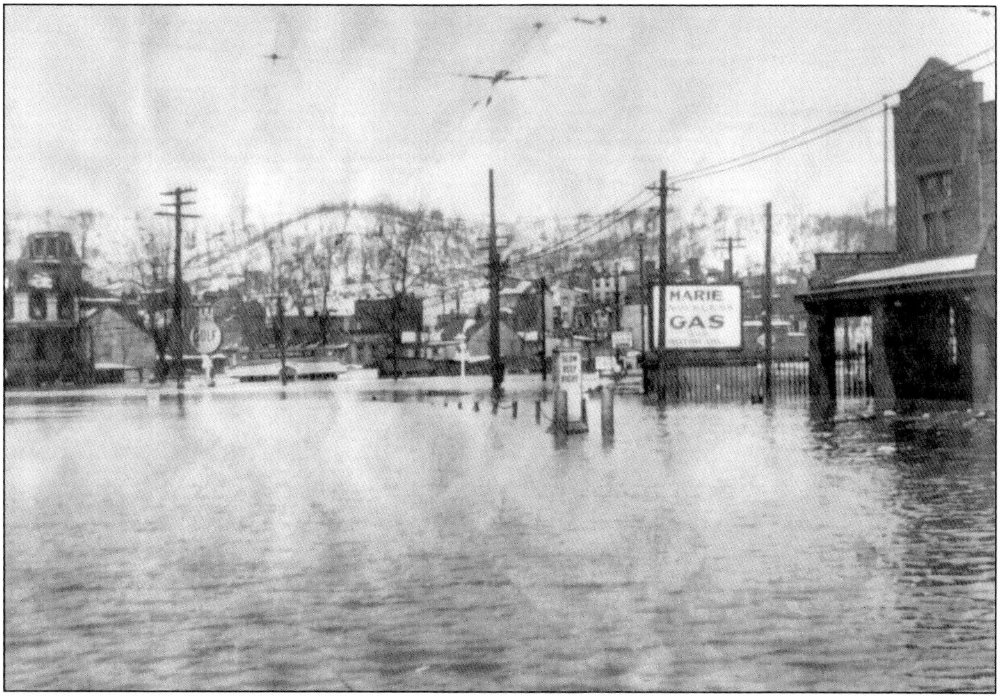

On March 17 and 18, 1936, Pittsburgh and its neighboring communities experienced the worst flood in their histories. Warmer-than-normal temperatures led to the melting of snow and ice on the upper Allegheny and Monongahela Rivers, causing water to rise to 25 feet on March 17. Heavy overnight rains dealt the final blow on March 18. Millvale's carbarn and train station experienced flooding first. (Jennifer Cohen.)

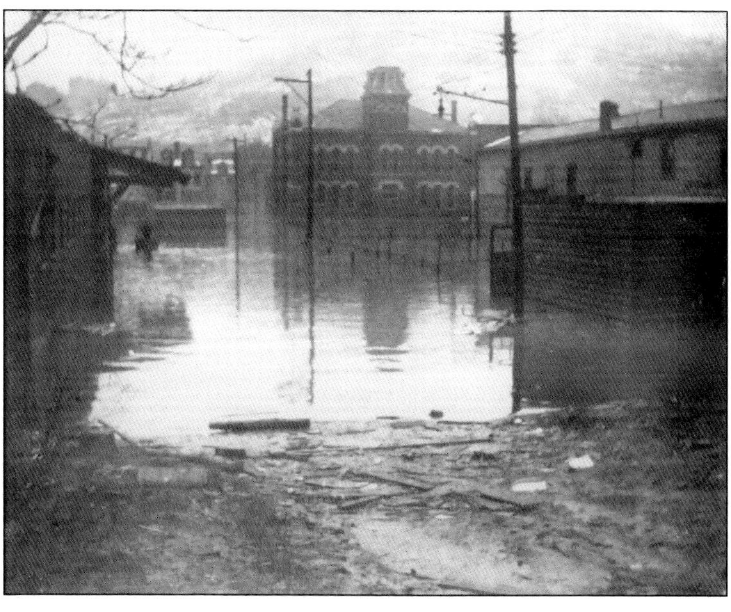

Although known as the St. Patrick's Day flood, waters actually peaked on March 18 at 46 feet, 21 feet above flood stage. Finally, five days later, water receded to 25 feet. Here, the First Ward School appears to float in a debris-filled lake. Though the building was refurbished, classes were no longer held there. It was sold to the fire department, to be used for meetings and events. (Michele Rheam.)

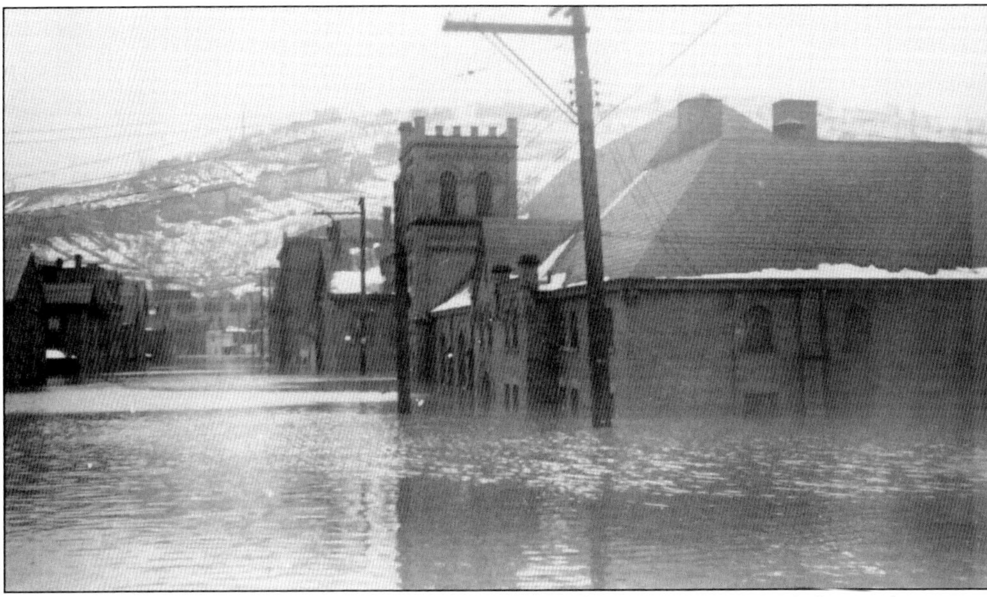

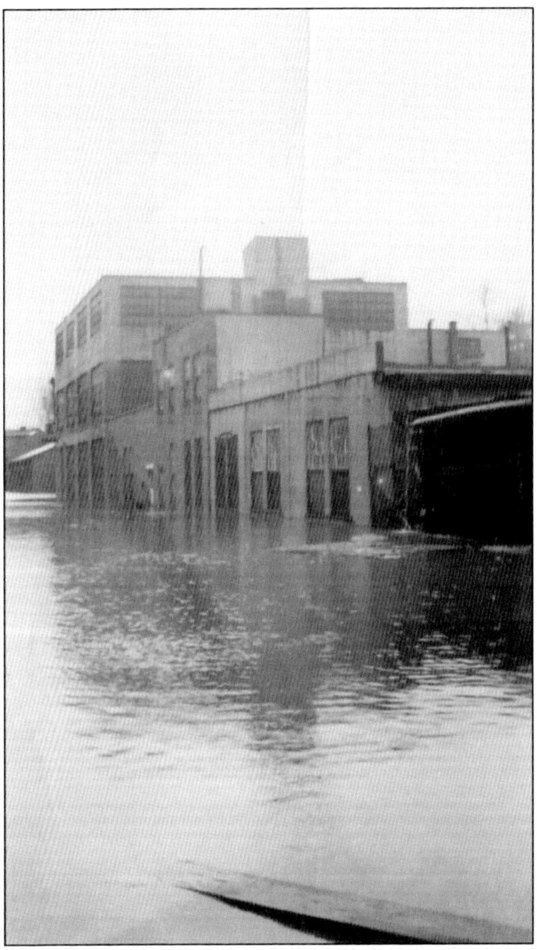

The Opera House and the Presbyterian church on Sheridan Street were flooded, as were all structures in Millvale's First Ward and part of the Second Ward. In fact, some of the buildings in the First Ward had water four to five feet above the second floor. Train tracks along the river were washed away or blocked with debris. Roads around the river were washed away or buckled. (Michele Rheam.)

McDowell Manufacturing, though located on Stanton Avenue, on the rise above Grant Street, was not spared the flooding of March 18, 1936. It would take weeks, even months, for Millvale's businesses to recover, but recover they did! (Flo Silbach.)

Located at 515 Grant Avenue, the Grant Theater was also flooded during the St. Patrick's Day flood. It was the site for special events, like the appearance of Dr. Milo, a London hypnotist, on November 21, 1952. Showing movies was its normal business. In January 1951, seven movie distributors sued the Grant and six other movie houses operated by Wilmer Enterprises for false attendance reports. (Barb Treusch.)

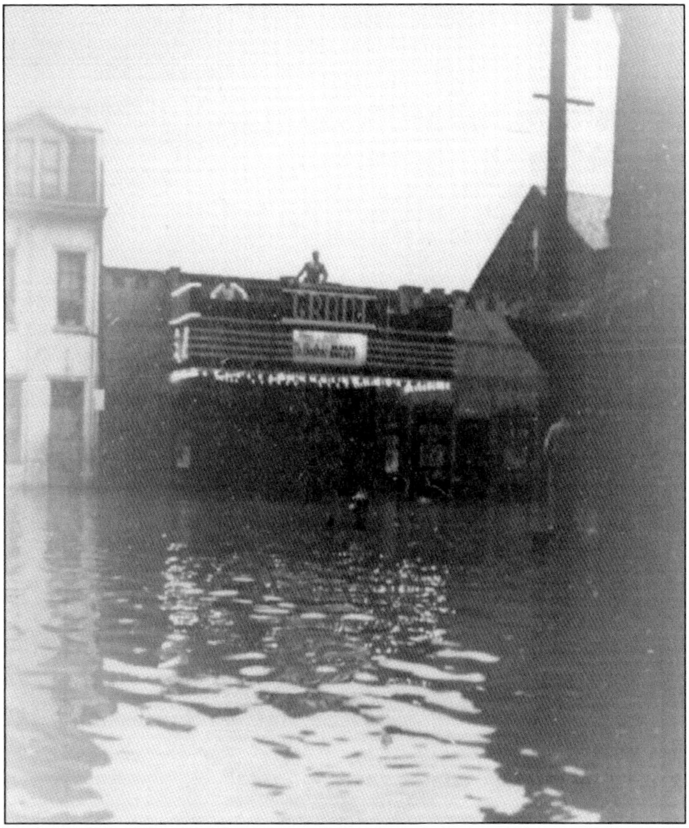

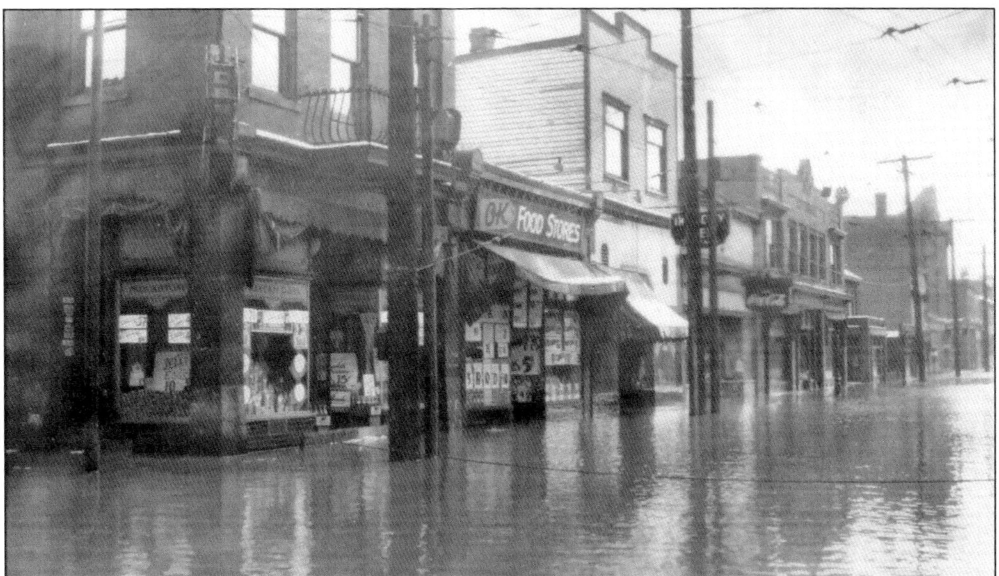

This photograph shows the deserted businesses, including Goodwin's Pharmacy, at the corner of North Avenue and Howard Street. Only the brave or the foolhardy tackled the floodwaters without the aid of boats. Electricity was out for eight days, and water was boiled for fear of typhoid fever due to contamination. (Flo Silbach.)

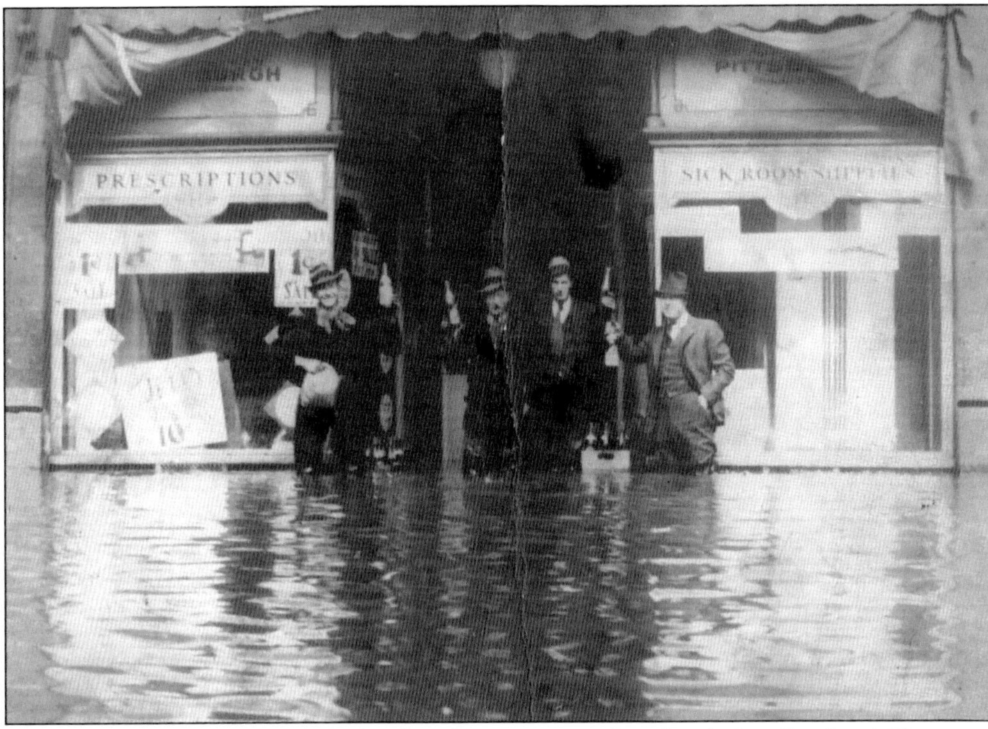

If the water was contaminated, the bottles of beer were not. Standing before Goodwin's Pharmacy, this group of men may be toasting to a better future, or perhaps just a week off work before the cleanup would begin. (Michelle Rheam.)

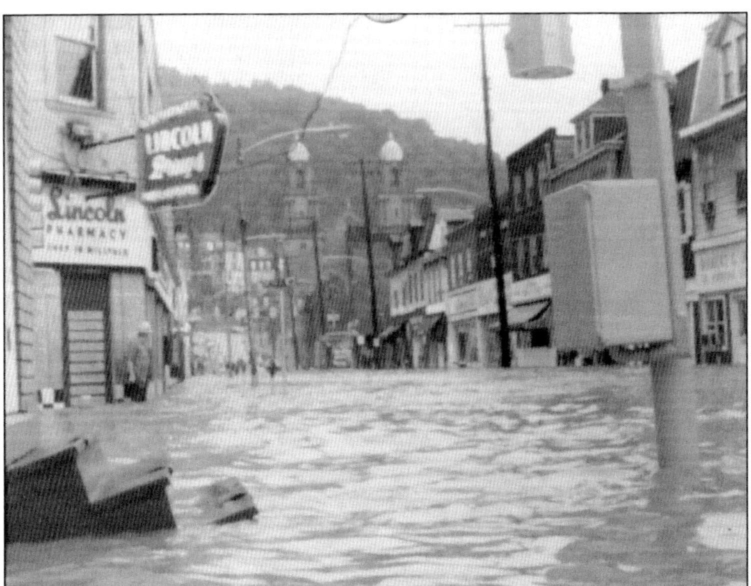

Though not to the extent of the 1936 flood, Millvale again found its First Ward flooded in the 1960s. As shown by this photograph, taken across from Lincoln Pharmacy, several feet of water can be seen all along North Avenue and extending toward St. Anthony's Church. (Jennifer Cohen.)

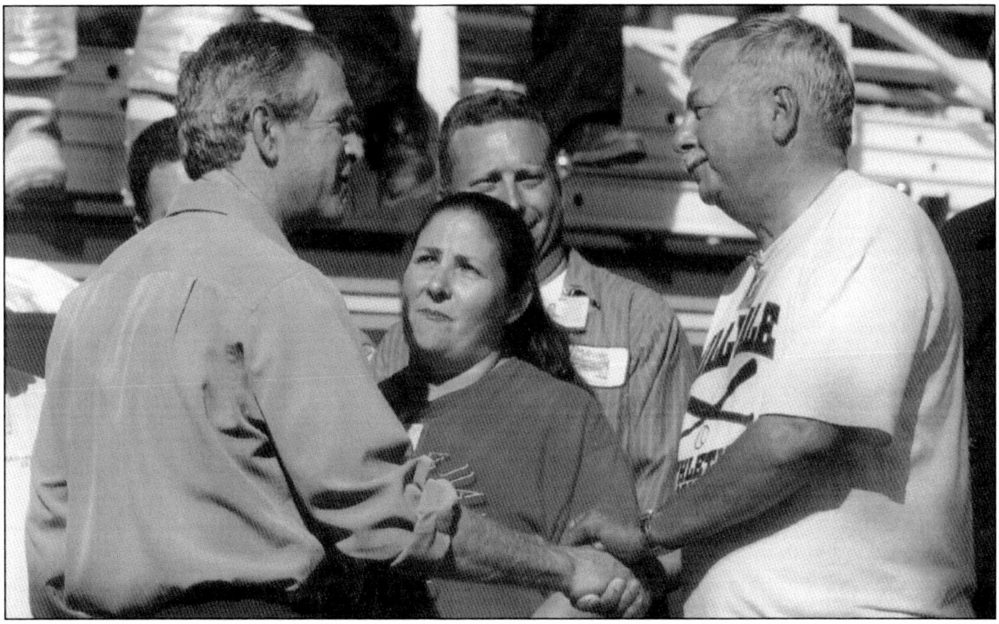

On September 22, 2004, Pres. George W. Bush (left) visits with Mayor Vincent Cinski (right) and Millvale residents following an aerial tour of flood damage caused by Tropical Depression Ivan. President Bush declared Allegheny County a major disaster site and ordered federal aid for Allegheny and nearby counties. Bush predicted that "within a reasonable period of time this town is going to be back on its feet, better than ever." (Vincent Cinski.)

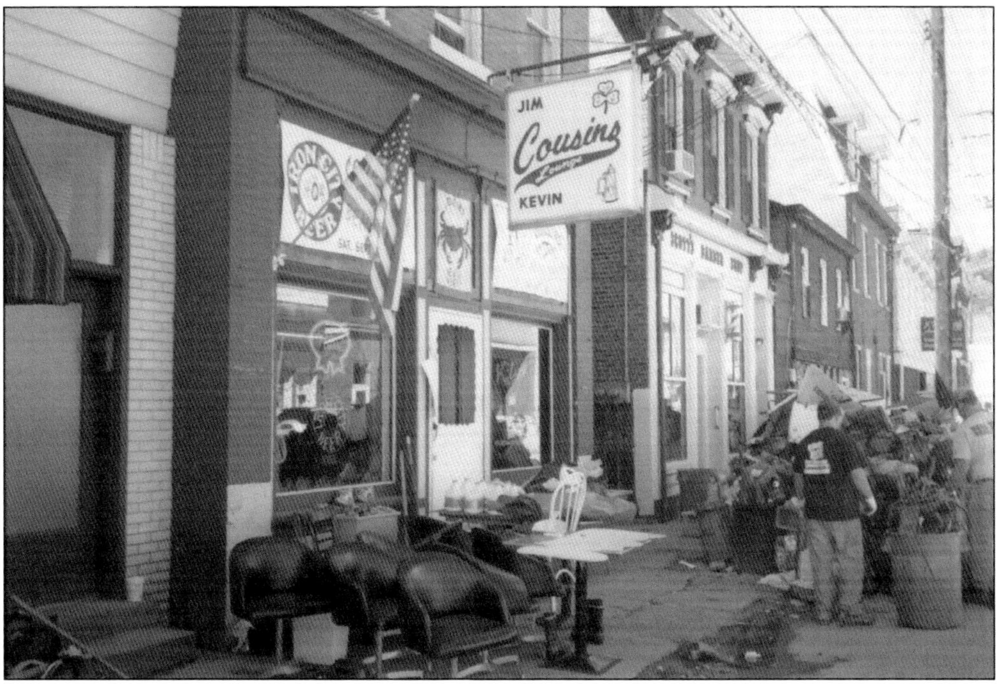

So rapid was the rise of water on September 17, 2004, that many families and businesses did not have time to move their possessions to higher floors. Streets piled with muddy furnishings, furniture, and business equipment was a typical scene in Millvale for weeks after the flood. (Bill Stout.)

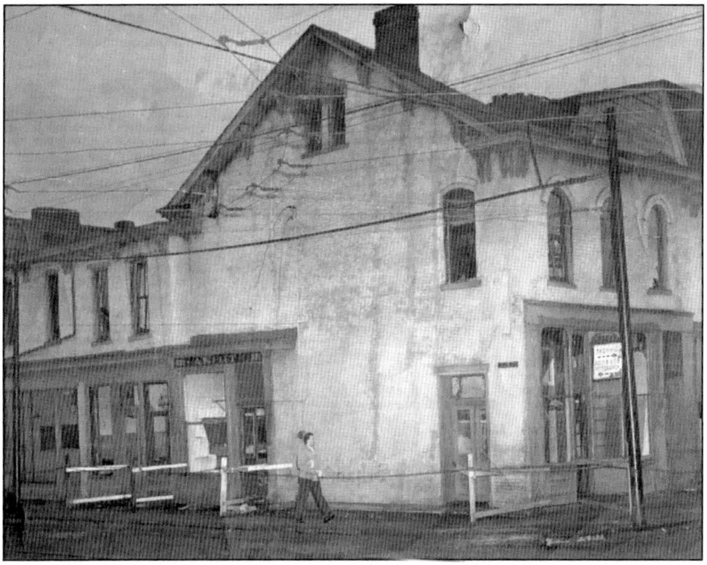

Hampered by near-zero temperatures, 10 volunteer firemen fought a fire on December 19, 1950. The blaze started at A.W. Plut Produce store and spread to Vecenie Beer Distributors, Pruney's Place, and Frank Mereci Shoe Repair. The fire did about $15,000 in damage to the four businesses and to several second-floor apartments in an old three-story brick building at Grant and North Avenues. (Frank Vecenie.)

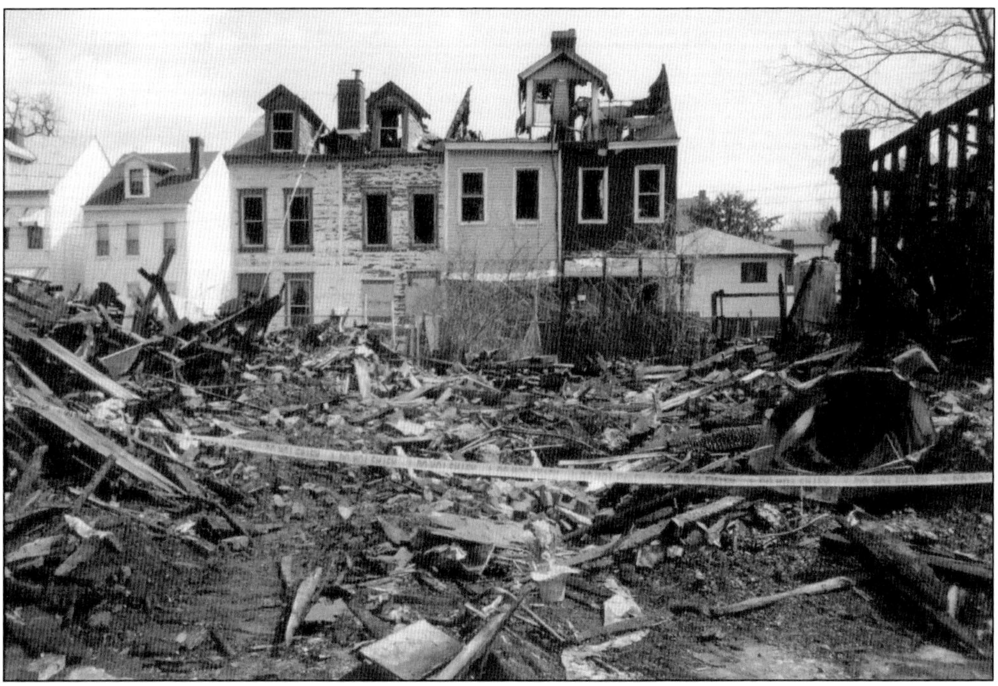

On March 31, 2002, a stubborn, fast-moving fire destroyed nine houses on Butler and Hays Streets in Millvale. As a result of the blaze, 23 people from six families lost their homes, but, luckily, no one was badly injured. Only three firefighters suffered minor injuries. (Jack Cavanaugh.)

Six

GOING SHOPPING

As an article published on Sunday, April 24, 1904, in the *Pittsburg Leader* describes Millvale's "streets alive with thousands of people, the stores brilliant with electric bulbs, and all is animation" each weekday at 8:00 p.m. Millvale was what would today be called a commuter town, or bedroom community. The streets grew quiet after the town's men boarded trolley cars to travel to their places of work.

Small businesses could be found all along North and Grant Avenues, providing virtually everything a family needed. There were grocers, meat markets, confectioneries, bakers, druggists, and tobacco and cigar merchants. There were dressmakers, shoemakers, tailors, barbers, dentists, physicians, realtors, and undertakers. The people who owned these businesses lived in the town and served their neighbors, often running tabs when cash was short. Sons succeeded fathers in businesses or sold out to apprentices when necessary.

Many fond childhood memories are associated with the town's businesses, like buying penny candy at Esther's, eating warm breakfast buns from Bergman's or Greb's, having an ice-cream cone, or, better yet, a sundae at Yetter's, getting a free slice of cheese or bologna at Johnny Diehl's, or buying half of a Popsicle for 3¢ at Stancati's. At Easter, the windows of Millvale's Five and Dime Store were filled with chicks dyed pink, blue, green, and purple, and yellow ducklings. Yetter's windows had milk and white chocolate crosses and bunnies, coconut, and fruit and nut eggs.

Millvale's floods have swept away all but the most persevering of businesses. Abandoned buildings with dilapidated storefronts can be found along Grant and North Avenues. And yet, for the nostalgic, there's still Lincoln Pharmacy, Jerry Kitman's Fine Furniture, Esther's Toys and Hobbies, Yetter's, and the Grant Bar. Jean-Marc Chatellier's Bakery and Attic Records have also stuck it out. The Draai Laag Brewing Company, with its Saints and Turncoats Tasting Room, is one of the town's newest establishments.

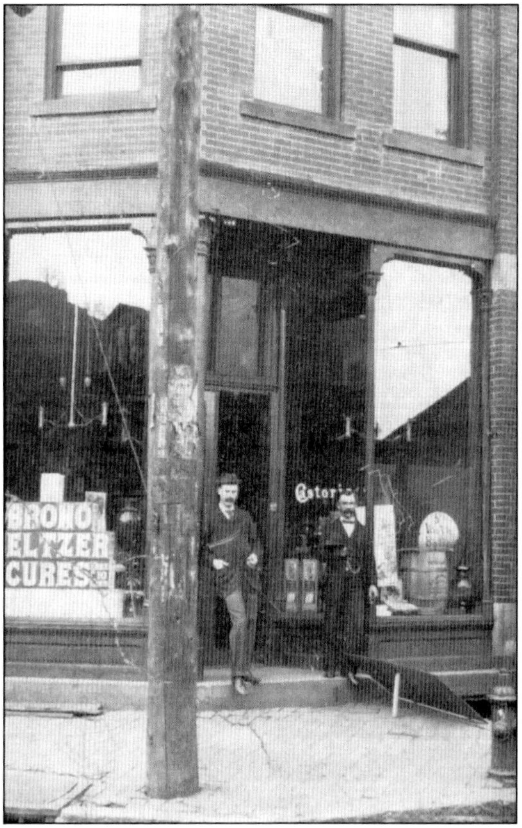

Established in 1873, Goodwin's Pharmacy commanded a prime spot in the center of Millvale, at the corner of North and Howard Avenues. In addition to selling medicines and supplies, Goodwin rented out the second floor of the building as an auditorium. This hall provided space for Sunday services for two years for the congregation of Christ Lutheran, until the completion of its church in 1903. (Jennifer Cohen.)

"Neatly done" shoe repair is the motto of James Guttilla & Brother, Millvale Shoe Hospital. The shop repaired items while the customer waited. Here, the shop's owner and his family await clients at their door at 133 Grant Avenue. (Millvale Borough.)

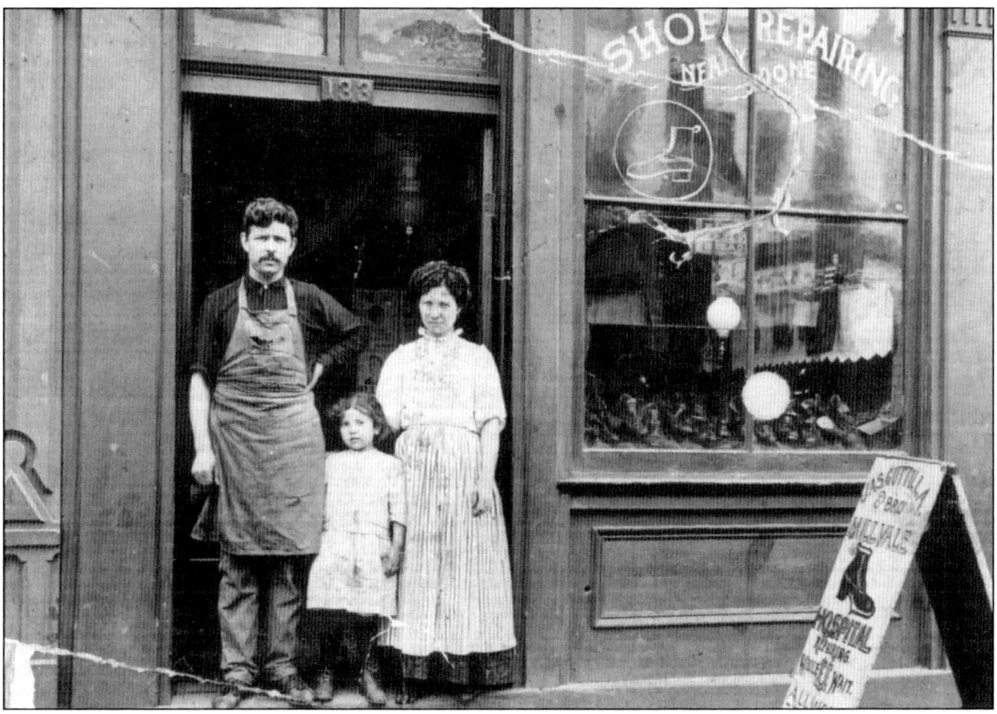

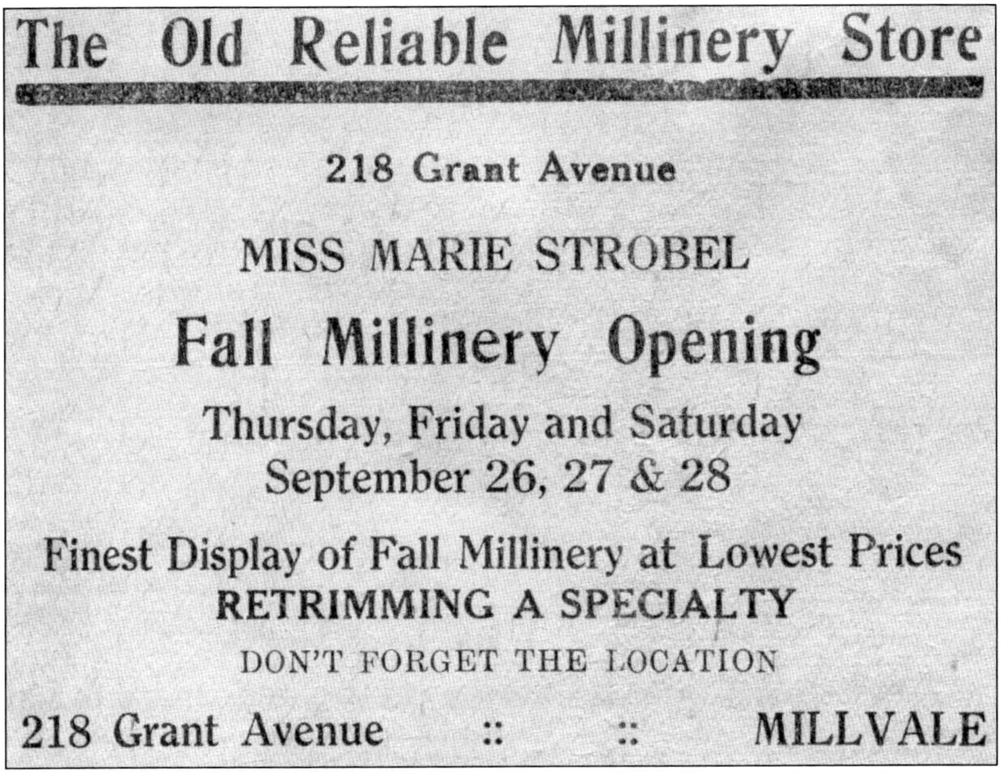

These advertisements ran in volume 12, number 30 of the *Valley Journal*, the official paper of Millvale Borough, on September 12, 1912. The *Valley Journal* succeeded the *Bennett Star*, the borough's first newspaper. But by 1924, it had been replaced by the *Millvale Press*. Miss B. Schmidt's millinery shop had competition, as Marie Strobel's millinery store also advertised its fall collection on the front page of the same paper (above). Typically, in 1912, there were no funeral homes where deceased loved ones could be viewed; instead, the deceased were embalmed in their homes, where respects could be paid in the front parlor. E.J. Pfeifer provided such services, as did his competitor, A.J. Haser, whose advertisement was placed directly beside Pfeifer's (below). (Both, Millvale Borough.)

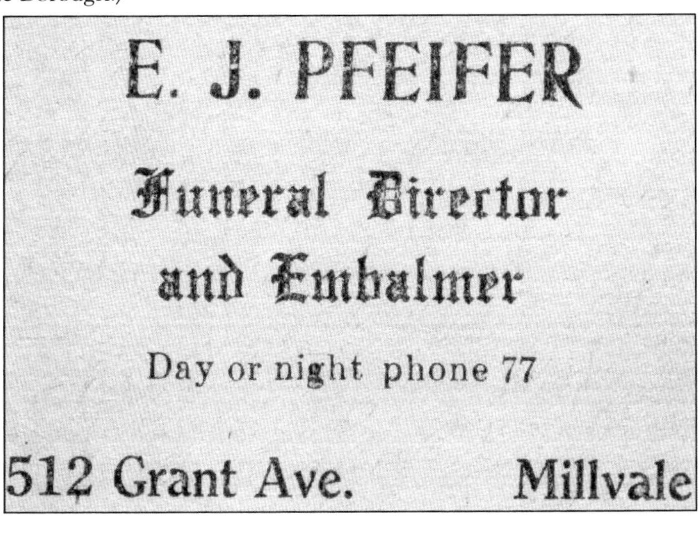

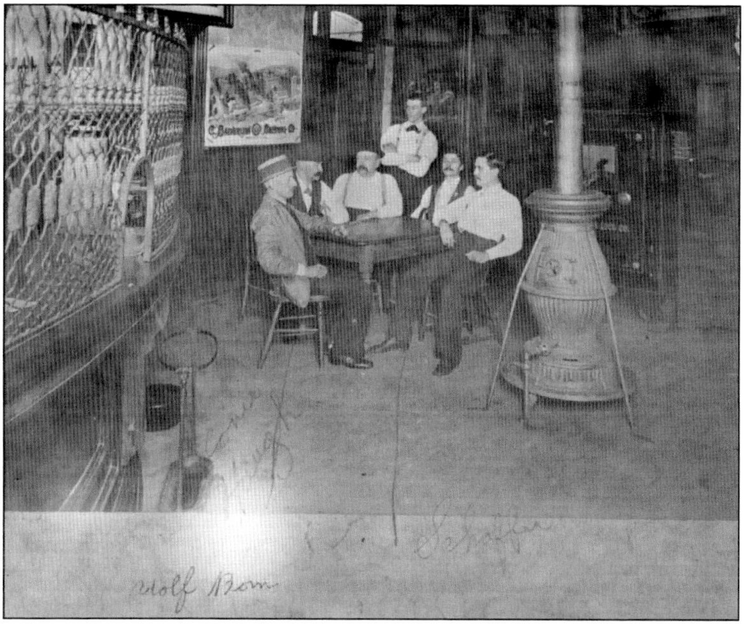

Lifting a pint or two of lager, a type of German beer, from one of Millvale's three local breweries was a daily pastime for the hardworking men of the town. In 1900, Millvale had 11 hotels serving meals and drinks. Note the advertisement for C. Baeuerlein Brewing Company, one of Millvale's local breweries. (Jennifer Cohen.)

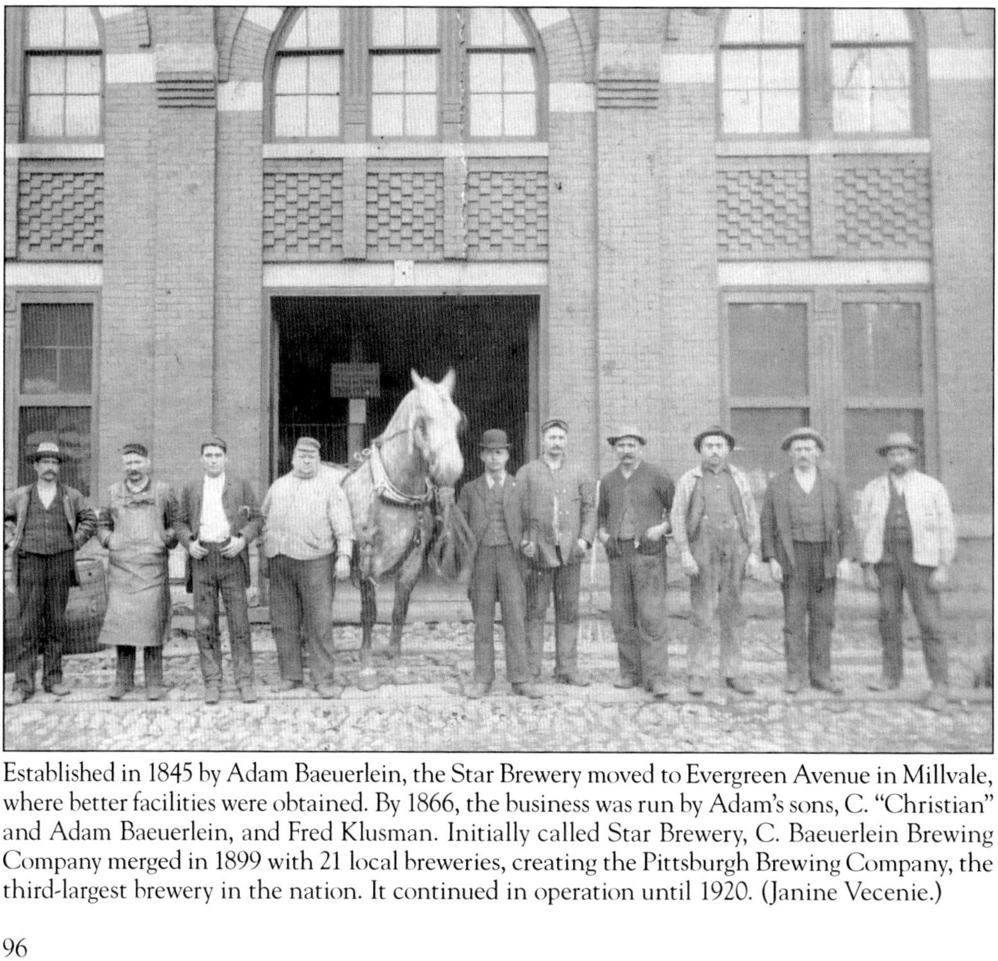

Established in 1845 by Adam Baeuerlein, the Star Brewery moved to Evergreen Avenue in Millvale, where better facilities were obtained. By 1866, the business was run by Adam's sons, C. "Christian" and Adam Baeuerlein, and Fred Klusman. Initially called Star Brewery, C. Baeuerlein Brewing Company merged in 1899 with 21 local breweries, creating the Pittsburgh Brewing Company, the third-largest brewery in the nation. It continued in operation until 1920. (Janine Vecenie.)

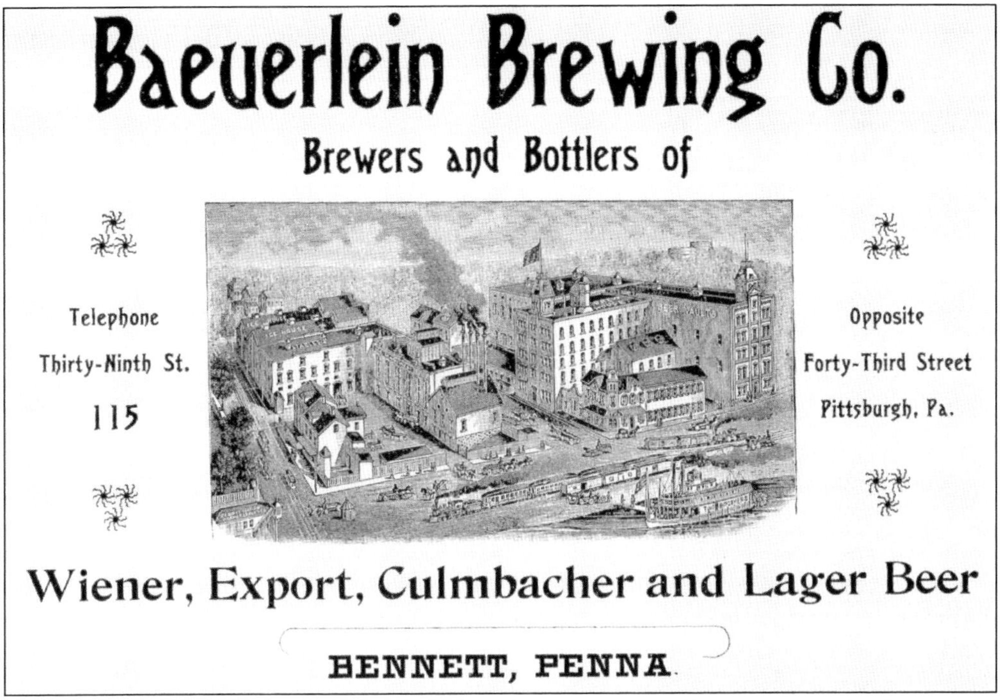

This advertisement, published in the *Proceedings of the Twenty-eight Encampment of the Grand Army of the Republic* in Pittsburgh, shows the extent of the Baeuerlein Brewing Company in Millvale. The company's annual sales reached $60,000 in 1879. The remaining building, the 1900 Stock House, can be found at the corner of Evergreen Road and East Ohio Street. (Archives Service Center, University of Pittsburgh.)

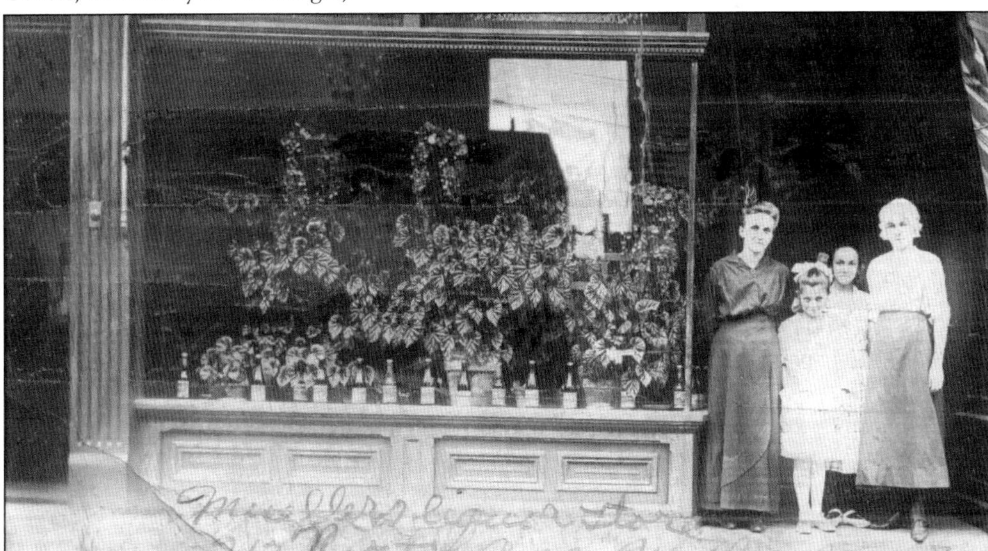

Mueller's Wholesale Liquor Store, at 213 North Avenue, is pictured here in 1918, which was 15 years before the establishment of Pennsylvania's Liquor Control Board. This location became Diehl's Meat Market. Later, John Diehl sold the business to his workers, William Roch and Charles Marlovits. Today, the building houses the bakery of Jean-Marc Chatellier. (Jennifer Cohen.)

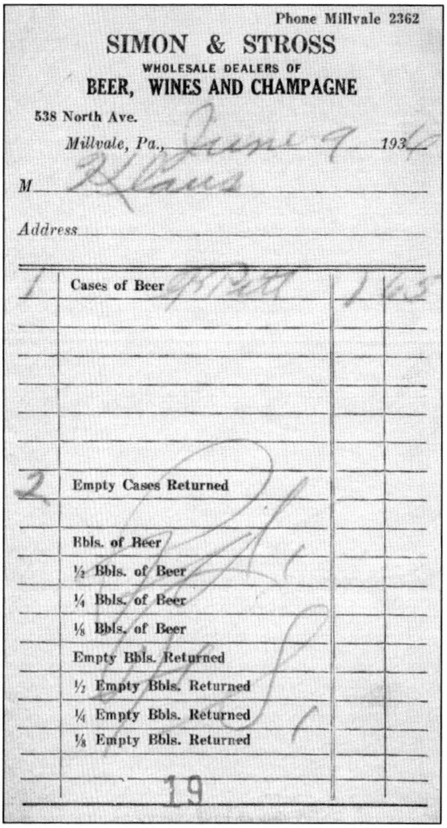
Phone Millvale 2362

SIMON & STROSS

WHOLESALE DEALERS OF

BEER, WINES AND CHAMPAGNE

538 North Ave.

Millvale, Pa., June 9 193

M Klaus

Address

1	Cases of Beer Ft Pitt	1	65
2	Empty Cases Returned		
	Bbls. of Beer		
	½ Bbls. of Beer		
	¼ Bbls. of Beer		
	⅛ Bbls. of Beer		
	Empty Bbls. Returned		
	½ Empty Bbls. Returned		
	¼ Empty Bbls. Returned		
	⅛ Empty Bbls. Returned		

19

Simon & Stross was one of the many beer distributors formerly located in Millvale. This receipt shows the price of a case of Fort Pitt beer as $1.65 in 1936. Fort Pitt Brewing Company was a major local brewer with plants in Sharpsburg and Jeannette, but it ceased operations in 1958. (Carol Szwedko.)

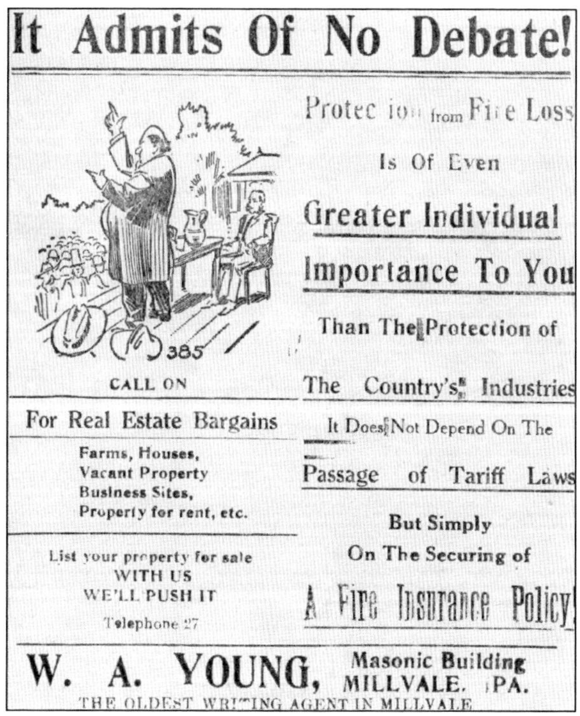

One of Millvale's many companies in 1912 was the W.A. Young Real Estate and Insurance Agency, located in the new Masonic building. The business offered real estate bargains and fire insurance policies. Young was "the oldest writing agent" in Millvale. (Millvale Borough.)

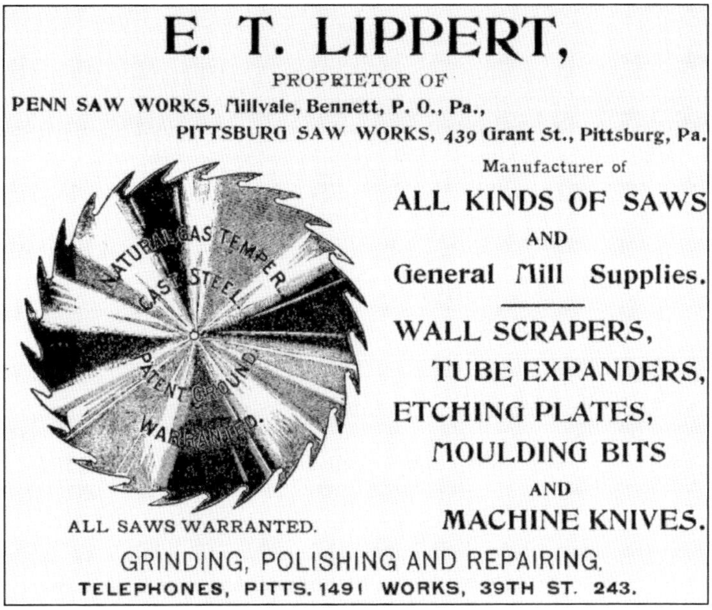

Ernest Theodore Lippert, born in Prussia, immigrated to Pittsburgh. After working for years in the saw factory of Lippincott, Bakewell & Company, he purchased the firm and named it Penn Saw Works. To accommodate increasing business, in 1896, he constructed a new plant in Millvale. Lippert was the inventor and patentee of world-famous patent ground circular saws. (Archives Service Center, University of Pittsburgh.)

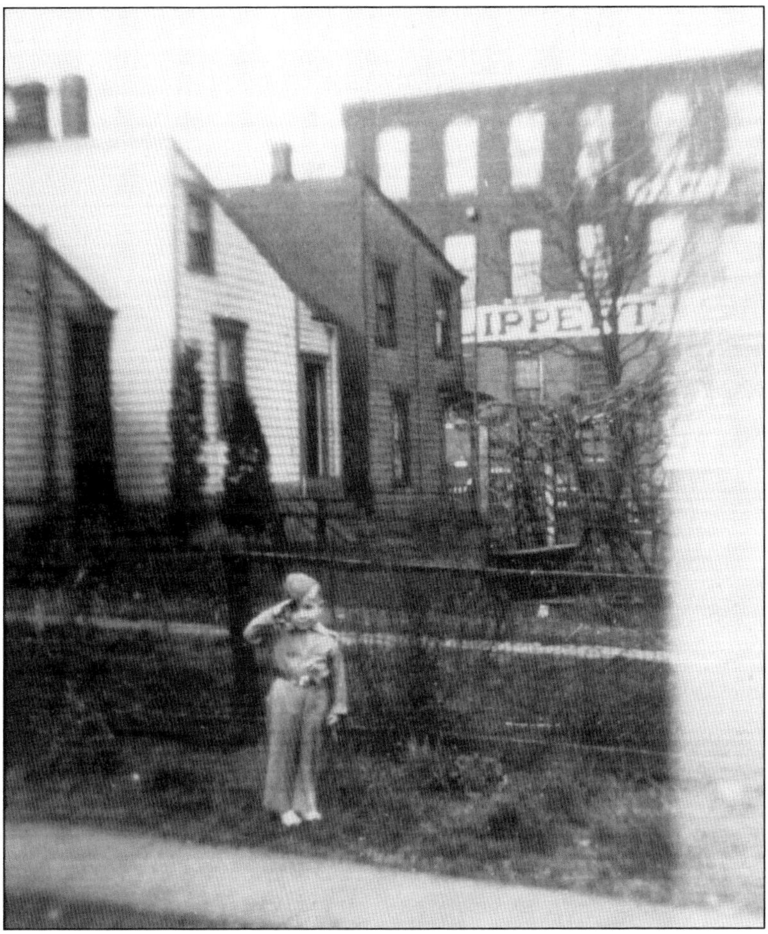

Built in 1900 by E.T. Lippert to house the Penn Saw Works, this building, shown here from Sample Street, was converted into apartments in 2004. Lippert, who resided in Millvale beginning in 1874, was a prominent member of the community, serving on its council from 1892 to 1908. He was a charter member of St. John's Evangelical Lutheran Church. (Bill Stout.)

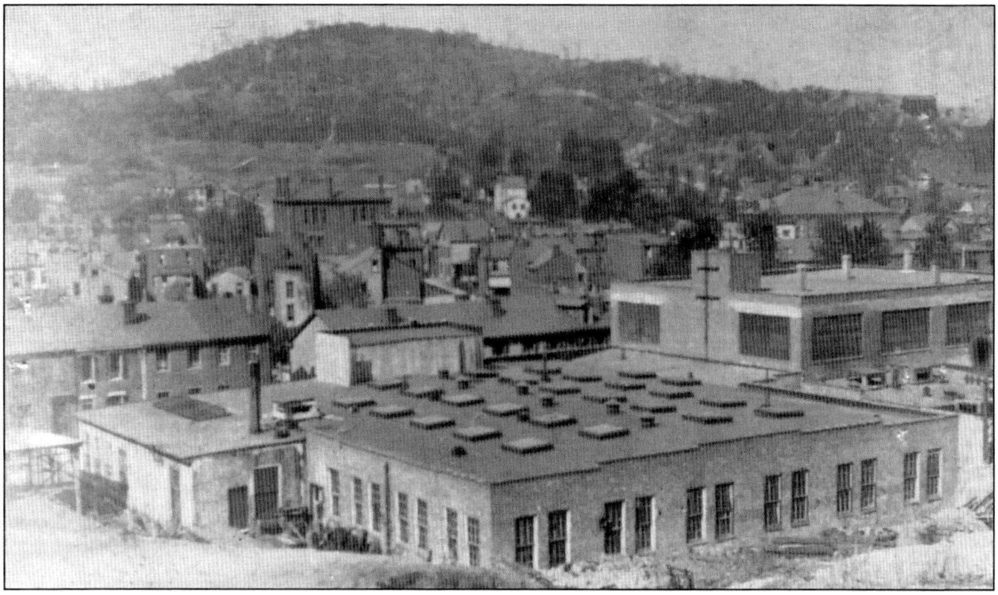

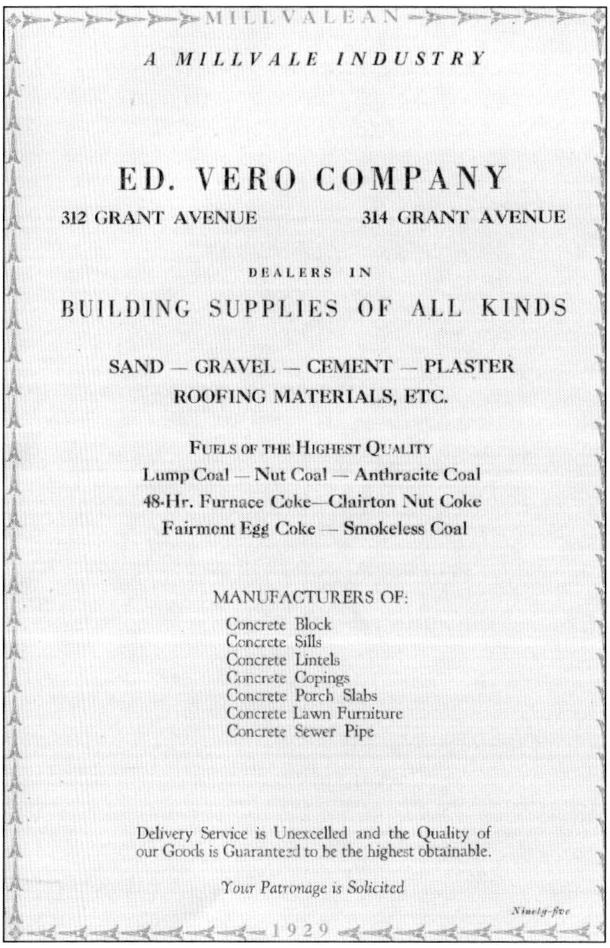

MILLVALEAN

A MILLVALE INDUSTRY

ED. VERO COMPANY

312 GRANT AVENUE 314 GRANT AVENUE

DEALERS IN

BUILDING SUPPLIES OF ALL KINDS

SAND — GRAVEL — CEMENT — PLASTER
ROOFING MATERIALS, ETC.

FUELS OF THE HIGHEST QUALITY
Lump Coal — Nut Coal — Anthracite Coal
48-Hr. Furnace Coke—Clairton Nut Coke
Fairmont Egg Coke — Smokeless Coal

MANUFACTURERS OF:

Concrete Block
Concrete Sills
Concrete Lintels
Concrete Copings
Concrete Porch Slabs
Concrete Lawn Furniture
Concrete Sewer Pipe

Delivery Service is Unexcelled and the Quality of our Goods is Guaranteed to be the highest obtainable.

Your Patronage is Solicited

Ninety-five

1929

Known for its innovative technology, McDowell Manufacturing, led by Birger Engstrom, general manager of the plant and president of Pittsburgh's chamber of commerce, made headlines with the development of an improved coupling for joining irrigation pipes in 1950. The device made it possible for one man to erect and dismantle a complete irrigation system without tools. McDowell finally closed its Millvale plant in the 1960s. (Jean Domico.)

Originally an ironworker, Ed Vero is best known as an ice and coal deliveryman, dealing in Champion coal and Connellsville coke. Later, he owned the Ed Vero Company, with a fleet of motortrucks and teams hauling building supplies, sand, gravel, and concrete blocks to every part of the city. He was a burgess from 1908 to 1909. (Mary Ann Knochel.)

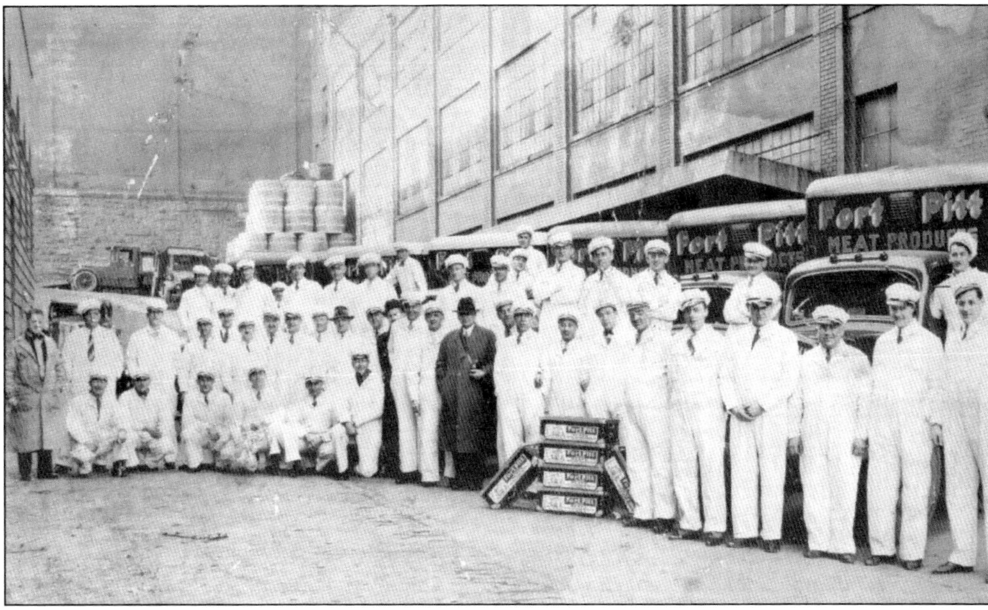

In 1921, the American Brewing Company, part of the Independent Brewing Company of Pittsburgh, sold its property to Fried and Reineman Packing Company, a substantial business that once employed thousands. Slaughtering houses, rendering houses, and processing plants dotted East Ohio Street, Spring Garden Avenue, and Herr's Island. Fried and Reineman remained in business for 40 years. (Jean Domico.)

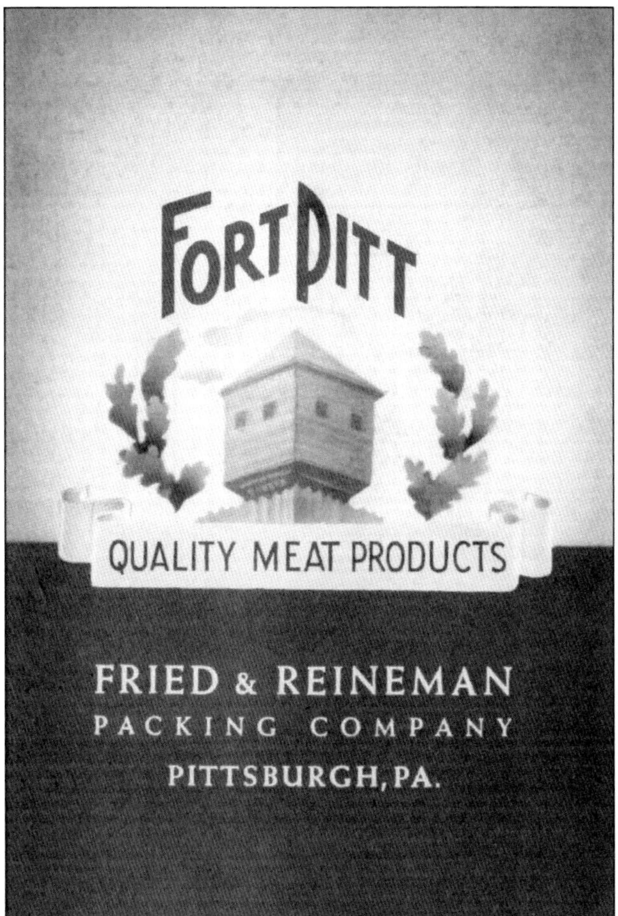

Fried and Reineman, who mainly slaughtered and processed hogs, specialized in Fort Pitt brand hams, bacon, lard, "fine bologna," and sausages. The company sold veal and lamb and distributed Blue Valley butter and dairy products. The Allegheny County Jail was one of its biggest customers for bologna and sausage. The company also appealed to housewives with a cookbook of Josephine Gibson's tested recipes and planned menus. (Jean Domico.)

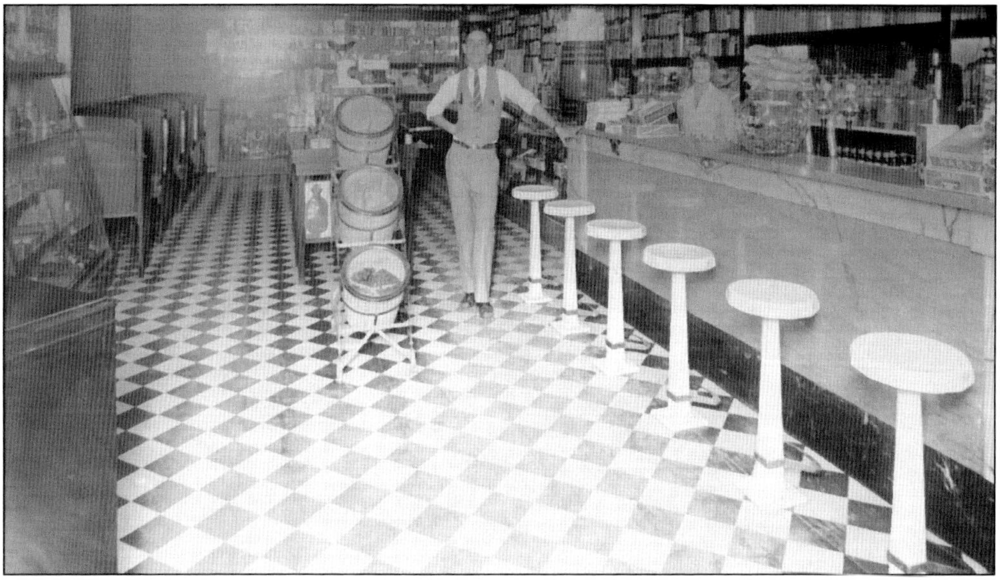

Frank Pschirer, pictured here, was a building contractor in Millvale, along with his father of the same name. Together, they built the white brick Pschirer Building on the corner of Lincoln and North Avenues, which houses Lincoln Pharmacy. Born in Austria, the elder Pschirer came to America in 1881 and, two years later, sent for his sweetheart, Mary Ann Boehm, and married her. (Jennifer Cohen.)

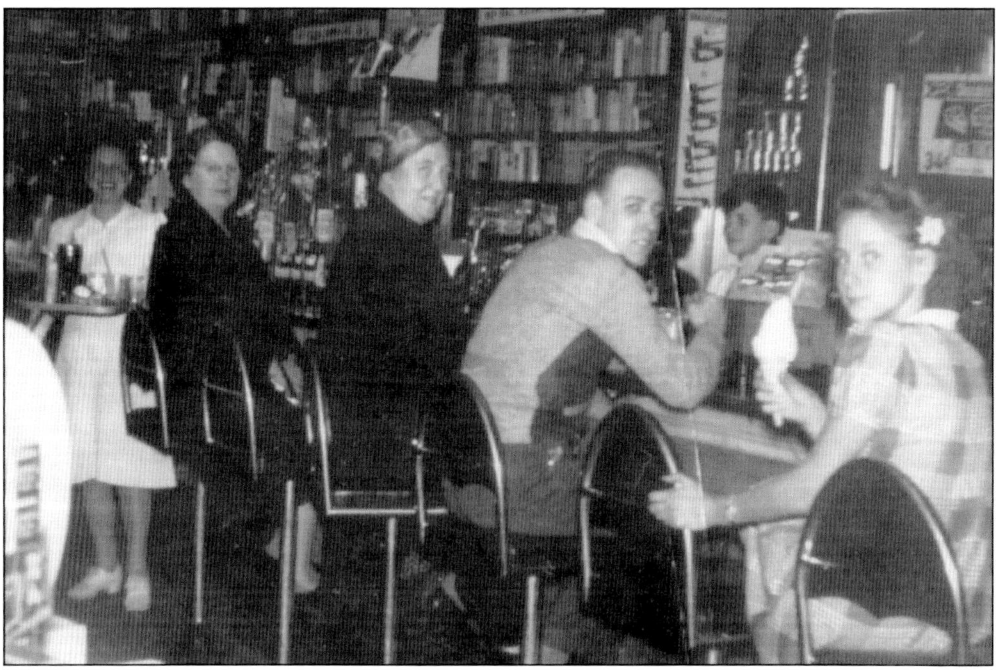

Patrons at the counter of the Lincoln Pharmacy take a break from shopping and schoolwork to enjoy a soda fountain treat. The Lincoln now houses Pamela's P&G Diner, whose other locations include the Strip District. Customers line up early on Saturdays and Sundays for one of Pittsburgh's best breakfasts at the diner, which has been owned and operated by Pamela Cohen and Gail Klinginsmith since 1980. (Jennifer Cohen.)

The Lincoln Pharmacy was established in 1928 by Oscar and Joseph Cohen. After Oscar's death in 1952 and Joseph's in 1954, Joseph's son, Stanford, returned to operate the pharmacy with his mother, Sadie. Later, Stanford asked Frank Rosenfeld and Michael F. Guido to join him. The Lincoln, always known for its distinctive checkered delivery car, is still serving the Millvale community after 85 years. (Jennifer Cohen.)

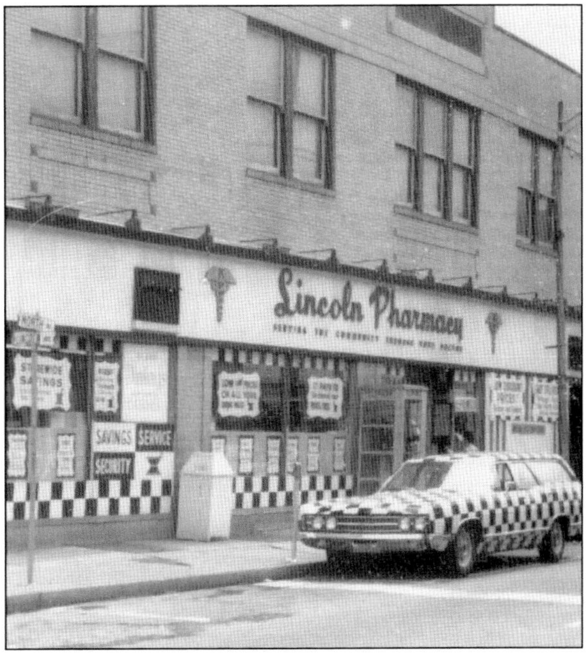

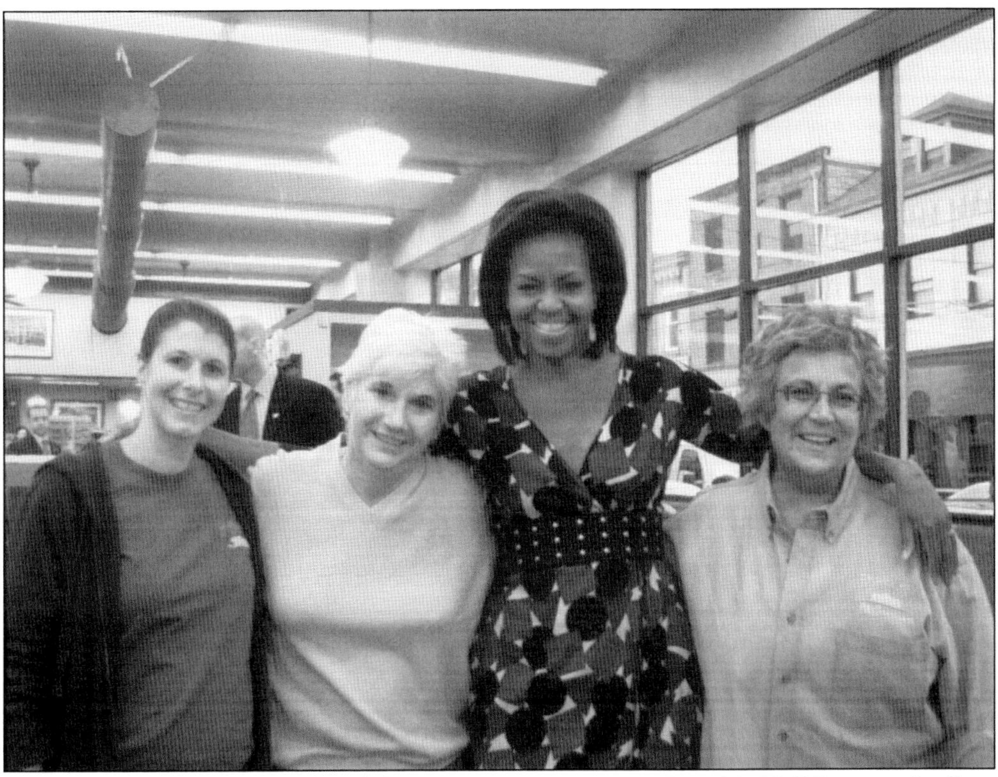

Although the president's schedule did not permit a return trip to Pamela's P&G Diner in the Strip during the 2009 G20 summit in Pittsburgh, First Lady Michelle Obama made a visit to Pamela's in the Lincoln Pharmacy on September 25 and ate some of its famous pancakes. The chair on which she sat now has a plaque commemorating her visit. (Patty Hachick.)

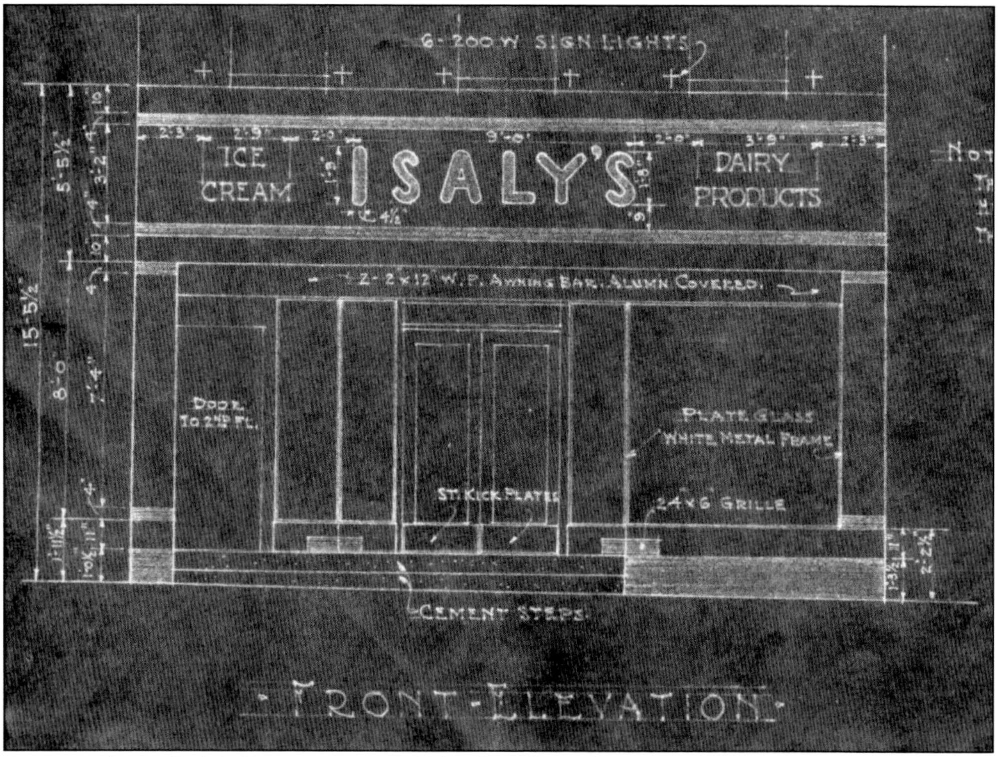

At its peak, an Isaly's Dairy Store could be found in almost every community in Pittsburgh and beyond. Designed by downtown architect Vincent Schoeneman, Millvale's store opened in 1938–1939 and became an instant hit. After all, who could resist those "skyscraper" cones, Klondike ice cream bars, or, better yet, barbecue made with Isaly's signature chipped chopped ham? (Millvale Borough.)

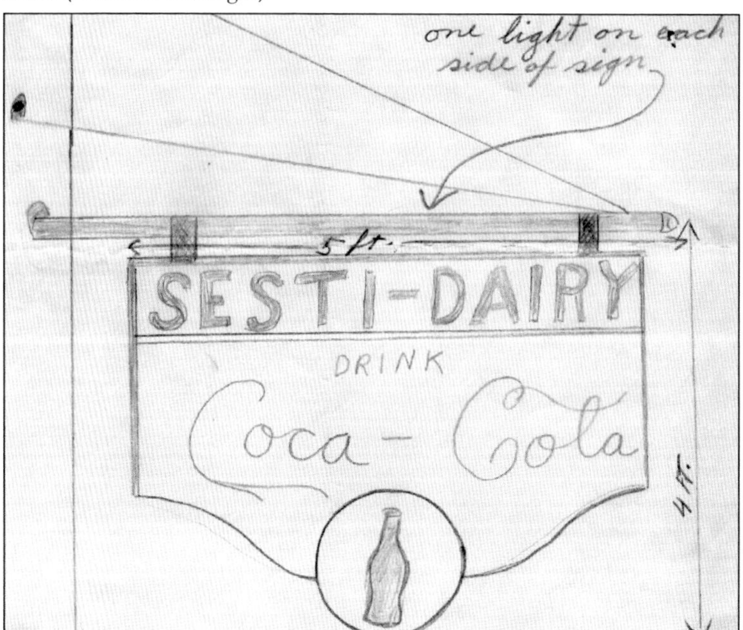

Sesti's Dairy, located at 131 Grant Avenue, upgraded its storefront in 1940 with borough approval. This sign, with the iconic Coca-Cola logo, was four feet tall and hung ten feet from the pavement. On a hot summer day, it was a beacon drawing young people for a cold soda. (Millvale Borough.)

Originally, Bennett Lumber & Manufacturing Company used a horse-drawn wagon to pick up lumber at the Pennsylvania Railroad station on Bridge Street and deliver it to the plant for further preparation. Arnold Bauer, president of the company, was also Millvale's fire chief for many years. (Mary Ann Knochel.)

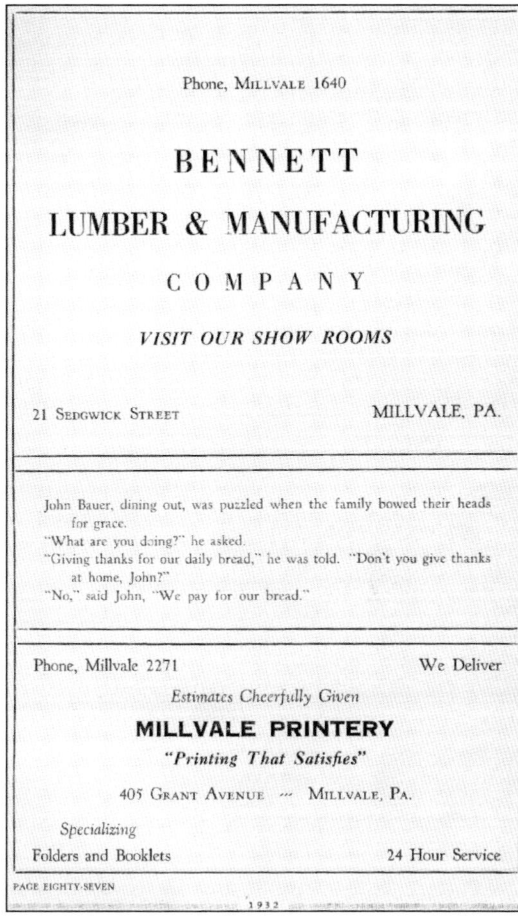

Phone, Millvale 1640

BENNETT

LUMBER & MANUFACTURING

COMPANY

VISIT OUR SHOW ROOMS

21 Sedgwick Street — MILLVALE, PA.

John Bauer, dining out, was puzzled when the family bowed their heads for grace.

"What are you doing?" he asked.

"Giving thanks for our daily bread," he was told. "Don't you give thanks at home, John?"

"No," said John, "We pay for our bread."

Phone, Millvale 2271 — We Deliver

Estimates Cheerfully Given

MILLVALE PRINTERY

"Printing That Satisfies"

405 Grant Avenue — Millvale, Pa.

Specializing

Folders and Booklets — 24 Hour Service

PAGE EIGHTY-SEVEN

1932

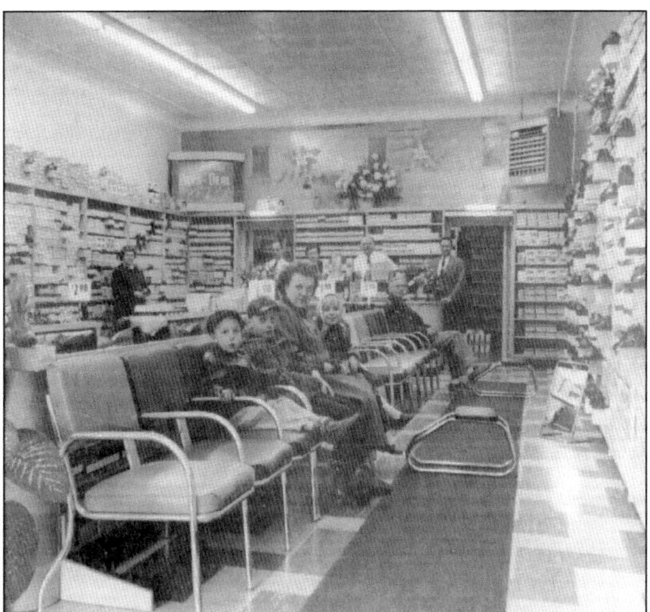

In this photograph, taken on March 11, 1955, from left to right, Jim Shanko, John Shanko Jr., Esther Shanko, and Judith Shanko await help in Michaels' Shoe Store. (Jean Domico.)

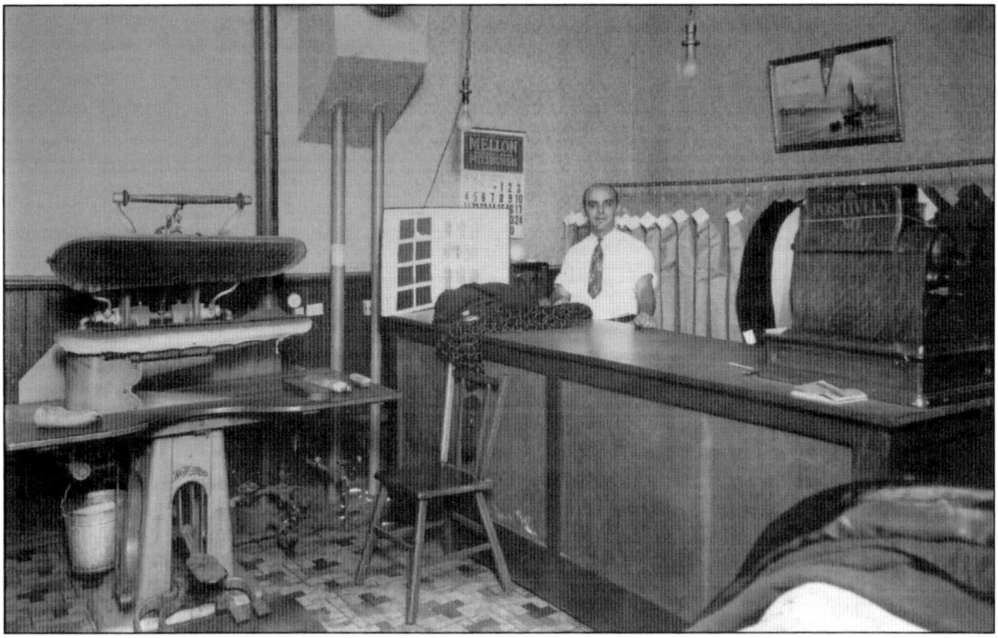

John Stancati is shown here in his cleaning and tailor shop, located at 146 Grant Avenue. The shop later became the neighborhood ice cream and candy store which he ran with his wife, Margaret. Popsicles cost 6¢ in the 1950s. Stancati sold neighborhood kids a "halfsie" until another 3¢ could be found. (Sudie Schindler.)

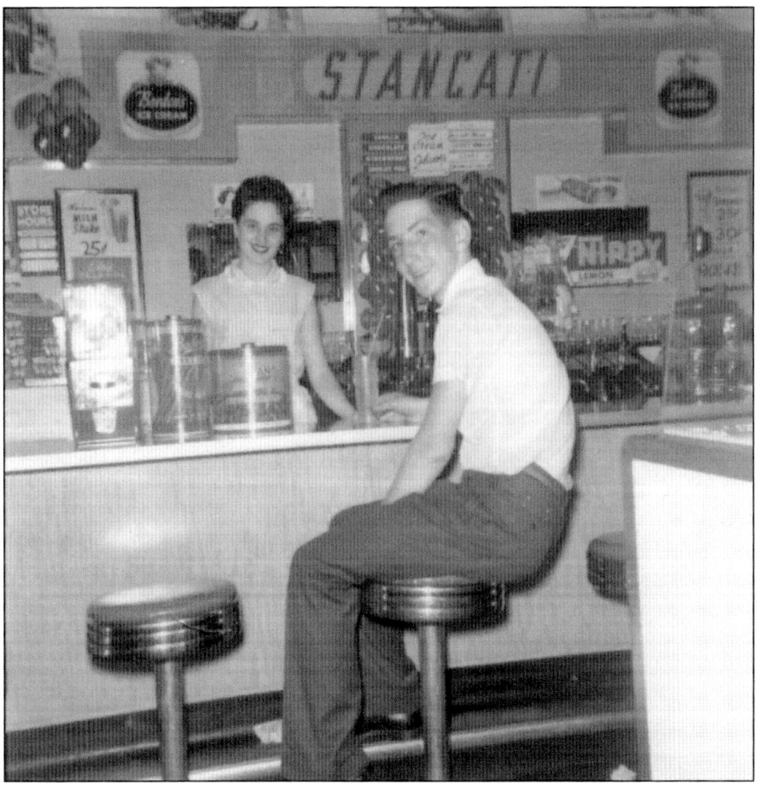

Josephine Stancati waits on Charles Gates Jr. at the soda fountain of Stancati's Ice Cream Parlor. (Sudie Schindler.)

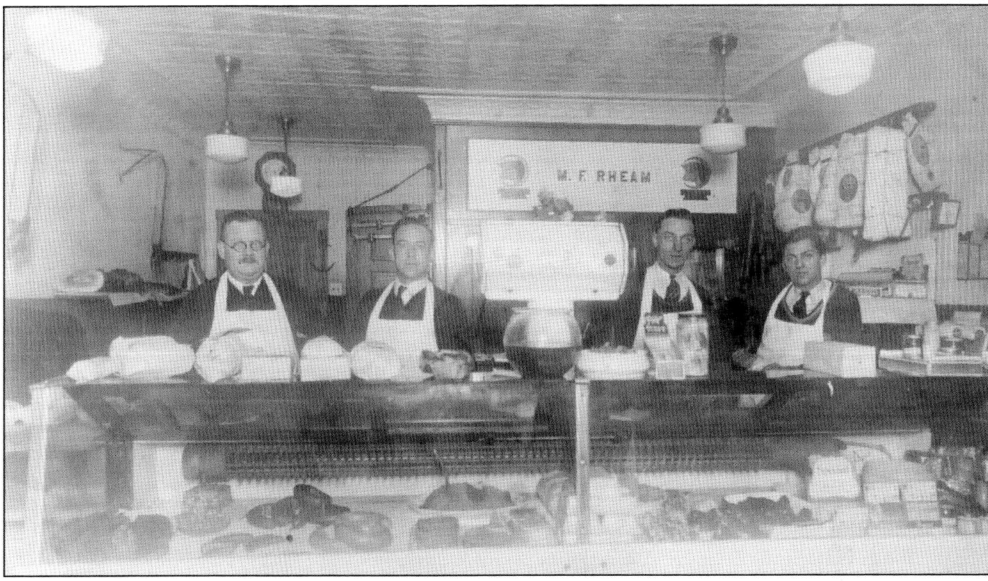

Located at 655 Evergreen Avenue, Rheam Butcher Shop served Millvale's citizens from 1931 to 1965. Pictured on the far left is Michael F. Rheam, the original owner, and next to him is his son, Michael J. Rheam, who inherited the shop. Brothers Al (second from right) and George Buchert are also shown. (Michele Rheam.)

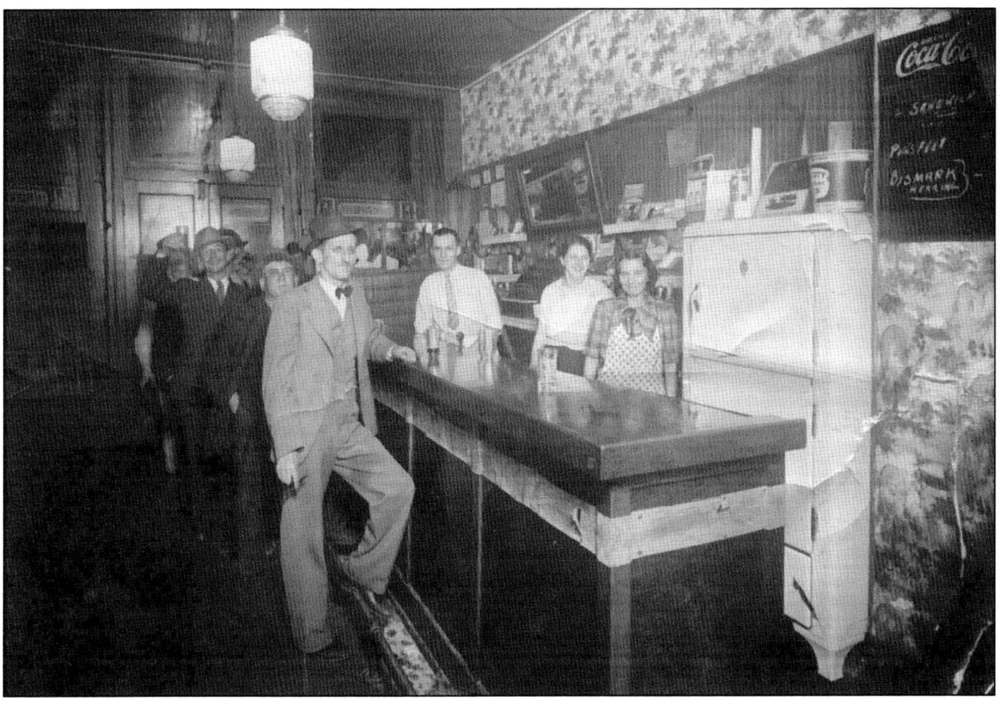

This is the interior of George's Place, at 307 Grant Avenue (presently Cousins' Lounge). George Marlovits (behind the bar, in necktie), owner, with Mary Marlovits (behind the bar, center) as a barmaid, serve locally brewed beers and daily specials, which include sandwiches, pig's feet, and Bismarck herring. Years later, Mary would marry Clarence Conlon and open Conlon's Tavern on North Avenue. (Ann Conners.)

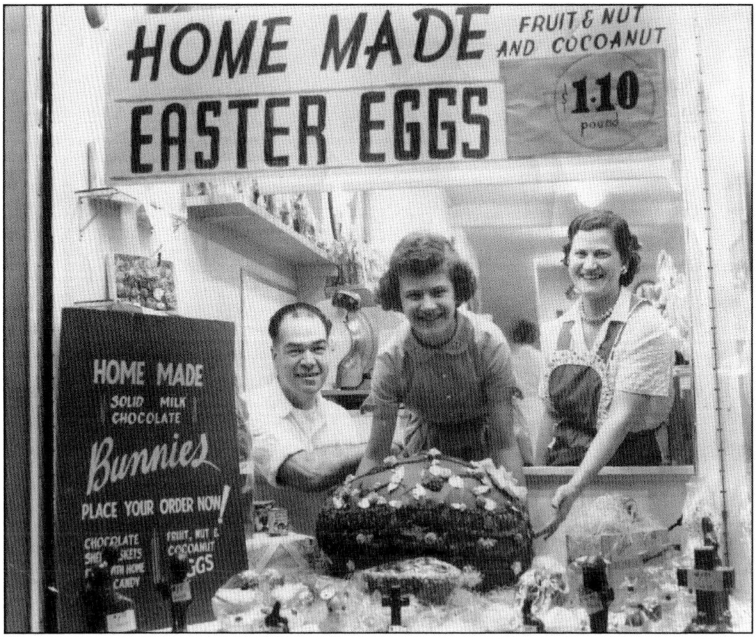

Gertrude and Elmer Yetter beam as their daughter, Arlene, places a huge handmade Easter egg in the window of their storefront at 504 Grant Avenue in 1952. No Easter basket would be complete without at least one fruit-and-nut or coconut egg and several chocolate bunnies and crosses from Yetter's. Arlene and her husband, Ed Carr, have run the store since 1976. (Arlene Carr.)

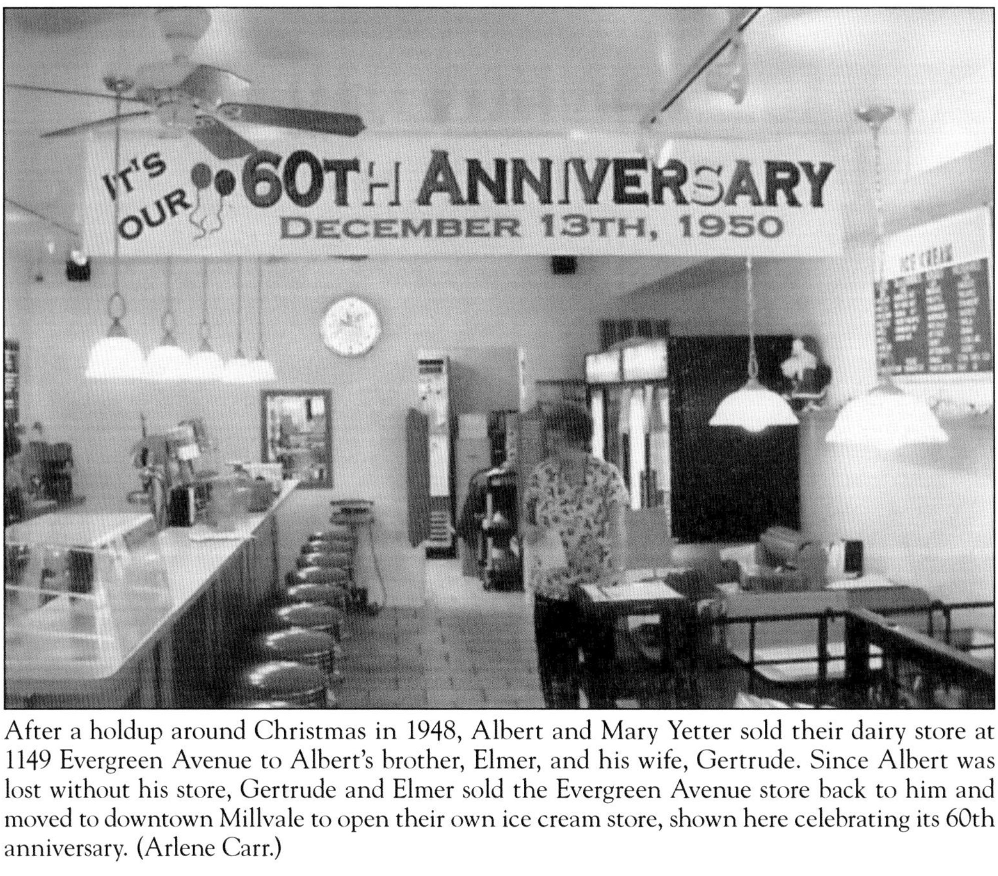

After a holdup around Christmas in 1948, Albert and Mary Yetter sold their dairy store at 1149 Evergreen Avenue to Albert's brother, Elmer, and his wife, Gertrude. Since Albert was lost without his store, Gertrude and Elmer sold the Evergreen Avenue store back to him and moved to downtown Millvale to open their own ice cream store, shown here celebrating its 60th anniversary. (Arlene Carr.)

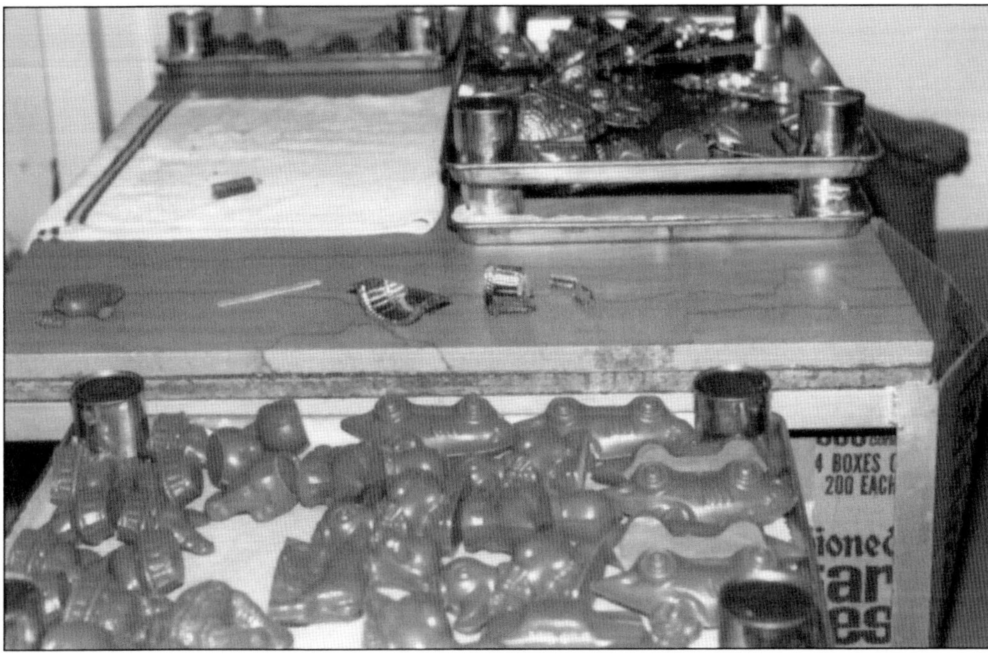

Yetter's candy business always boomed around the holidays, especially Easter. Chocolate novelties, including cars, chickens sitting in baskets, and rabbits, are shown here on the counter, awaiting trimming after being extracted from their molds. Make no mistake, these treats were not hollow, but were solid milk chocolate handmade by Yetter's. (Arlene Carr.)

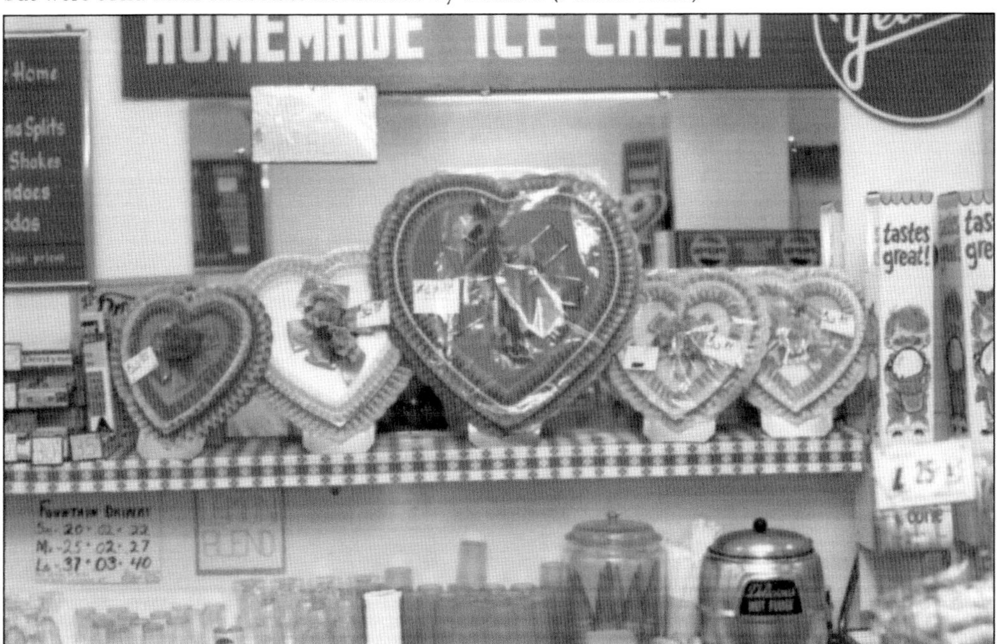

Valentine's Day hearts filled with handmade chocolates line the back of the soda fountain at Yetter's. Besides chocolates, Yetter's was known for its homemade ice cream, including the vintage vanilla-with-cherries Whitehouse. The 2004 flood destroyed the store and all of its equipment. It reopened, but no longer makes its own ice cream. (Arlene Carr.)

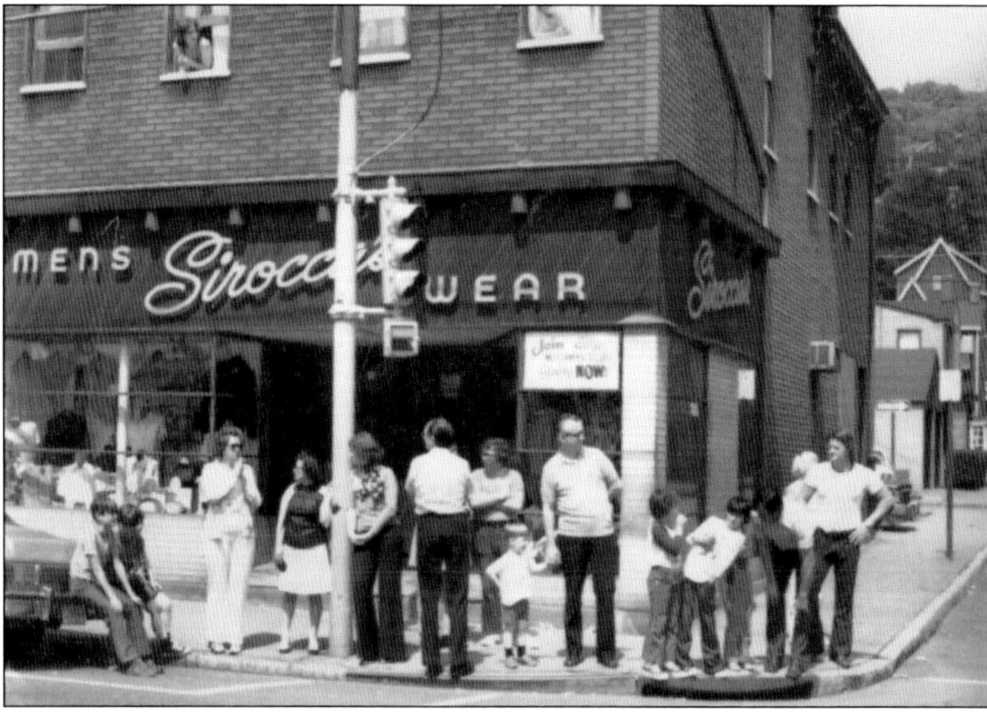

On the corner of Lincoln and North Avenues, with Sirocco's Men's Wear (referred to by residents as a haberdashery) behind them, residents wait for one of Millvale's parades. This was the only men's store for suits, sport coats, shirts, ties, and hats in town. There were two stores for women. (Jennifer Cohen.)

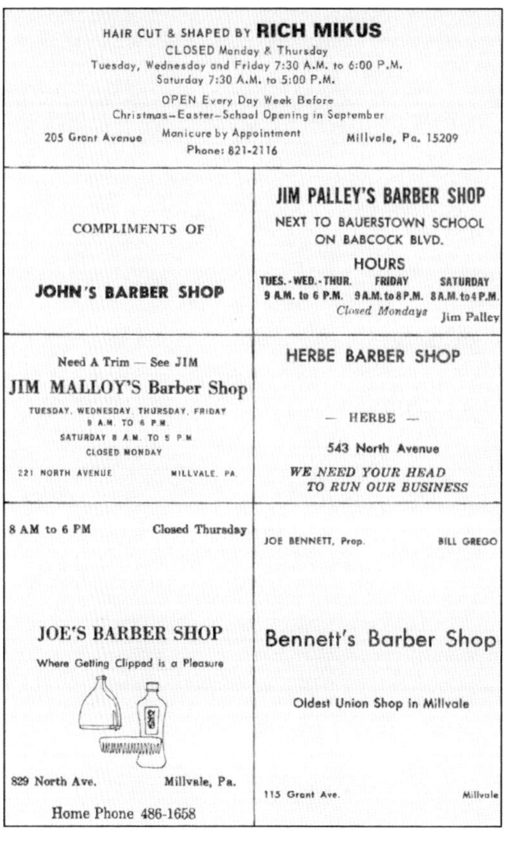

Starting in the late 1890s, barbershops have been among Millvale's businesses. In 1900, there were eight: William Brown, John Freidt, John G. Haser, Max Herbe, John Hoffarth, Charles Rebel, William F. Sachs, and Edward Tillman. This advertisement from the 1972 Millvale Boy's Club brochure lists seven, including a Herbe Barber Shop. (Jack Cavanaugh.)

Known as "Coonie," Conrad Accetta stands behind the counter of his North Hills Hardware at 217 North Avenue. Located between Isaly's and Esther's, the store opened in 1952 and was in operation for approximately 13 years. Accetta had been in the hardware business with his brothers in South Hills, at Mount Lebanon Hardware, before opening the Millvale store. (Suzanne Accetta Salhany.)

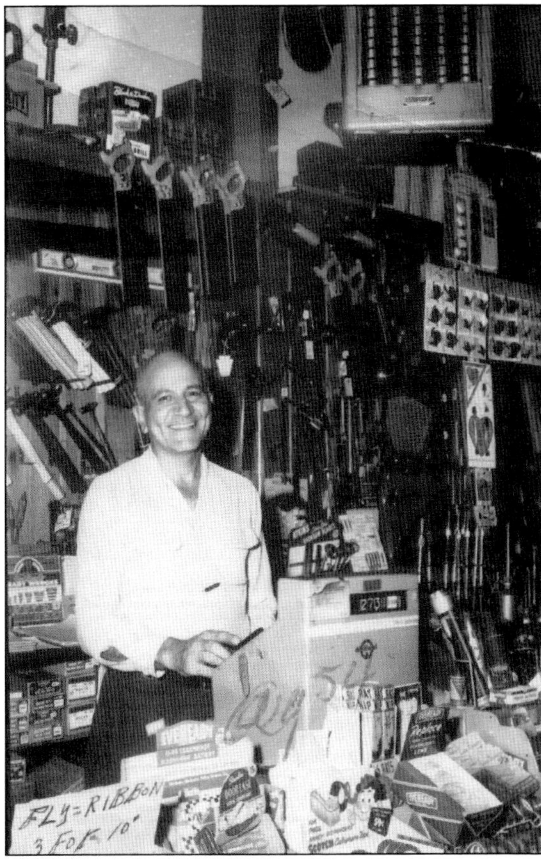

This May 1998 photograph, taken from Williams Street, shows Lippert Saw Company and St. Anthony's Roman Catholic Church. Lippert Saw Company produced circular saw blades in a variety of sizes and armor plating for military vehicles. On this section of the Lippert property now stands a senior apartment complex. (Bill Stout.)

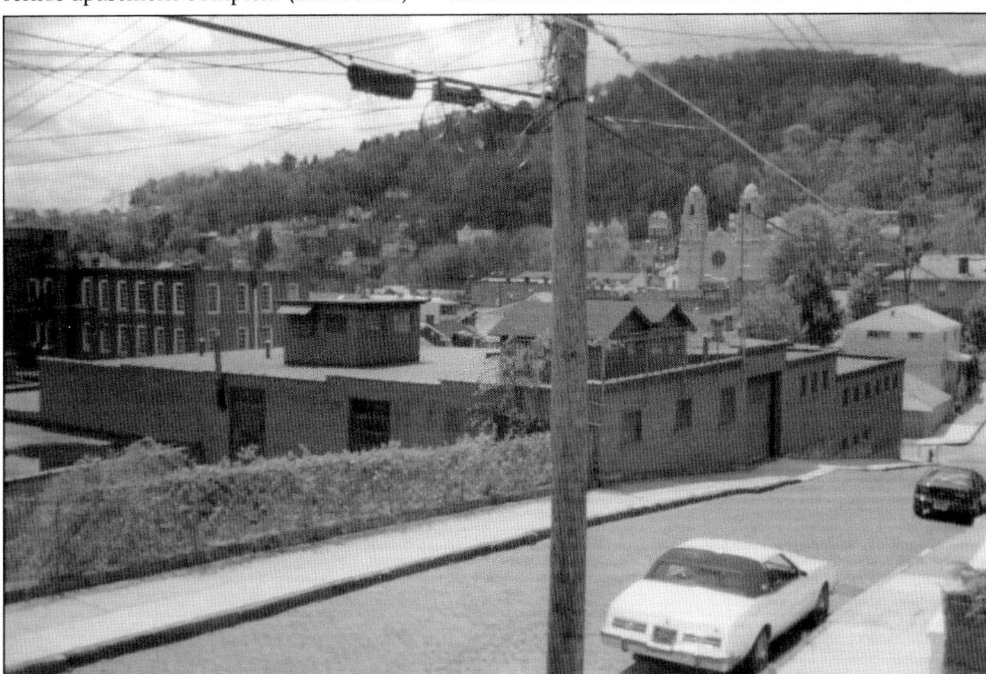

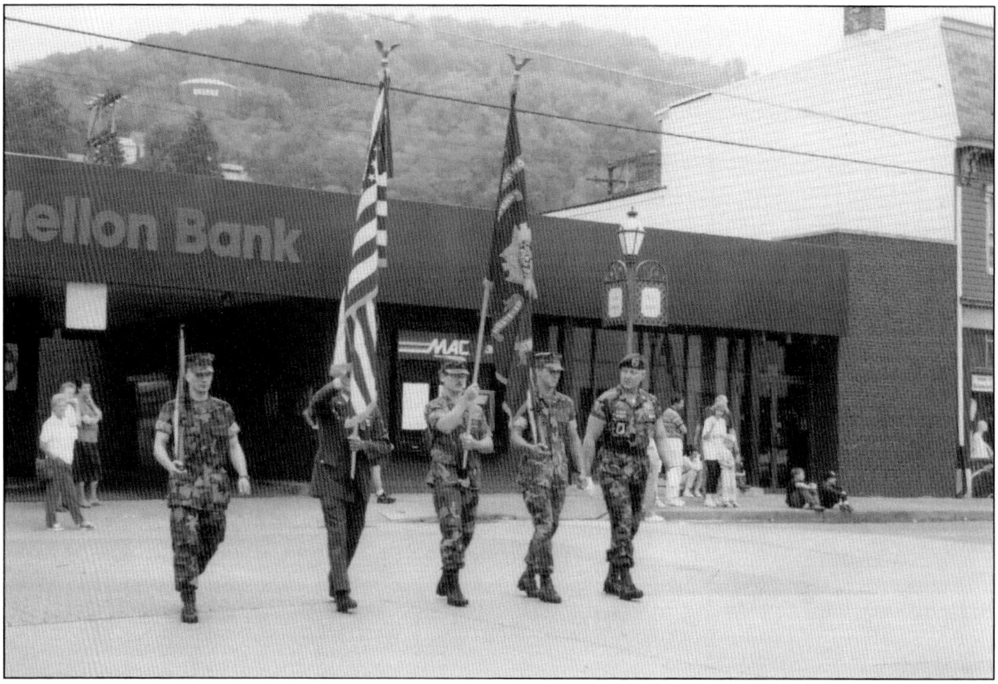

This picture, taken in 2000, shows the Mellon Bank along North Avenue during one of Millvale's many parades. Mellon Bank was founded in 1869 by Thomas Mellon with his sons Andrew W. Mellon and Richard B. Mellon. Millvale's five-and-dime store stood here at one time. Today, the drive-through is gone, and the building is now used by the Elemental Church. (Bill Stout.)

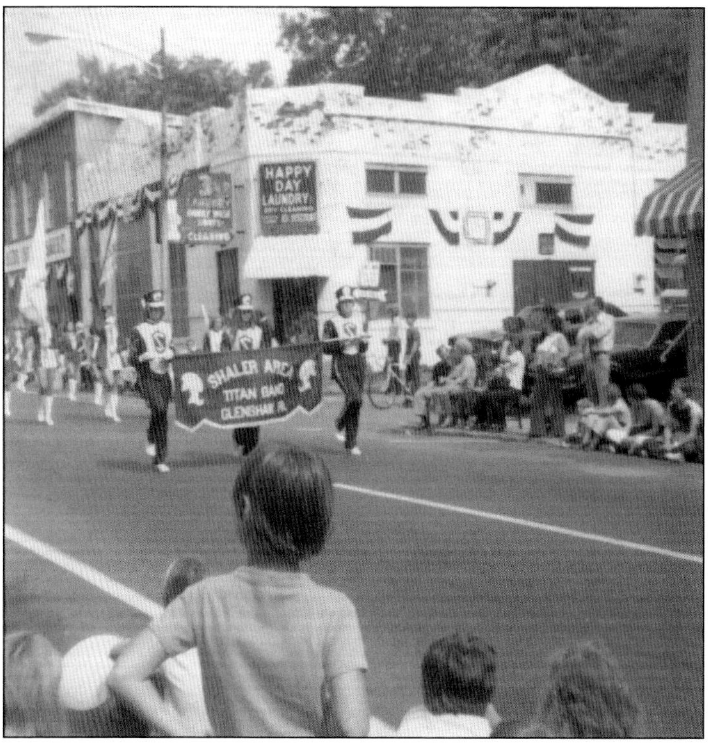

In the days when families did not have washing machines and there were no Laundromats, Happy Day Laundry, located on the corner of North Avenue and Fremont Street, was considered a blessing to housewives. (Al Atkinson.)

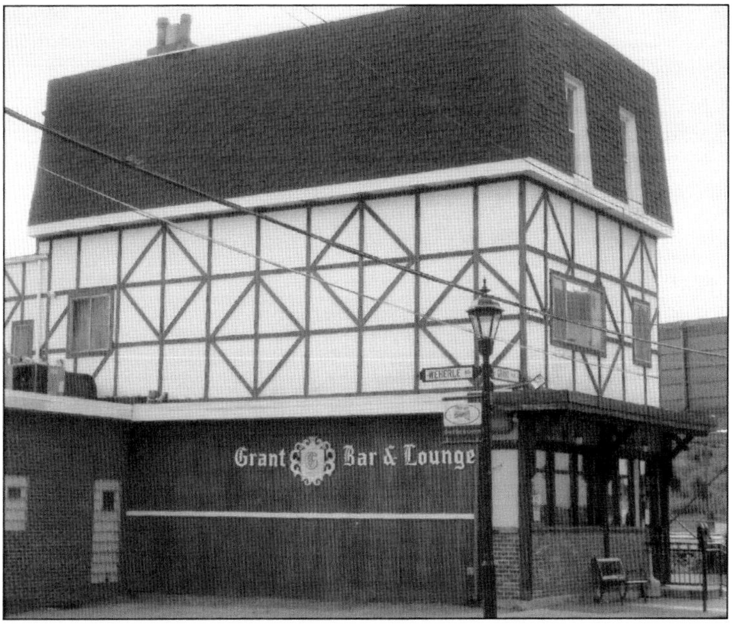

The Grant Bar was purchased by Matthew and Maria Ruzomberka from Anton and Sophia Kacherak on December 4, 1925. At the time, it was called the Grant Hotel and provided rooms for the railroaders and mill workers who worked along the Allegheny River. After Prohibition, it became a restaurant and bar. Still in business, it is renowned for its fried shrimp and homemade cream pies. (Bill Stout.)

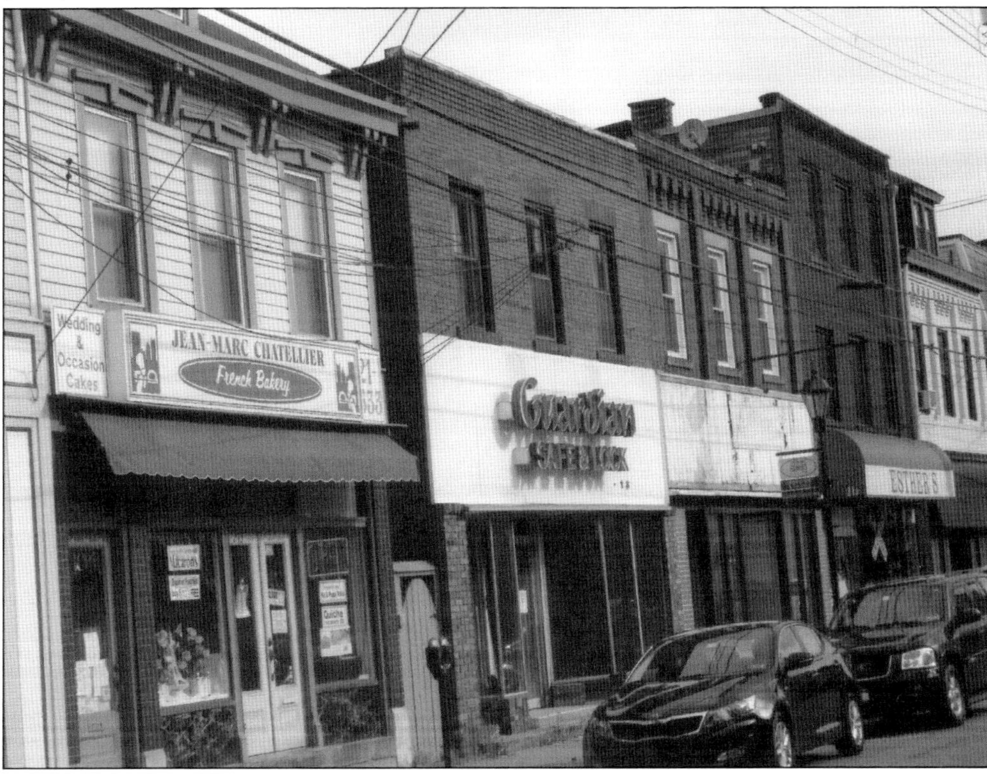

In 1938, Esther Mehler started Esther's Coffee Shop at 303 North Avenue, selling ice cream and candy. The shop moved to its present location in 1954 and later expanded to include hobbies and toys. Esther's Hobby Shop celebrated its 75th anniversary in 2013. Also visible is the establishment of a third-generation French baker, Jean-Marc Chatellier. Open since 1992, the store sells wonderful *macarons* (French for "macaroons") and croissants. (Bill Stout.)

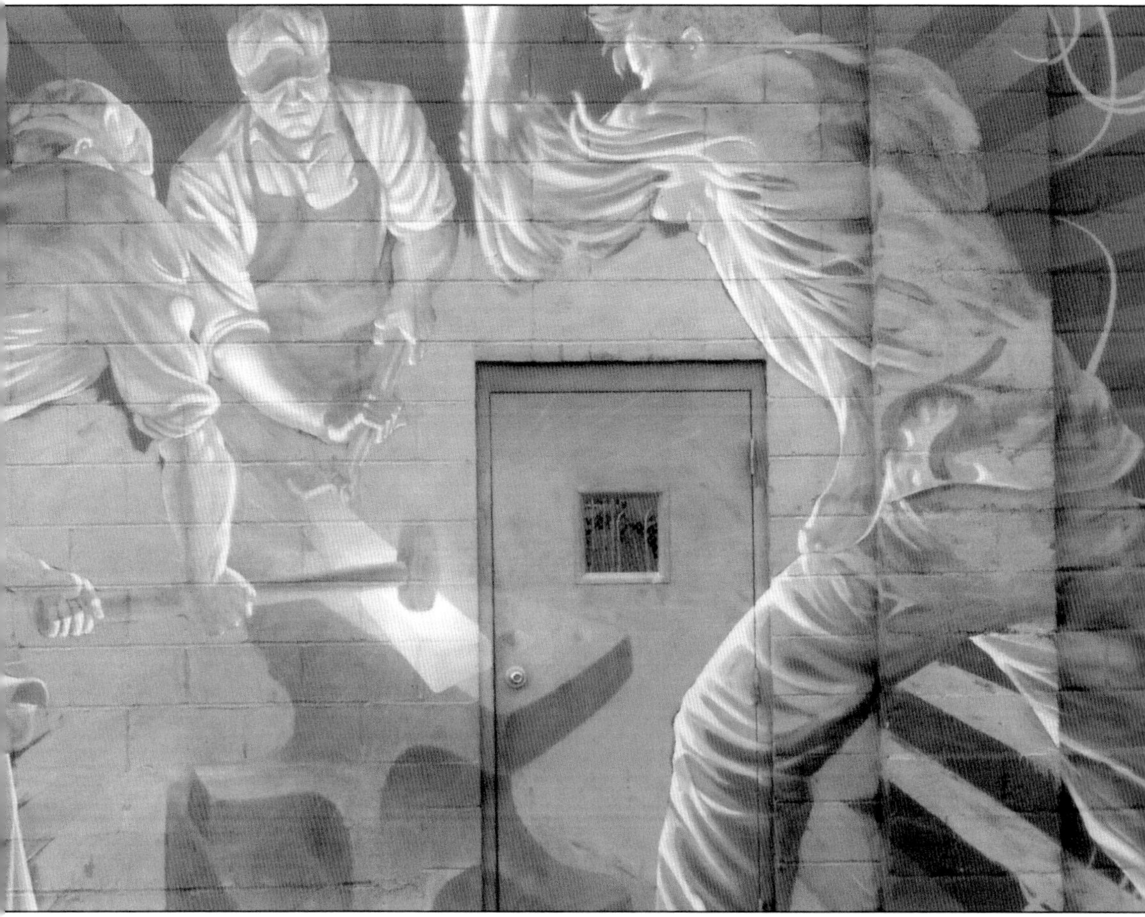

Red Star Ironworks, which specializes in hand-forged decorative and architectural metalwork projects for industrial and residential clients, was begun by Peter Lambert around 2000. Along with eight others, Lambert, who parlayed his passion for ironworking into a business, received the 2008 SBA Young Entrepreneur of the Year award from the US Small Business Administration. Red Star's projects have included a sign for the BRGR in Cranberry, falcon statues for gravestones, an ornamental gate like the one in Grant Avenue Park, the iron balconies at the Willow Restaurant, and the chandeliers at Café Zao. Lambert and others from Red Star have worked with Allegheny Grows to plant urban gardens in vacant lots in Millvale. (Bill Stout.)

Seven

PLAY BALL!

One of the things that can be said about Millvale citizens is that they are joiners. At times, they created nationality-oriented societies, joined athletic teams, established religious organizations, and joined fraternal orders.

A charter was granted to a small group of German men interested in choral singing on May 5, 1890. Showcasing its members' talents, the Franz Abt Liederkranz Club traveled across the United States from its headquarters on Sedgwick Street, now home to Panza Gallery. Another group of German men created a vocal and instrumental music society in 1904. Known officially as the St. Anthony's Musical and Beneficial Society of Millvale, it is more fondly called the Goose Hall, after the geese raised in the neighborhood. The hall was often the destination for parties, weddings, meetings, and other social engagements.

Sports became increasingly popular, and folks traveled to Millvale to watch baseball and football games and even professional boxing. The high school sponsored award-winning teams, as did many local bar owners and organizations, such as John Wukits and Walt Bavanovich, the American Legion, and Millvale's Merchant Association. Hickey Park, just over the line in Bauerstown but listed as in Millvale, was the destination for baseball games and boxing matches featuring Billy Conn. During the 1950s and 1960s, Millvale had its own Boy's Club run by a small group of volunteers and paid for by booster book advertisements and donations from local businesses. Even today, a bowling alley operates in town.

The various Catholic churches sponsored the Christian Mothers, the Knights of Columbus, and the Holy Name Society. Protestant churches such as Christ Lutheran sponsored youth-oriented groups, including the Boy's Club and Boy Scouts. The Opera House, another venue for socializing, was home to many organizations before they could establish permanent homes. Fraternal orders included the Corinthian Lodge, which moved into the new Masonic Hall building on January 4, 1911, and Millvale Moose No. 68, which met in its now defunct building on Sherman Street. VFW Post No. 118 has been aiding soldiers, sailors, and Marines since the beginning of the 20th century. Its building has been the scene of dances, meetings, and even race nights.

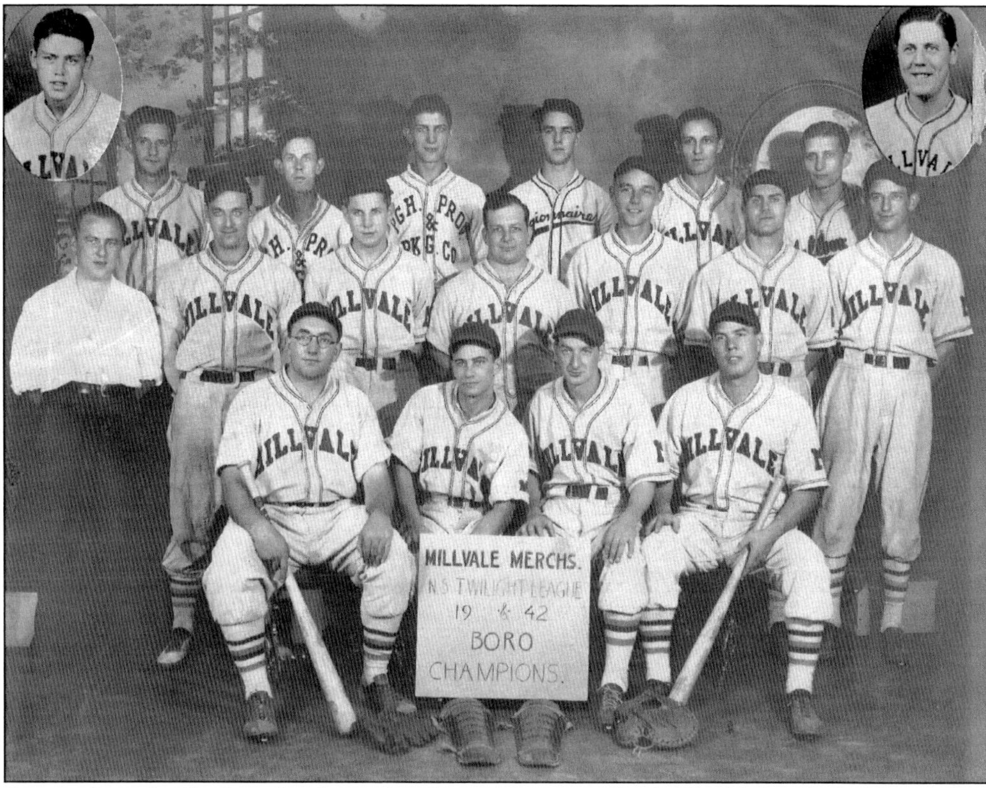

An article in the *Pittsburg Leader* on April 24, 1904, states that Millvale's baseball club is a glory, plays before thousands of fans, and "walloped" the Homestead team. Burgess D. Edgar Hickey was the manager, and the club had a park by the borough line. In such tradition, the Millvale Merchants, a semipro baseball team that played on Sample Hill, poses for a photograph (above) after becoming borough champions in the Twilight League in 1942. Walt's, composed of local citizens, was sponsored by Walt Bubanovic's Bar on Grant Avenue, currently Sweeney's. The team, seen in the below photograph, became league champs in 1953. Almost directly across the street was a friendly rival, sponsored by John Wukits' Bar. Fans filled the bleachers at the Millvale ball field to watch friends and relatives and to hear the latest gossip. (Above, Becky Rakers Stout; below, Nancy and Vince Jaksic.)

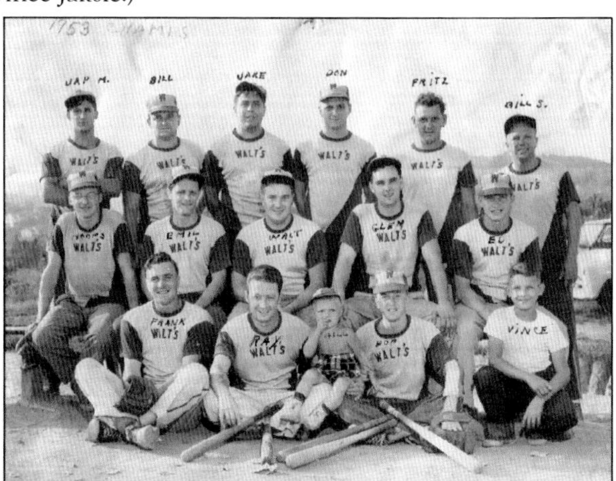

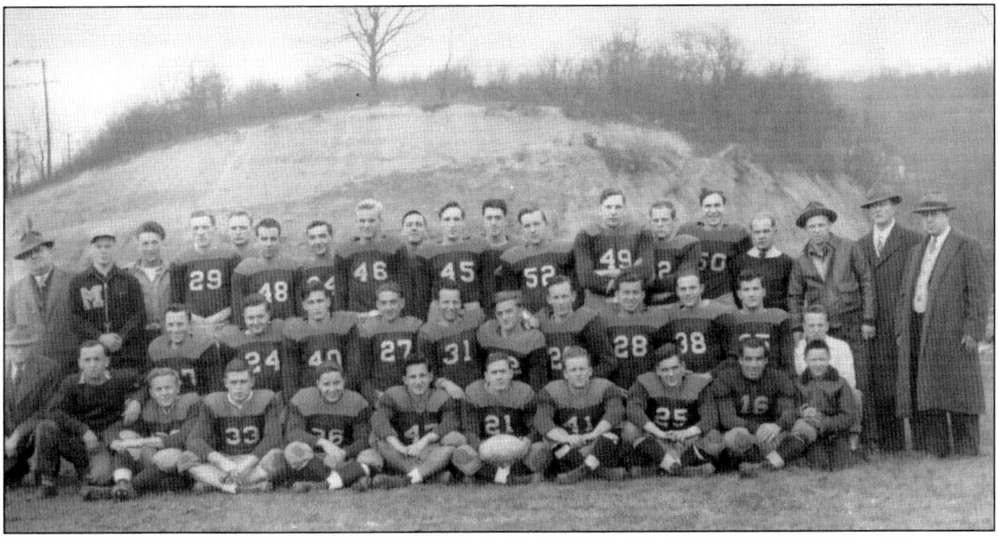

High school football was very popular over the years. Even today, former teams and individuals are recognized by the Shaler Area Athletic Hall of Fame. The champion 1941 team was inducted in 2006, and Bob "Popeye" Stout in 2012. The American Legion team pictured above had a successful 1947 season, winning eight games and losing only to the Etna Vets, 12-6, and the Bloomfield Civies, 26-14. Its home field was on Sample Hill. In the gridiron action seen in the below photograph, former mayor Jack Cavanaugh (10) plays for the Millvale Indians in the late 1940s at the high school field. The semipro Millvale Amici team played the Allegheny County circuit, even the County Workhouse in Blawnox. The Millvale Cardinals was another local team that joined the circuit. (Both, Bill Stout.)

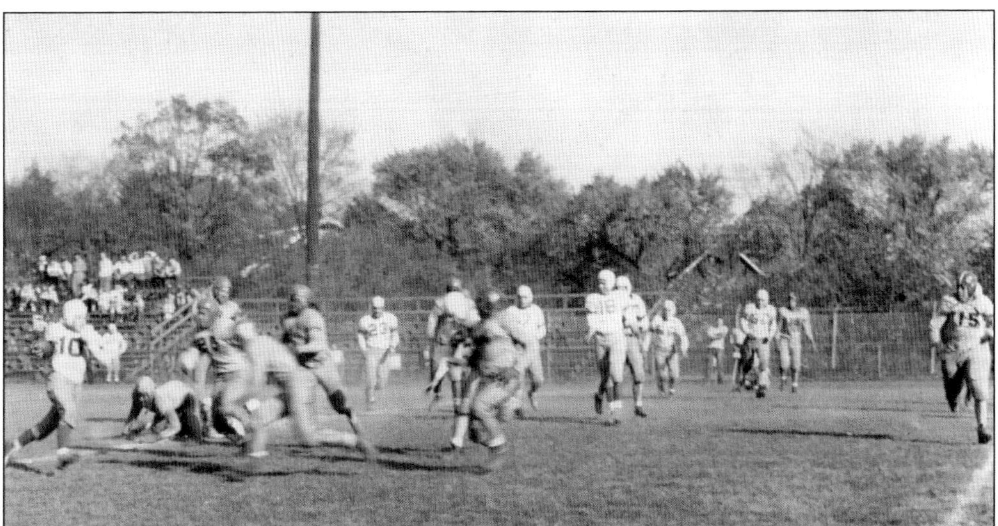

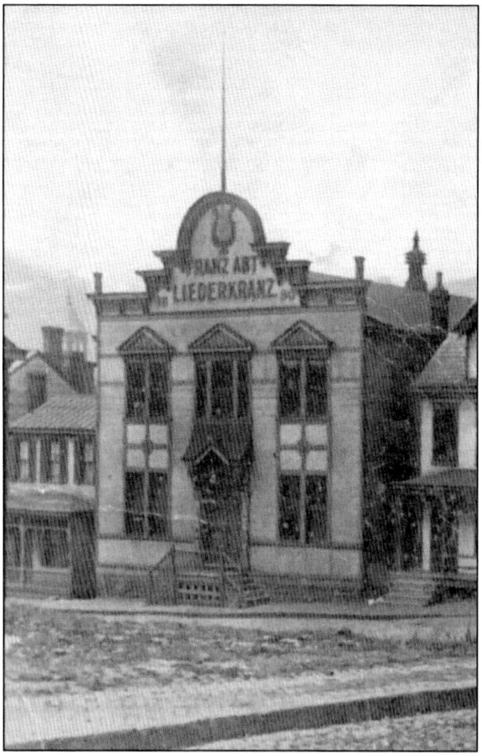

Millvale had its share of men's clubs. Following the Civil War, veterans organizations were created. Millvale had the Grand Army of the Republic Post No. 545 General A.A. Humphreys, which disbanded before World War I. On Sedgwick Street stood the headquarters of a German music society, the Franz Abt Liederkranz Club (seen here in a close-up of the image shown at the top of page 49), which was chartered on May 5, 1890. (Panza Gallery.)

The three Catholic churches of Millvale and several local organizations held bingo nights, which proved so popular that players at times could visit four different locations in one week. Ladies also had religious groups, such as the Christian Mothers, and auxiliaries to fraternal orders. For many women of the borough, these were the only respectable outlets available after a day filled with housework and children. (Bill Stout.)

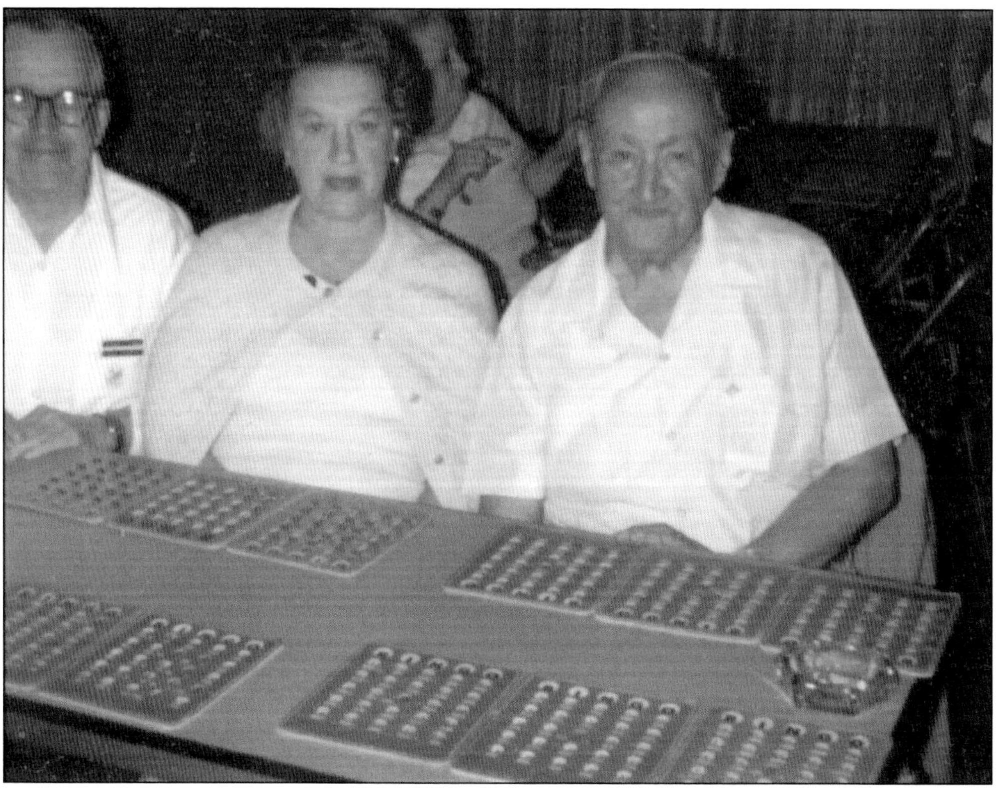

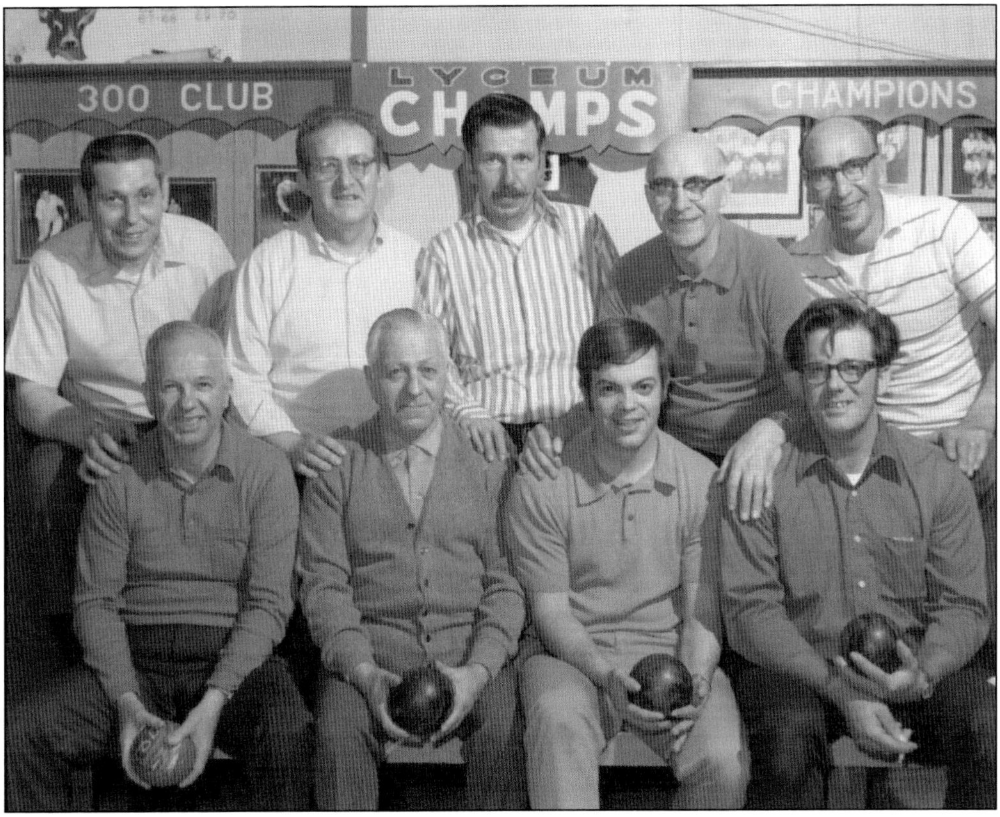

The new St. Anthony's Lyceum, dedicated in 1925, replaced a previous one destroyed by fire in 1923. It was a popular place for students and young adults because in the basement were duckpin lanes, a basketball pit, and many pool tables. An auditorium was located on the ground floor. It was a popular destination on Saturday nights for the Early Bird Bowling League. Duckpins were set up by pinboys. Posing in the above photograph are, from left to right, (first row) Bill Stout, unidentified, D. Brunfleck, and Bill Watson; (second row) Nick Grubic, Herman Abt, Ross Urban, Bill Pfund, and Bob Pfund. Every year, Bob Pfund prepared a review (right), which included highlights, for the members. At one time, there were three full-size pin lanes in the borough: McCarthy Lanes (currently Millvale Lanes atop the Lincoln Pharmacy), Eidenmiller's (now Jack's Discount Videos), and Kiefer's Bowling Alleys (occupied now by a BP service station). (Both, Nick Grubic.)

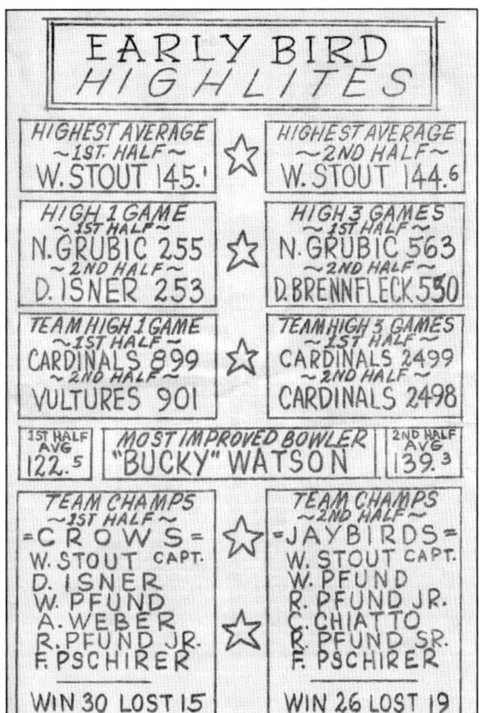

EARLY BIRD
HIGHLITES

HIGHEST AVERAGE ~1ST. HALF~ W. STOUT 145.1 ☆ HIGHEST AVERAGE ~2ND HALF~ W. STOUT 144.6

HIGH 1 GAME ~1ST HALF~ N. GRUBIC 255 ~2ND HALF~ D. ISNER 253 ☆ HIGH 3 GAMES ~1ST HALF~ N. GRUBIC 563 ~2ND HALF~ D. BRENNFLECK 550

TEAM HIGH 1 GAME ~1ST HALF~ CARDINALS 899 ~2ND HALF~ VULTURES 901 ☆ TEAM HIGH 3 GAMES ~1ST HALF~ CARDINALS 2499 ~2ND HALF~ CARDINALS 2498

1ST HALF AVG 122.5 | MOST IMPROVED BOWLER "BUCKY" WATSON | 2ND HALF AVG 139.3

TEAM CHAMPS ~1ST HALF~
=CROWS=
W. STOUT CAPT.
D. ISNER
W. PFUND
A. WEBER
R. PFUND JR.
F. PSCHIRER
WIN 30 LOST 15

☆ ☆

TEAM CHAMPS ~2ND HALF~
=JAYBIRDS=
W. STOUT CAPT.
W. PFUND
R. PFUND JR.
C. CHIATTO
R. PFUND SR.
F. PSCHIRER
WIN 26 LOST 19

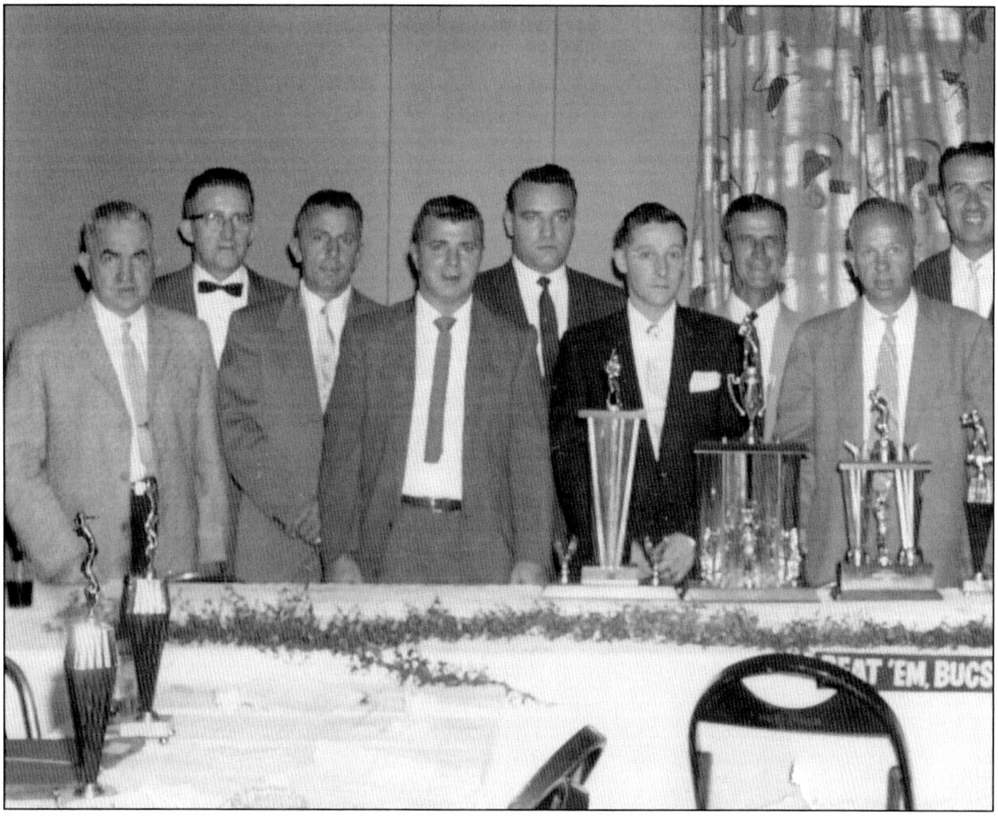

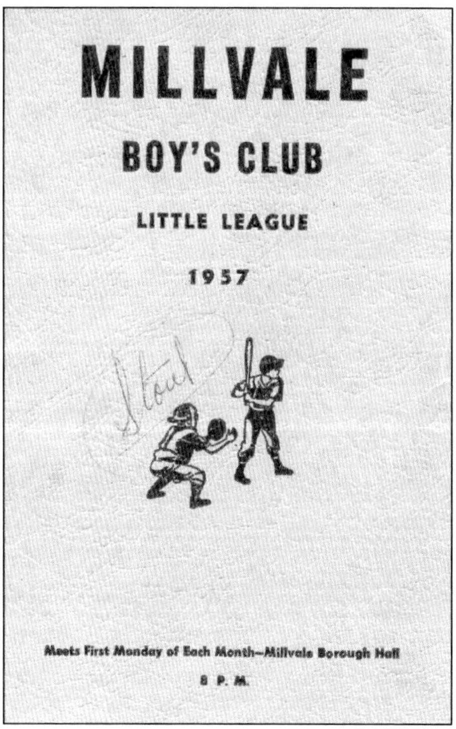

Started in 1954 by a group of dedicated citizens meeting Monday nights at the high school, the Millvale Boy's Club received its nonprofit charter in 1957. Financial backing was provided by a small group of civic-minded businesses: Millvale VFW, Millvale Moose, Millvale Rotary Club, Bennett Lumber Company, Millvale Luncheon Club, Bergman's Bakery, E.T. Lippert Saw Company, and McDowell Manufacturing. Annually, the club published a booster book filled with paid advertisements to help with expenditures. In the above photograph, members gather at the Star Lite Lounge in Blawnox in September 1960. Receiving trophies on behalf of the club are, from left to right, Ducky Hill, Herman Abt, Rip Ropper, Markus "Syki" Stohovic, Joe Coko, Jack Kavanaugh, Rocky Mikus, Bill Stout, and Al Andiorio. At a picnic in North Park at the end of each season, every Little League player received a small trophy commemorating his accomplishment. (Both, Bill Stout.)

With the aim of hosting sports for the school-aged children of the borough, the Boy's Club grew from just Pony teams in 1956 to include basketball in 1959, boxing in 1964, and bowling and girls' softball in 1965. Baseball games were held during the week at the high school field, basketball and boxing took place on Saturday mornings at the high school, and weekly bowling matches were held above the Lincoln Pharmacy. (Bill Stout.)

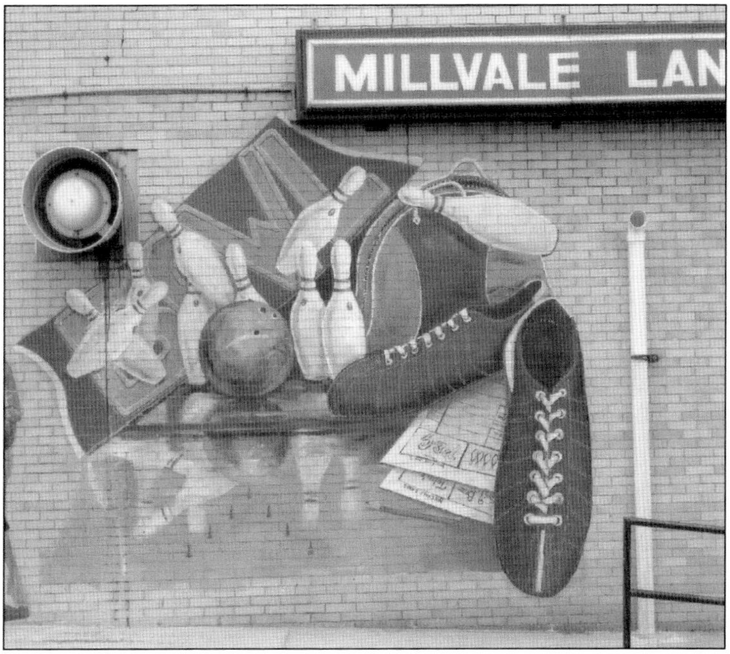

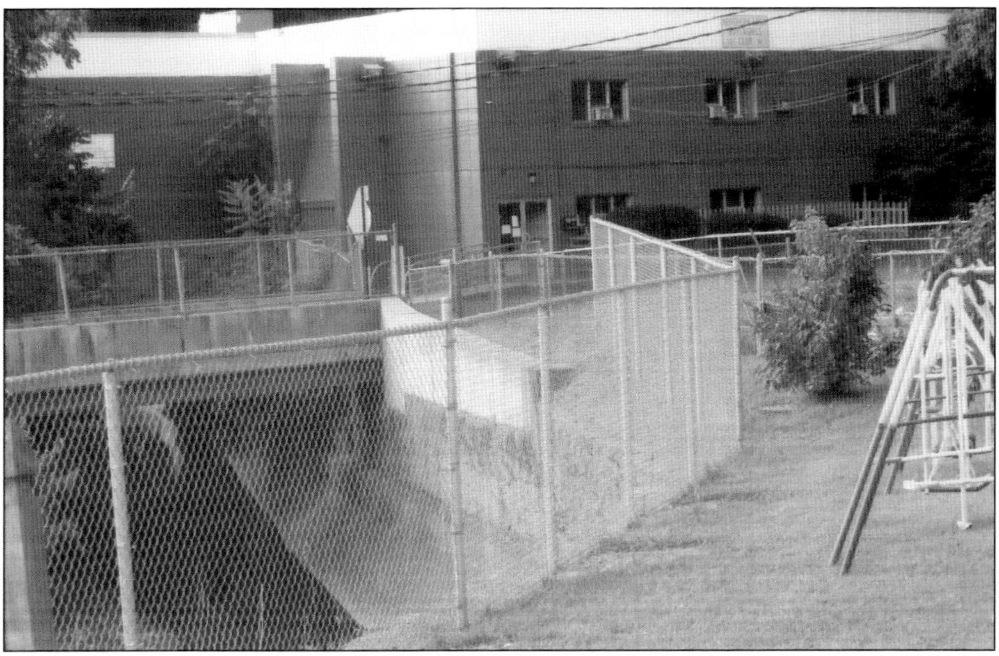

In May 1969, the Millvale Boy's Club was accepted by the Boys Clubs of America as a provisional member. Land at the foot of Sedgwick and Farragut Streets was purchased in 1968. The building opened in 1972 after years of fundraising, including the promotion "A Nickel A Week Will Cover The Creek." As seen here, Girty's Run passes under part of the building, a fact true of many of Millvale's buildings. (Bill Stout.)

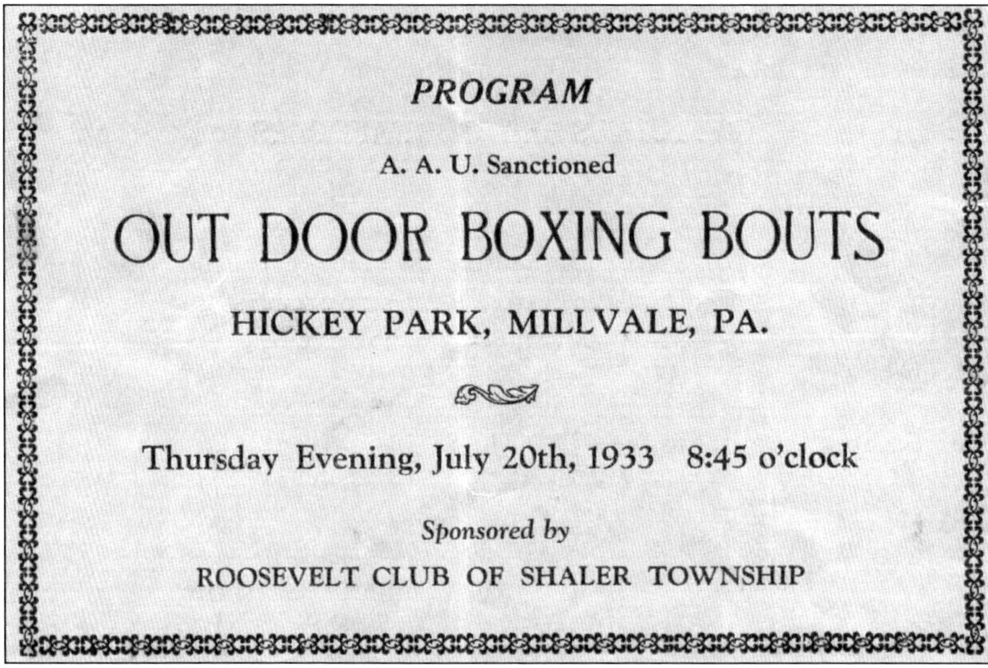

PROGRAM

A. A. U. Sanctioned

OUT DOOR BOXING BOUTS

HICKEY PARK, MILLVALE, PA.

Thursday Evening, July 20th, 1933 8:45 o'clock

Sponsored by

ROOSEVELT CLUB OF SHALER TOWNSHIP

An easy trolley ride to the borough limits and a short walk took one to the recreational destination Hickey Park, the place to be on Monday nights for boxing fans during the 1930s and 1940s. Born in Lawrenceville, Fritzie Zivic, known as the "Croatian Comet," had many early fights here. The aggressive fighter remained in Pittsburgh until his death in 1986. Local Croatians made up his large fan base. (Millvale Borough.)

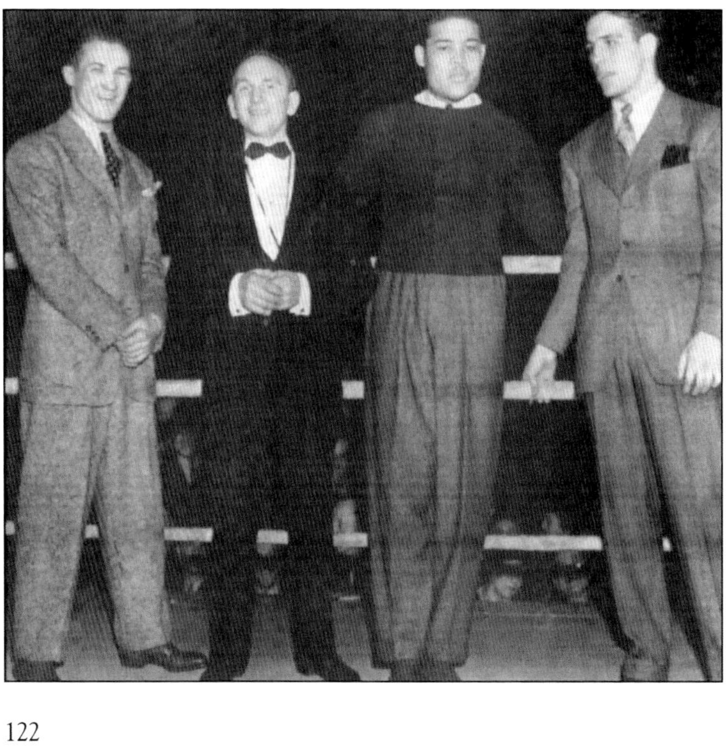

Another popular draw was heavyweight Billy Conn, known as the "Pittsburgh Kid." He unsuccessfully challenged Joe Louis for the title in 1941. Pictured, from left to right, are Fritzie Zivic, Harry Klaus, Louis, and Conn. Hickey Park originated as a ball field for an early-20th-century Millvale sports club managed by burgess D. Edgar Hickey. Pittsburgh-area teams played and fans gathered here from near and far to support their favorites. (Jean Domico.)

This undated matchbook cover from the Hickey Park Tavern, later the Brown Jug, mentions the "fight bowl" and gives Millvale, Pennsylvania, as its location, even though it was in Bauerstown, across from the fire station. The reverse reads, "The screwiest place outside an asylum. Yes, it's 'Kernel' Al. Mercur's (original) Nut House at Hickey Park Tavern opp. Fight Bowl Millvale, PA." (Bill Stout.)

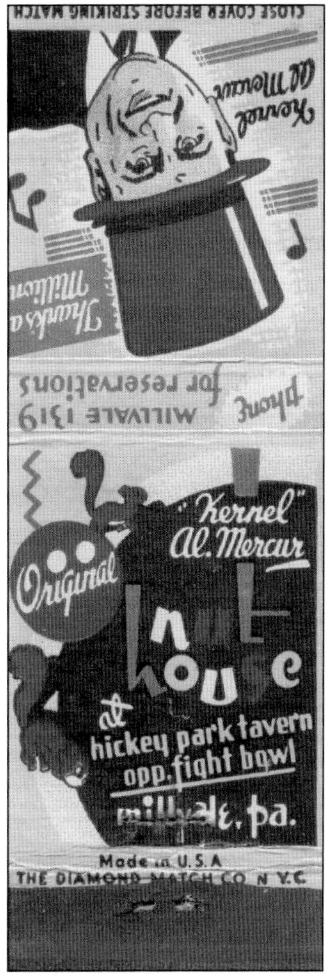

Ever popular in Millvale, the Moose band marches in a 1927 parade. The now defunct Millvale Moose had a large building on Sherman Street that included a rentable hall, meeting rooms, and a bar. The Loyal Order of Moose started a branch in Millvale in 1908. It sponsored child-oriented programs, including a Christmas party with Santa Claus, who gave out stockings filled with oranges and boxes of candy. (Flo Silbach.)

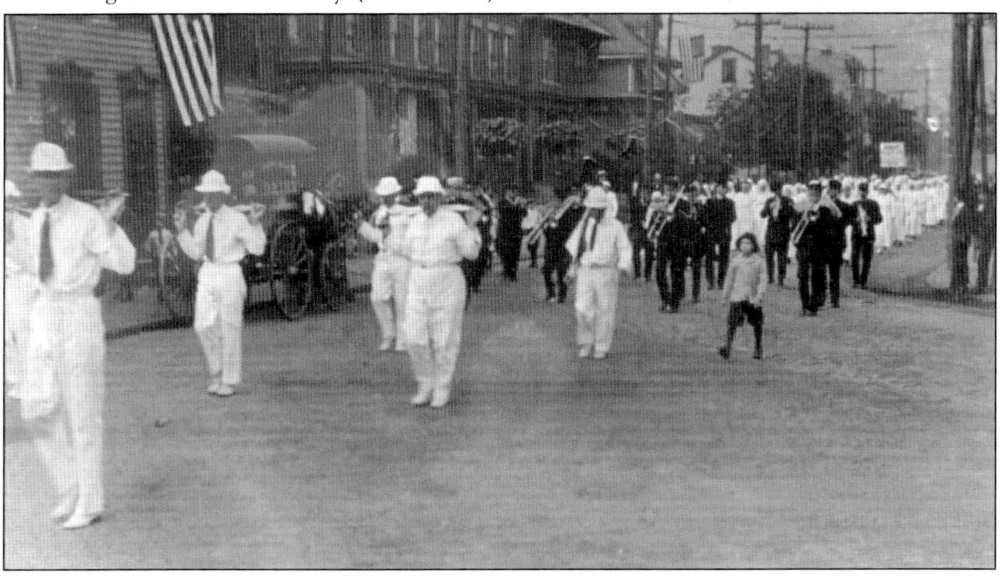

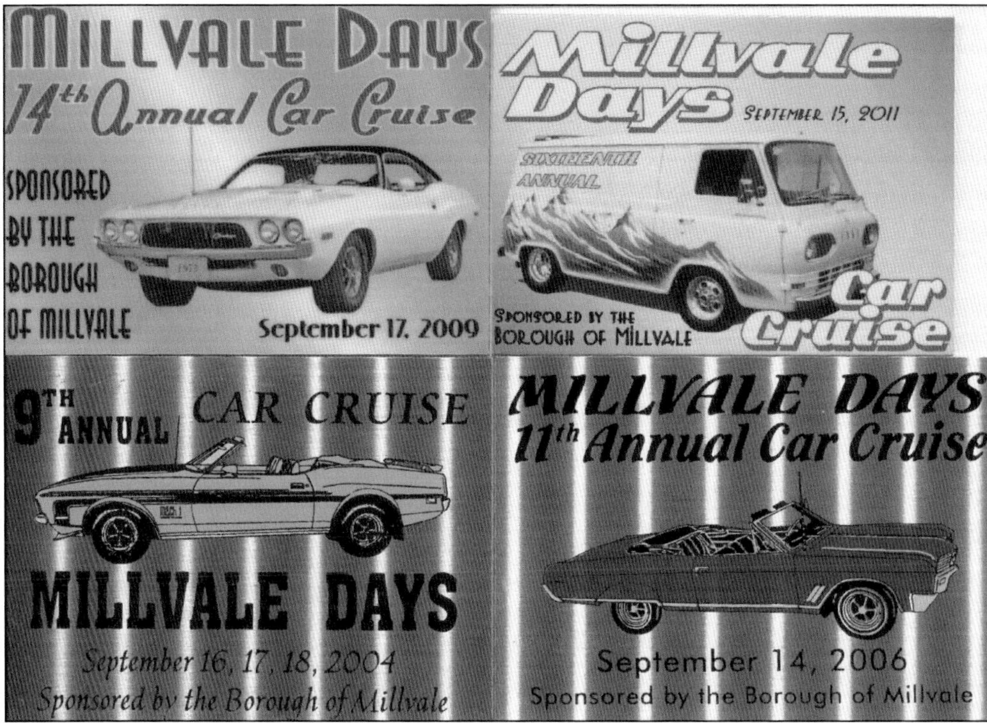

Millvale's centennial festivities spanned eight days and included recognition dinners; dances; business, industrial, and professional displays; and both a civic and a grand parade. The festivities for Millvale's 125th anniversary were so successful that, annually since 1993, a three-day celebration called Millvale Days is held in September. On Thursday night, car enthusiasts are invited to display their vehicles after a parade from the borough line to the corner of North and Grant Avenues. They are presented with that year's Car Cruise plaque. The majority of Grant Avenue is sectioned off from noon on Thursday until Sunday for rides, games of chance, wrestling, bands, and food and merchandise booths. A large Saturday morning parade of bands, dance ensembles, clubs, organizations, and local and Allegheny County dignitaries travels the length of the borough. The year 2013 marks Millvale Days' 20th anniversary. (Both, Bill Stout.)

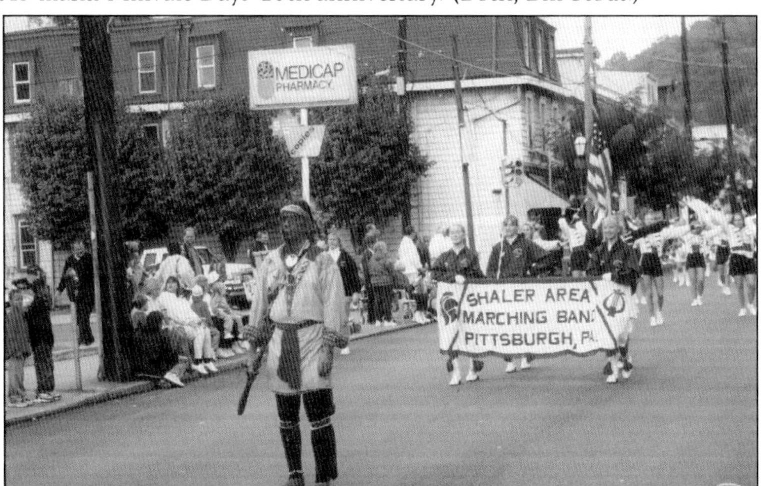

On February 1, 1888, Millvale's Corinthian Lodge No. 573 was constituted. Before the Masonic Hall building on Grant Avenue was constructed and the Corinthian Lodge was able to move in on January 4, 1911, its meetings were held at the Opera House. Over the years, many buildings in Millvale had their cornerstones laid by the lodge. At the top of this thank-you plaque is the Masonic logo. (Debra Stoltenberg.)

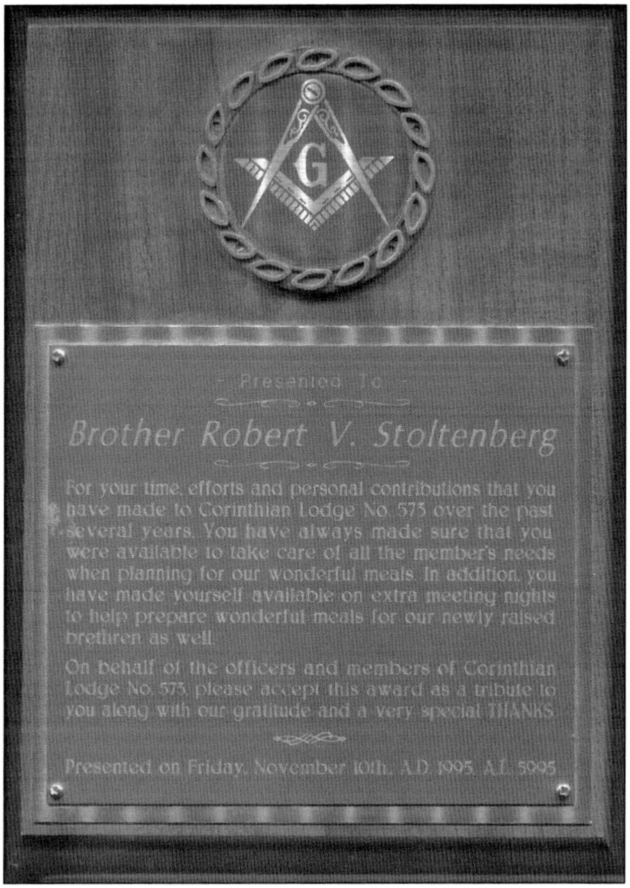

It was unusual for people to move away from Millvale, not only due to civic pride, but because of the proximity of friends and relatives. While they saw each other often at local stores, Millvale High School classes held reunions over the years, giving those who moved to Florida an excuse to return. Seen here celebrating its 30th reunion is the class of 1940. It appears that almost everyone attended. (Bill Stout.)

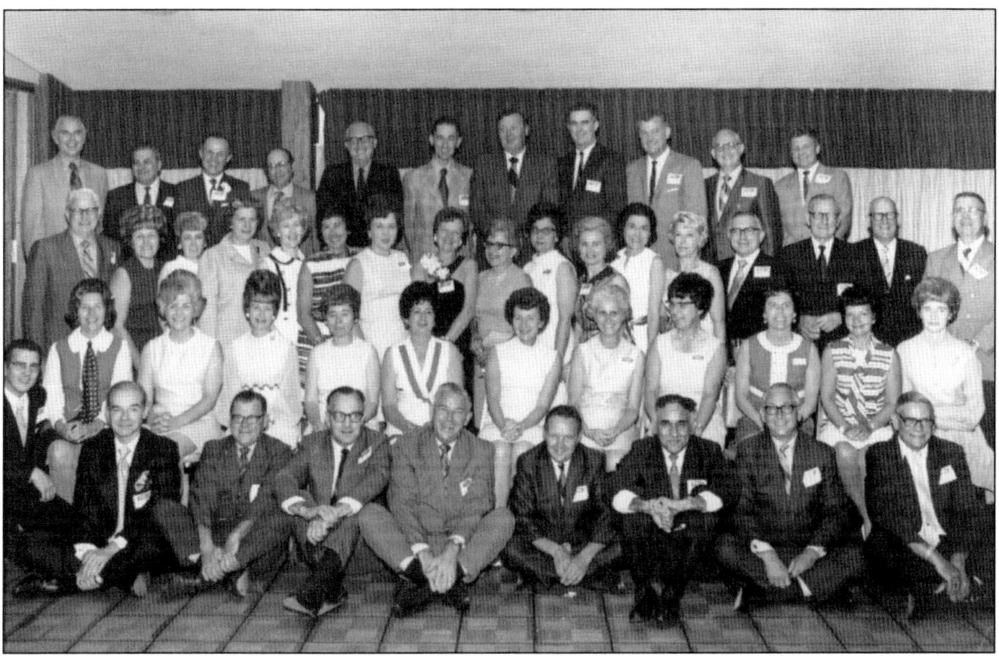

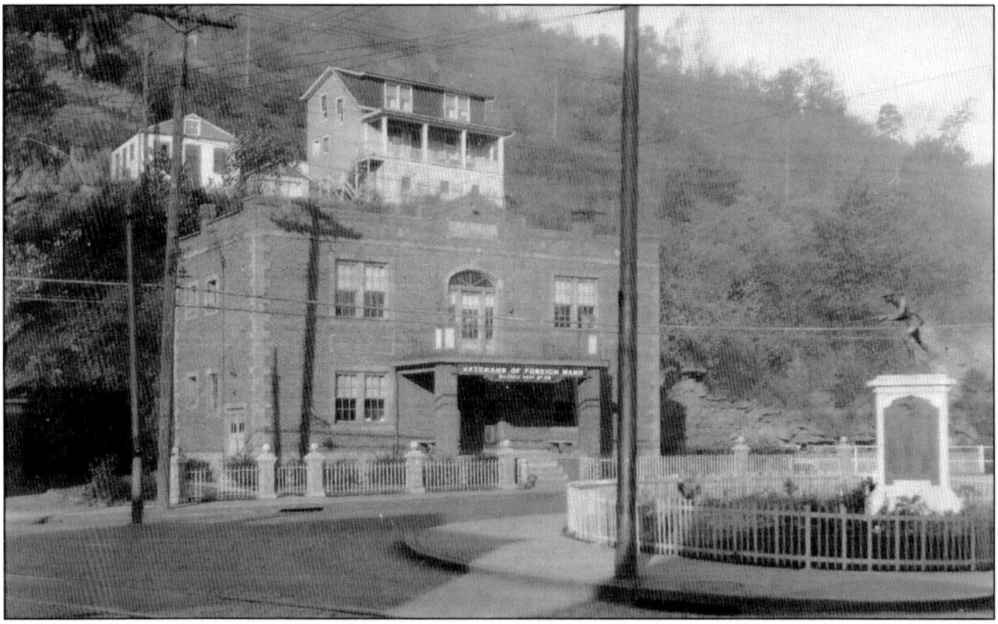

Since its formation in 1919, the Veterans of Foreign Wars Post No. 118 has been active in Millvale. The post home was completed in 1926, and the Soldier Monument was moved from Fountain Square to Memorial Park in 1931. The VFW has helped with local disasters, from the 1936 flood to those occurring today. Meetings, events, and a welcoming bar keep the post home an active place. (Jack Cavanaugh.)

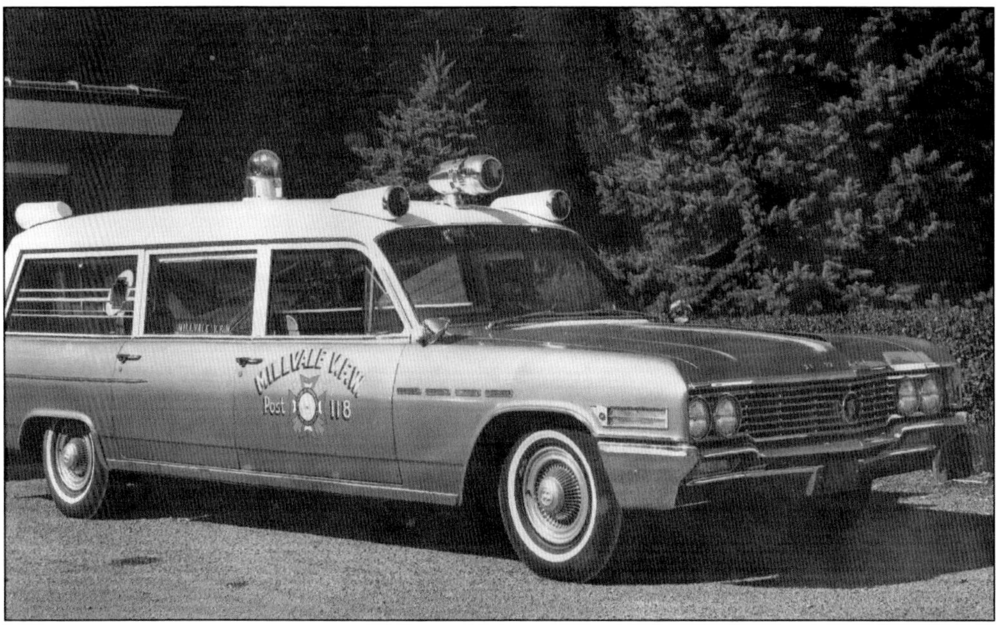

The citizens of Millvale could breathe easier knowing that at the meeting on January 10, 1952, VFW Post No. No. 118 voted to purchase an ambulance for use by members and local citizens. At the time, no immediate ambulance service was available. A committee was appointed to operate an around-the-clock service, and a LaSalle ambulance was purchased the next day. Today, the Ross-West View EMS Ambulance service covers the town. (Jennifer Cohen.)

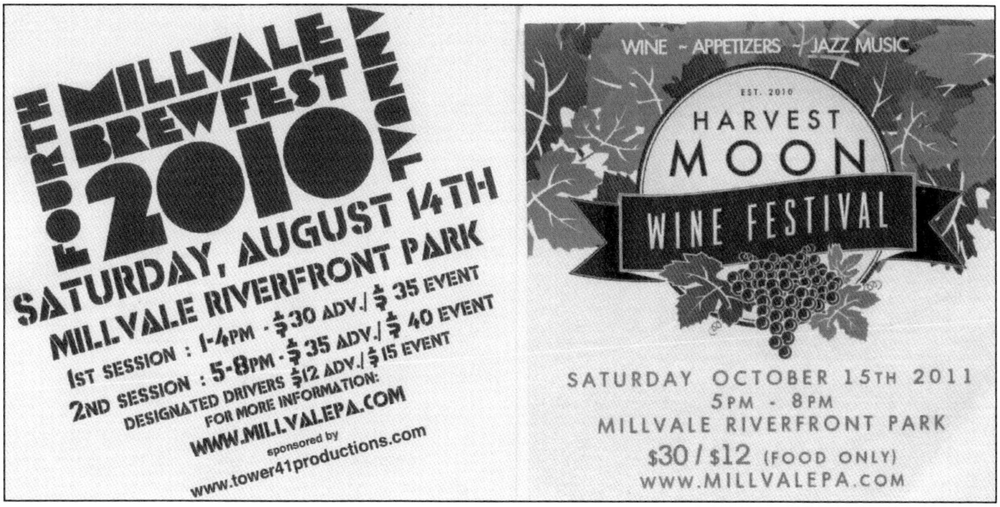

The property along the river where the mills operated is now Millvale Riverfront Park, Kayak Pittsburgh, and the Three Rivers Rowing Club. Two very popular events held at the pavilion annually are the BrewFest and the WineFest, where local businesses can display their products and provide samples in the souvenir glass provided with paid admissions. A walking and bicycle path winds along the river to Pittsburgh. (Bill Stout.)

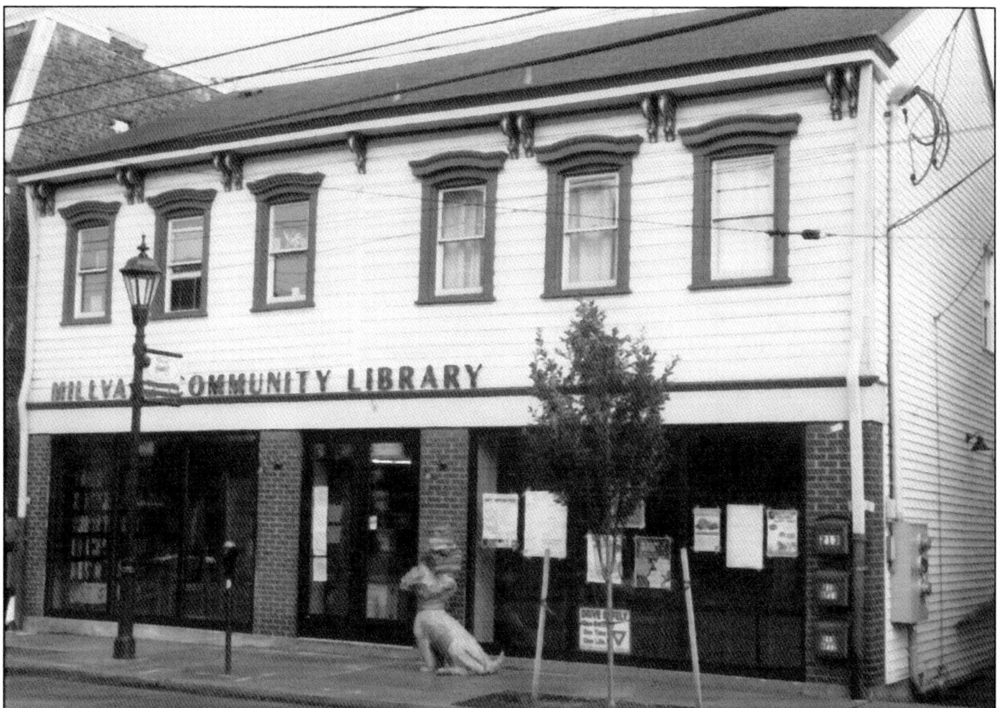

One thing missing from Millvale's 145-year history was a public library. Residents had to leave the borough for that service. On August 18, 2013, the Millvale Community Library on Grant Avenue was dedicated. A building ravaged by the 2004 flood was basically rebuilt by a small group of volunteers. Book donations were accepted from citizens and from Mount Alvernia, and many, many grant applications were submitted. (Bill Stout.)